EVIL
MUST NOT HAVE
the LAST WORD

THE LIFE OF MARY WYGODSKI
HOLOCAUST SURVIVOR, MOTHER, TEACHER, & WITNESS

Tom Burke

VETERANSCRIBE PRESS
Boston, Massachusetts

Copyright ©2021

Printed in the United States of America
Cover Photo: Matthew Burke
Book & Cover Design by Mary Meade.
Edited by Frances Woods

Evil Must Not Have the Last Word, Tom Burke —1st ed.
ISBN 978-0-57833-409-7

To Mort Wygodski,

without whose love this story

would not have been told.

And to Mary Ellen Burke,

without whose love this book would

not have been written.

"Go home from this place and tell your children and your grand-children that you have looked into the eyes and have shaken hands with people who have survived the greatest cataclysm mankind has unleashed on mankind. Tell them to tell their children and their children's children, because these people will be mourned and spoken about and wept over for 10,000 years. For if they aren't, we are all done for."

—PADDY FITZGIBBON,
On the Occasion of the Dedication
of Irish Shoah Memorial, Listowel, Ireland, 2010

Contents

Foreword

EVER SINCE I was a little girl, I wanted to be like my mother. And I have wanted to be the same kind of mother to my own children that she was to me.

"My little girl yesterday. My daughter today. And my friend forever." That was one of her favorite sayings. And mine.

She had so many wise sayings that I still remember and repeat when I walk the streets at night. I talk to her, and I talk to my family. They were taken away from me so long ago. Blessed be their memory.

"Yesterday is history. Tomorrow is a mystery. And today is a gift."

"You don't criticize other people's children in their cradles."

"The alum is a galum." [The crowd is stupid.]

And many more. I don't know why, but this is one that always made me afraid:

"There is not a bad experience that you cannot overcome."

I would like to tell you the story of my life, of that bad experience that my mother's words foretold.

I survived and overcame what has become known as the Holocaust. The Shoah. As I write this, I have outlived Adolf Hitler by seventy-six years. I have outlived his fellow traveler and mass murderer Joseph Stalin by sixty-eight years.

May their names vanish. They did not defeat me. I am still fighting them. I have lived to tell my story.

My story is mine alone. But it is also the story of millions of people who endured the most monstrous evil ever perpetrated by man. Our stories must be told. The truth must prevail.

Adolf Hitler and Joseph Stalin are long dead. But the evil, the lies, and the hatred that drove them and their minions have not died. They are abroad in the world, in many guises. They will be with us until the last day.

So too will goodness, truth, and love. Evil must not have the last word.

𝒱𝒾𝓁𝓃𝒶

Great-grandfather Rabbi Mordechai Eliezer Kovner,
Vilna Gaon in the 1860s

*J*WAS BORN IN Vilna, Poland, in 1925. The city is now
called Vilnius. It is once again the capital of the country of
Lithuania, as it had been the capital of the Grand Duchy of Lithuania in 1323. It is also the exact geographical center of Europe. French
scientists have calculated that point at about six kilometers north of
Vilnius's Old Town, at 54° 50' North and 25° 18' East.

My beautiful mother, Chasia Suchowski, was born there, too, when the city was called Wilno. It was then a part of Tsarist Russia. My father, Faivusz Tabachowitz, came from Swienciany, a *shtetl* that is about fifty miles northeast of Vilna, almost on the border of present-day Belarus. He served in the Lithuanian army during World War I. Then he came to Vilna, met and married my mother, established his leather business, and started our family. I am the oldest of four siblings and the only member of my immediate family to survive the Holocaust.

Legend has it that Napoleon Bonaparte marveled at the Jewish culture of our city and dubbed Vilna "The Jerusalem of Europe." He may or may not have said those words while on his way to attack the Tsar in Moscow. But Jewish folk throughout Eastern and Central Europe have long called Vilna Yerushalaim d'Lita. Though a relatively small city, it was the nerve center of rabbinic learning and Jewish culture.

Eliyahu ben Shlomo Zalman, who lived from 1720 to 1797, had a peerless scholarly reputation and was better known as the Gaon of Vilna. The Gaon was the undisputed authority on all Jewish religious law throughout Eastern and Central Europe. The Vilna Shas, or Babylonian Talmud, was printed in Vilna in 1886 by the Widow and Brothers Romm.

Jews have been in Poland and Lithuania for at least seven hundred years. The once-mighty Polish-Lithuanian Commonwealth came into being in 1386 when Lithuanian Grand Duke Wladislaw Jagiello married Queen Jadwiga of Poland. In 1388 Jagiello's cousin, Grand Duke Witold, granted Jews a charter of rights that ensured economic opportunities and freedom of religious exercise. Their rights included freedom of transit, freedom of trade, and freedom of financial operations such as lending of money and receiving mortgages on the estates of the nobility.

The Jews were exempted from the jurisdiction of religious and municipal law courts. Their jurisdiction was entrusted to two high-ranking dignitaries, who were representatives of the King in the various provinces and towns. The charter contributed to the increase of Jewish emigration from Germany into Poland and Lithuania. The Union of Poland and Lithuania preserved the charter in spite of anti-Semitic and reactionary objections of the Polish parliament (Seym) and the Catholic clergy.

The lives of Jews were seldom easy in Eastern Europe, no matter what rulers held sway over the country. The Cossack Rebellion of 1648–1658 swept Jews out of Vilna for six years. The Jewish Quarter of Vilna was burned, and most of its inhabitants were expelled or slaughtered, by Russian and Cossack troops in 1655. During the reign of King Jan Sobieski, who was nominally friendly to Jews, riots, killings, and pogroms by Christian religious fanatics were common. Under the last Polish king, Stanislaw Poniatowski, Jews had to pay a heavy tax. Poniatowski was a former lover of Empress Catherine the Great of Russia. The Jews of Vilna supported the unsuccessful revolt of Tadeusz Kosciuszko in 1794–95 and fought against the Russian army in defense of Vilna.

The Polish-Lithuanian Commonwealth went out of existence in 1795. Vilna came under the rule of Tsarist Russia. Before the annexation and three partitions of Poland, there were relatively few Jews in Russia. All at once, Empress Catherine had millions of Jewish subjects. By decree, she created the Pale of Settlement in order to restrict Jewish migration to other parts of her empire. The Pale was roughly the size of the old Commonwealth lands. The Jews came to refer to the area as Lita. The tsars never trusted the Jews. Pogroms against Jews were regular occurrences in many parts of the Russian Empire in the nineteenth and early-twentieth centuries.

Those travel restrictions inhibited the ability of Jews to assimilate into Eastern Europe's wider society. There were three legally defined estates in Russia: the gentry, the peasants, and the citizens. Jews belonged to none of them. We had no voting or civil rights. On the other hand, the concentration of so many Jews within the Pale brought forth a flourishing of Jewish society.

Lita became the heartland of Ashkenazi Jewry. Hassidism and Zionism developed. Yiddish was the vernacular language. The Jews of Lita were known as Litvaks. Along with their distinct dialect, they had a penchant for learning, distinctive customs for cooking, and a sense of cultural superiority.

In 1859, the Maskil and scholar Rashi Fin published *Kiryah Ne'emanah,* a history of Vilna and its community. The book's title means "Faithful City." This is probably where the name Yerushalaim d'Lita came from.

Young people from the smaller towns, shtetls, in the region would come to study at the Rabbinical Seminary or Yiddish Teacher's College. Then they would return to their towns or emigrate to Palestine or to the west. Jews of Vilna took immense pride in their status as a center of worldwide Jewish culture.

Warsaw, with more than 350,000 Jews, was the political capital of Poland. Vilna, with just 60,000 Jews, was the second Jerusalem and the spiritual capital of the Jewish nation that Hitler and Stalin destroyed.

Age Meyer Benedictsen, the Danish historian, visited Vilna at the beginning of the twentieth century. He called the land a "fourfold divided country." He wrote that Vilna had its Russian government officials sent by the Tsar, its Poles once again able to speak their language and longing for past glories, its Lithuanians whose land and properties had been taken away by the Russians, and its Jews. Benedictsen himself was the son of a wealthy Jew. He wrote:

But the busy crowds in Vilna who trade and throng the streets, who hurry and slave are the Jews, for Vilna more than anything is the town of the Jews.

The Jews have been in Lithuania from the earliest time of which we have any reliable record, but they have been neither willing nor able to assimilate with the natives of the country. . . . The many centuries have rather estranged them from the native race rather than united them with the latter, they do not speak the language of the country among themselves, but use their own Hebrew-German dialect. . . . The have neither friends nor enemies nor interests in common with the people . . . they have never been able to make real friends for fear thereby of making enemies. . . .

The Lithuanian Jews feel themselves as strangers, half homeless amongst a people who shun them, their whole existence is one continuous endeavor to keep a position of balance in the easiest way, to find the necessary bread. . . . Humble and wretched as the Jew often appears to be, the pride of race still dwells within him. . . . What does he care for the roughness and contempt of the infidels . . . the Jew still possesses the gold of the soul which can glitter at the proper time, and if one can approach him without any stupid prejudice one can see what is good in him, then the best human qualities, sympathy and helpfulness become apparent.[1]

The Jewish writer Cecile Kuznitz observed, "If Vilna had a specific Jewish geography, it was largely created through the use of a distinct language. While the city changed from Vilna to Wilno to Vilnius, Jews called the city Yerushalaim d'Lita, a name that never appeared on any official map. . . . Some streets also had their own names in Yiddish, such as St. Nicholas Street, known to Jewish residents as Gitkes-toybes zavulek [Gitke-Toybe's Alley]."[2]

To outside observers, though, we were a people that stood apart through our own choices. Such an attitude would make anti-Semitism easy to justify or rationalize. An American Catholic named Robert McBride wrote the following about Vilna in 1938:

In every Polish city, save those of the extreme west, the ghetto is an integral part of the community. In Wilno it is more proportionately an entity than in any other important town. Here forty percent of the population is Jewish and here, as elsewhere, they prefer the seclusion and exclusively racial character of the ghetto to life elsewhere. In these modern days, no attempt had been made at segregation; the Jews prefer to live together in their huddled quarters in the same way as they dress in their orthodox black and allow their faces to remain unshaven. Their racial characteristics and orthodoxy are carefully guarded and they enjoy no social intercourse with their Polish neighbors. Seemingly unassailable, if present customs hold they will continue to remain a race apart and be regarded by the Poles as a foreign element in their community. . . . The Hebrew population in Wilno engages in all the trading occupations—shopkeeping, vending in the market places, and I doubt not, taking in each other's washing.[3]

After World War I ended, and Tsarist Russia was no more, Vilna remained a chaotic battleground and an increasingly dangerous place for Jews. We were there in great numbers but were outside of any political power structure.

In a brief period of two years (1918–1920), the city had experienced a stream of occupying armies, everything from the Red Army to Polish legionaries and Lithuanian volunteers. . . . The Lithuanians claimed Vilnius as the rightful historical capital of independent Lithuania; the Poles rejected such claims on the basis of the cultural and linguistic affinities of Wilno to Poland. The Soviet regime, in diplomatic isolation, voiced its opinion that although Vilna had been a part of Russia, the Bolsheviks were ready to share it with the oppressed people (mostly peasants) of Lithuanian and Byelorussian origin. Nobody asked or wanted to hear what Vilne meant to the Jews.[4]

This was the world in which my parents grew up. This was the world into which I was born.

One more thing about Napoleon. His second visit to Vilna foreshadowed the horrors that would befall us a century and a quarter later. His Grande Armée had initially numbered approximately 680,000 soldiers. Of these, some 400,000 passed through Vilna on the way to Russia in 1812. Students of history know that the French entered Moscow, burned and looted it, then started their long march back to France. Pursued and harassed by the Tsar's Cossack troops and starving in the descending winter, they had lost thousands of men by the time they reached Vilna.

It was on the killing fields of Vilna that the fleeing French army met its last and most devastating defeat. At Panerai (Ponary) Hill, on the western outskirts of the city, Cossack troops slaughtered the ragged, leaderless remnant of Napoleon's legions. That battle, on December 9, 1812, took place in temperatures that dropped as low as fifteen degrees below zero.

There were forty thousand unburied French dead in and around Vilna after the carnage. Only eight thousand members of the Grande Armée who left the city straggled back to France. Napoleon, the little coward, had bypassed Vilna before his army got there. He left in disguise, by carriage, on the night of November 24, 1812, and hastened back to raise more troops for even more wars. He never gave his soldiers the order to retreat from Vilna.

Those mass killings of French soldiers began the infamous history of Ponary. As the Nazi war machine drove into Poland, Ponary became the site of mass shootings of Jews from Vilna and the surrounding towns. Beginning in July 1941, Lithuanian police under German supervision marched my friends and neighbors to the edge of large pits and then shot them, one by one.

By September 1943, when they liquidated the Vilna ghetto, over seventy-five thousand people, mostly Jews, but also Soviet prisoners of war and other political prisoners, had been murdered at Ponary.

My Family

My parents, Fivel (Faivush) Tabachowitz and Chasia Suchowski

M Y NAME IS Mera Tabachowitz. I was called Merczia. I was named for my grandmother. For a while, during my youth, I became Mila Kovner. I will tell you about that later.

As I look back on my happy childhood, I have only one regret. I never learned to play the piano.

My mother wanted me to learn to play. I tried once, then stopped my lessons. The second time I took lessons, I didn't do any better. The teacher told my mother, "She's just not ready yet. Give her time for other things first."

She didn't say that I wasn't smart enough. But maybe I felt that I wasn't. So I did not go back to it again.

I always appreciated music. How could I not? We had a piano, a mandolin, and a violin in our house. My father played the violin. He loved the opera, too. He was always singing or whistling the arias. Especially the ones from *Tosca* by Puccini.

My father's leather business was quite successful. He had started it with the help of my uncle, Yisroel Kovner. The shop was at 13 Klazcki Street in Vilna, not far from our house. They sold both fine finished goods to individuals and raw, uncut hides to other businesses.

But I don't believe that my father was a brilliant businessman. He was more a man of culture, of art and music and religion. Sometimes he would not go into work, but would go off to a ball game instead, and my mother would have to go to the store to watch over things.

I recall one time when people came and took back some of the furniture we had in the apartment. Too many of my father's customers were not paying their bills as promised, and he couldn't understand why. He had bought the furniture on credit, and could not pay some of his own bills. Eventually, though, we got our furniture back.

The Shares and the Millers – my cousins

My father was active in our Jewish community. Every morning before he went to the store, he would read the Jewish newspaper, so he was well informed on events that were taking place around the world. He liked to tease me and share secrets with me. In return, I would not tell my mother when he would sneak a cigarette on Shabbat.

We lacked for nothing material. Our apartment at 8 Niemiecka Street, in the heart of the Jewish quarter near the Great Synagogue, had five large rooms. We had luxurious furniture; we had crystal and silver for holidays and other special occasions. Relatives would often come to celebrate Shabbat with us. In the evening of Shabbat my parents liked to serve our guests tea from our large silver samovar.

My uncle Honah, my mother's brother, was one of my favorites. Before he got married, he frequently came to visit and would entertain us with his mandolin-playing.

Another uncle, Loveh, was a barber. His shop was on the other side of town. It was one of the many stops we would make on Purim while we carried on the tradition of Mishloach Manot. We fulfilled this *mitzvah*, or obligation, as mentioned in the Book of Esther, by loading up our Purim baskets with sweets and treats to be given to others. My mother would pull us through the snowy streets on our sled so we could deliver them. There were many uncles and aunts we would visit in addition to Uncle Loveh. They would give us treats in return, and we'd always return home with more good things than we had when starting out. We waited for that holiday the whole year. It was such a happy time.

Batia and sons Bill and Jesse Share

We had a live-in housekeeper, and later on we had a governess, or *nania*. Our house was not far from the Ostra Brama, the city gate that was adjacent to some large Christian churches. The gate is also a place where Christian pilgrims used to go and kneel on both sides of the street. One time our nania, who was not Jewish, took us for a walk there, and we joined the people who were kneeling down near the gate. My mother was not pleased when she heard where we had been. She had to explain to the nania that kneeling is not a part of the Jewish tradition.

Even though we always had domestic help, my mother ran the household. I followed her about constantly. The kitchen, especially, was her domain. She didn't like me to hang around in the kitchen with her. Perhaps that is the reason that I never became a good cook.

My father had six brothers and two sisters. His brothers Yankel, Meyer, Berel (Borys), and Moshe Tabachowitz died in Vilna during the war. The rest of my paternal aunts and uncles left Poland and its climate of anti-Semitism for the United States in the 1920s. My aunt Sadie married Isadore Greenberg and had five children. My aunt Feigel, or Fanny, married Solomon Miller. They had three children.

When my father's brother Wolf came to America, he married Chaifagel Share and took her last name. They had three children. The other surviving Tabachowitz brothers also changed their surname to Share. Shmuel married Mary Share and became Sam Share. Shimon had been married in Europe, to Batia Malarowitz, before coming to America in 1923. They had five children.

Sam Share and his wife settled in Syracuse, New York. In 1936, these Shares came back to Vilna for a visit. They brought us presents of clothing—suits, dresses, and shoes—from their new country.

Bill, Shimon, and Jesse Share arriving at Ellis Island, 1923

My father also took Sam out to Swienciany, the shtetl where they had grown up and where other family members still lived. It was about fifty miles from Vilna. I don't know for certain why my father didn't emigrate as well, but it was probably because of his business and our comfortable life. The Jewish grownups of that time surely knew all about prejudice and discrimination. They and their parents and grandparents had endured it all before.

But there was no way to predict, no way to imagine, what was in store for us.

Even though they didn't emigrate, my father and uncles and cousins were all Zionists. The Zionist movement, advocating a homeland for the Jewish people, began in the late nineteenth century. Waves of emigration, called *aliyahs*, from Europe to the land of Palestine actually began in 1883. The newly arriving Jews were not welcomed, initially, by the Old Yishuv Jews who were already there.

The Kishinev Pogrom in Russia prompted the Second Aliyah that began in 1904. About forty thousand Jews made it to Palestine over the next ten years. Then in 1917 the British government issued the Balfour Declaration, which endorsed the idea of a Jewish homeland in Palestine. As we will see, the British proved to be more antagonists than allies of Jews despite that first favorable proclamation.

My father was a man of book learning. My mother was a woman of worldly wisdom. She had little formal education. But that didn't matter to me or to any of our relatives. Especially not to my cousins. When their parents didn't understand them, my cousins would turn to her for advice.

My mother had five brothers—Chaim, Honah, Chone, Meir, and Moshe—and one sister, Genia. My maternal grandmother died at birth of another child, and about six months later my grandfather died. A friend named Basia Riva took the baby in and raised him.

I was born in August of 1925. Chaim followed me, 18 months later. I was told my mother got very sick when pregnant with Chaim, her second child. My aunt Genia sat with her twenty-four hours a day, never leaving her side, until she recovered. Genia's hair turned gray during that difficult and stressful time—a most unusual phenomenon.

Chaim was my opposite; he was outgoing, outspoken, and energetic while I was quiet and shy and very attached to my mother. Chaim had a favorite toy, a wooden horse. He would sit on it for hours. One day, when I was about eight years old, I was out somewhere with my parents. When we came home, the horse was on the floor, in two pieces. There were some tools lying around. Chaim told my parents that he had wanted to see what was inside the horse. I can recall my father being quite upset with him.

Another brother, Benia, was born in 1930. His death from meningitis, when he was about four years old, was the first family tragedy that I can recall. For a long time, I did not comprehend what had happened. I did know that Benia was very sick, and my parents sent me to live with my aunt Genia during the last stages of his illness. When I returned home, he was gone. The only indication of mourning was black sheets covering all of our mirrors and pictures.

My mother took Benia's death very hard. Soon after, in 1935, my sister Lila was born. She restored much of the joy that had been lost from our household. My youngest sister, Sala, was born some time in 1939, after the war started. I don't know the exact date of her birth, and I am sad to say that no pictures of her exist.

Vilna was not only a center of Jewish religious devotion. It was also a hub of the printing industry and of book learning within the Jewish world. Jews revere learning and education, and as a young girl I took full advantage of my opportunities. I was good at languages and social studies but I struggled with mathematics and needed a tutor to keep up with my classmates. I loved school. I had thought of becoming a nurse or a teacher.

My school was the Oswiata, which was a private, Polish-language gymnasium. My brother, Chaim, went to Perlman's Heder, a Hebrew school for boys. My parents had first sent me to a Jewish school too, but I didn't like it. I had to repeat a school year and was therefore a year older than my classmates.

The Oswiata would be the equivalent of a high school in America. It was well regarded by Jewish families of Vilna. Vilna also had many libraries and was home to the YIVO, the Yiddish Scientific Institute, which was established in 1925. Its mission was to preserve and teach the cultural heritage of Jews throughout Eastern Europe.

The schoolmates who were my closest friends were Bella Klok and Tanya Fisher. We spent a lot of happy times in each other's homes, and we enjoyed riding our bikes and skating during the winters. We would often spend our holidays at Tilatnik Park in Vilna. Two other girlfriends from the neighborhood were Putzia Katzenelson and Kela Rachman. They did not survive the war.

Bella was an only child. Her father was an executive for a big firm, the Electrolux Corporation. Her mother was a dentist. That was unusual for the times. Bella's mother was the family's breadwinner because the business climate of the 1930s was not good.

Bella played the piano. Unlike me, she took lessons and stayed with it. We sat together in school, on the same bench, for six years. We wore school uniforms, and sometimes the teachers were unable to tell us apart.

Tanya's father owned a large stationery store. The family was wealthy enough so that the parents were able to protect their three children from the Nazis. All three survived the war. Tanya was hidden in a Catholic monastery. Rita, who was the oldest, lived with her husband in a Christian neighborhood. Dora lived for a time with a Polish family, but she became lonesome and returned to the ghetto.

Later, when all of the troubles befell us, Bella and Dora became my new family members. I would not have survived without their love and support; I believe that they would say the same of me.

I want to tell you a little more about two of my cousins, who were both members of the Hashomer Hatzair Zionist youth group. Abba Kovner and Ber Kovner—two more different people you cannot imagine. Both survived the Holocaust and made it to Palestine when that land was still under British rule. Both played significant roles in the establishment of the new state of Israel. I will return to them as my story unfolds, but I want to introduce them here.

I was close to Ber, as our mothers were sisters. Ber was a bookworm. He was my first cousin, the one who most adored my mother and looked to her for support and advice. In order to graduate high school, you had to pass a test. Ber would read and read, to the point where his mother, my aunt Genia, would turn out the light. She said that reading so much would ruin his eyes.

Ber Kovner, before he left Vilna to study in Jerusalem

At first, Ber got a candle and kept up his reading. When my mother heard about this, she insisted that he come and stay with us. He did so, until graduation. But even before the end of high school, he fell victim to anti-Semitism in an incident that probably ended up saving his life. Some of the boys in school, who Ber thought were his friends, beat him up because he was Jewish. They struck him on the head with some kind of club or truncheon that they held in a hard rubber glove. The blow permanently damaged his hearing.

That attack was what made Ber leave Vilna to continue his education in Palestine. His situation was typical of all the Jews in Poland, actually. We could never tell who our real friends were. His parents were also convinced that it would be the best decision for him.

Ber and his girlfriend, Esther Novick, who left for Palestine with him in 1938, planned to work at an immigration farm, study at the University of Jerusalem, and earn their immigration permits upon graduation. Ber's parents were not happy about his relationship with Esther. They had hoped that his leaving the country would end that relationship, but they were powerless to stop her from going too.

At the University of Jerusalem, he studied history. In 1940, he and Esther joined the Communist Party in their new country and eventually became its leaders. They changed their names to Vilner and Vilenska in honor of their native city.

Abba was a few years older, born in 1918. I didn't know him as well as I knew Ber. Abba was a more distant relative; his father was the cousin of Yisroel Kovner, Aunt Genia's husband. Abba was born in Sebastopol, Russia. When he was four years old, his father, Israel, was arrested and imprisoned by the Russian secret police for the crime of conducting private commerce. After a few months his mother and uncles collected enough money to get him released. In 1926, when Abba was eight years old, his family moved to Vilna to rebuild their lives.

Abba was an artist and a writer. His parents would come around to our apartment, and in summer would join us for out-of-town gatherings. Abba was one of the few younger Jews who saw through the

Nazis' deceptive tactics and understood the horrible reality of what they were doing. Abba would become a leader of the underground resistance in Vilna. He barely escaped with his life and led a group of partisans who operated in the forests.

Those summer family gatherings still bring the fondest of memories. Every year we would rent a *dacha*, or summer home, at Pospieszki. It was a resort community about a day's journey away by *droschka*, a horse-drawn carriage with balloon tires for travel on cobbled city streets. We would go there for the whole summer until school began, and many members of our extended family would also rent homes there. My father and uncle Yisroel would work in the city during the week and spend Friday night through Sunday morning with us.

The Kovners, Uncle Yisroel and Aunt Genia, brought their four children: Ber, Mania, Cila, and Mila. Also, there were my mother's cousins, the Sinuks—Pola, Boris, Chasia, and Moishe. The Sinuks all emigrated to Canada and survived the war.

We children filled those summer days with carefree fun: roaming through the nearby forest and picking flowers and berries; milking the cows and goats and drinking their warm, fresh milk; swimming in the sparkling clean Neris River; and collapsing, exhausted, into our hammocks in the forest during the long afternoons.

This was my life until 1939. I was fourteen when it all ended.

No, my first life did not just end. It vanished, for me and for millions of other people. Just because we were born Jews.

My Early Years

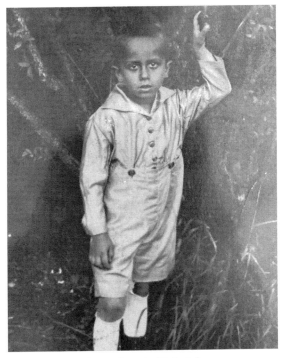

At age four, in Bialystok

MY FAMILY NAME, Wygodski, comes from the Slavic noun "Wygoda," meaning "convenience." My forefathers were most likely innkeepers, providing convenience to travelers in the region of Eastern Europe that was known as White Russia. My great-grandfather's family was from the city of Bobrovsk, which is about nine hundred miles east of Bialystok, Poland.

My mother's family name was Niewswiczewski. They lived on a ladifundium, a landed estate, near the town of Nieswiez in Eastern Poland. The Jewish community there dated back to the sixteenth century. Nieswiez was first taken over by Russia during World War II. The Nazis overran the town when they invaded Russia, and by July 1942 they had murdered all of its Jews.

My grandfather Mordechai, from whom I derived my name, was manager of the ladifundium. He died in the early twentieth century. My grandmother Perl and some of her children, including my mother, moved to Bialystok at the beginning of World War I. Perl took good care of my great-grandfather and raised my mother and her four brothers and four sisters—or perhaps they raised each other. Perl was heavily involved in many kinds of volunteer work and spent a lot of time outside the house. She died in 1917.

Some of my mother's family members emigrated to the Americas between the two world wars. They survived the Holocaust. Todros (Theodore) and Hirshl (Hirsh) came to the United States. Weloc (Wolf) and Heine Feige went to Chile. Hillel went to Peru. Leible, Gershon, and Yankel made it to Argentina.

My grandmother, along with her sisters Shaina and Myrym, all perished in the Holocaust along with their families. So did my father's brothers, Abram and Michael. I survived only because I had gone to Israel in 1938 to continue my education.

I am third from left in front row of this family gathering. My
parents are at the left end of the third row.

Bialystok was a city of about 80,000 people—Poles, White Russians,
Germans, and Jews. The Jews made up about 50 percent of the population. The new Republic of Poland and Russia were in a constant state
of war in the years following World War I. The area around Bialystok
changed hands several times. Marauding soldiers from both sides
used to plunder and steal from the residents. My grandmother used to
keep them at bay by yelling "Fire! Fire!" When I was a child, if people
asked me how did Gramma cry, I'd answer "Fire! Fire!"

We lived in a mixed neighborhood; a Pole and a German were our
next-door neighbors. My great-grandfather Itzhak Wygodski owned
our six-unit apartment house and an adjacent textile plant. It was on
Jana Kelenesa Branickiego at the corner of Electryczma, across the
street from a beautiful park on the grounds of Count Branicki's estate.
Itzhak Wygodski was an ordained rabbi, but he did not practice his
profession.

A family story held that he once helped Polish revolutionaries
back in 1863, and in return he was protected by Polish authorities. If

that was true, it didn't help very much later on. In the 1930s, he was sitting in the park and a bunch of anti-Semitic men came along and cut off his beard. The police did nothing and said that he should not have provoked them.

I was born in a local hospital on January 13, 1919. It was a cold morning. I am the first-born son of David and Tzipeh Wygodski.

My earliest childhood memory was my brother Chaim's circumcision. He was born when I was four. His cut-off prepuce somehow found its way to one of the beautiful plants that we had around the house.

My mother, Tzipeh Wygodski

Not long after that, we had to give up many of those plants. I contracted pneumonia after I had a bout of whooping cough. The Jewish doctors misdiagnosed me and treated me for typhus. I almost died. My mother took me to a Polish specialist, Dr. Levitt. He diagnosed my illness correctly. It took me about six months to recover. The plants were using up a lot of the oxygen in the house, we were told, and so they had to go. We gave many of them to the doctor to thank him for his outstanding job on me.

I guess that I wasn't the most cooperative child. I wasn't the healthiest either. But at least I was a good student—when I decided to be.

When I was six, my great-grandfather insisted that I go to a Hebrew Cheder, which was quite some distance from our house. Walking to school in the cold Polish winter interfered with my recovery. I didn't like the school either, so I refused to go. Then they enrolled me in a Yiddish-language school a few blocks from the house. I didn't care for that one either, so I wouldn't go.

With my brother Chaim, center, and my mother

My father kept trying, and after a few months he enrolled me in a private Polish-language school run by a Dr. Gutman. The age for the first-grade students in that school was nine, and I was seven at the time. The year of my birth got changed, somehow, at registration. It said 1917 though I had been born in 1919. That little falsehood cost me a year later on.

But I did well in school, my health improved, and I didn't mind walking to school when the temperature dropped to minus-ten degrees Celsius. Most of the subjects came easily to me. I especially loved mathematics, algebra, and geometry. By the upper grades, five through seven, I used to solve my math problems at home, as soon as I arrived. I was anxious to keep proving my skill.

I was also a pretty good soccer player, and I liked to read books in my spare time—authors like Victor Hugo, Karl May, Henryk Sienkiewicz, and others. I was less interested in my two hours a week of Hebrew with a teacher named Mr. Shkolnik, but I mastered it and it helped me later when I went to Israel.

Half of my classmates used to come to my home and copy my math homework. The other half went to Sara Narawcevicz's house and copied hers. But despite my good grades all the way through school, the Polish Commission for graduation would not let me graduate after I had completed the eighth grade. I was fifteen and a half, and the minimum age for graduation was sixteen. They would not let me take the final exams, the MATURA, which led to graduation. I had to repeat a year and make a whole set of new friends. It was humiliating.

In the upper classes we wore uniforms and hats, along with colored armbands that had the number of the school. When we entered the seventh grade, the armband color changed from blue to red. I was only fourteen then, and many people used to look at my red arm band with disbelief.

In both the sixth and seventh grade, male students belonged to Army Preparation groups that were similar to ROTC in the United States. At the ages of fourteen and fifteen, I was one of the youngest and smallest members. But I was also a good marksman, so I was not at all out of place.

I am reclining in the front row of this photo of my Army
Preparation Group

After seventh grade, in the summer of 1934, they sent three hundred of us to a three-week camp near the city of Grodno. We lived in tents, performed military exercises, took courses in military strategies, and underwent a fifteen-mile march in full gear. Even there, while serving our country in a military setting, we felt the sting of Polish anti-Semitism. You would see things like "Jews to Palestine" and "Don't Buy from the Jew" in Polish newspapers. At that camp, the night before we all graduated, some of the Poles tried to invade the Jewish tents. We had to fight them off.

During that extra academic year, I fell in love for the first time. Gacia Becer, a plump Jewish girl in the sixth grade, was the only child of Russian-speaking parents. Gacia's mother doted on her and spoiled her. When we were together, Gacia also had some affairs with Gentiles. I knew about them, I was jealous, and that didn't help matters. We finally broke up—painfully—after a year and a half. Later on, her mother died and her father forced her to marry a cousin who was twenty years older than she. Gacia died in the Holocaust.

I went through another rite of passage shortly before graduating. I got drunk for the first time. My old classmates had a party at the beautiful home of a girl named Sally Rivkind. That's another experience that I never forgot.

Vilna, 1939–41

At left, Chaim, Lila, and me with our parents. At right, Lila.

W HEN I THINK back on the many years I have lived on earth, I tell myself that I have led two lives. The first one was the years of my carefree youth in Vilna. The second was my adult years that began when I stepped ashore in British Mandate Palestine in 1946.

So, what do I call those years that began in September of 1939 and ended in August of 1946? A transition? A bridge? A dark valley?

The Book of Exodus tells the famous story of Joseph interpreting Pharaoh's dream with a prediction of seven lean years and a warning to prepare for famine and hardship. Maybe I should think of it in that way—six, rather than seven, lean years when I learned hard lessons that prepared me to face the world alone.

Those years were a part of my life, to be sure. I remained among the living. I learned just how precious life is and just how precious are our family and friends. There were many occasions along the way that death brushed right past me and turned the other way. My son, Avi, often remarks that "the coin kept coming up heads" for me. I will tell you about those occasions.

But I must also say that I did not make it through those six lean years alone. I lost my entire immediate family to Adolf Hitler's band of mass murderers. But I had friends who became my second family. Benevolent strangers stepped in for me at critical moments. So, too, did people who were on Hitler's side but did not do exactly as he would have wanted.

And when I was finally ready to launch my second life, there were more family members—people from my extended family and then the man who would become my husband—to hold my hand and accompany me the rest of the way.

During those six lean years I often felt lonely. At times I felt that God had abandoned me. But I wasn't alone. It has taken me many years to realize that.

World War II began, officially, when Germany attacked Poland on September 1, 1939. Adolf Hitler's planes and tanks and trucks loaded with soldiers overwhelmed the ill-equipped Polish army. They called it *blitzkrieg*, or "lightning war." Conquest was swift and brutal. The Jews of Vilna, and throughout Lithuania and Poland, suffered some of the consequences immediately. We had no idea of what was in store for us, of course.

What happened to us in Vilna during the early years of the war must be understood in context, both of the era's political agreements and of the ancient animosities among the peoples and nations of Eastern Europe. Those animosities always included hatred of Jews.

One week before the attack on Poland, the Germans and the Russians made a compact of thieves, the Molotov-Ribbentrop Pact. They agreed not to go to war against each other and divided Poland into two areas of domination. The dividing line was the Bug River, to the west of Vilna. That meant that Vilna was in the Russian sphere.

Hitler never meant to keep his nonaggression promise to Stalin. Ever since coming to power in Germany he had lusted for the lands to the east: the wheat fields of the Ukraine, the oil fields of the Caucasus, the mineral riches of Silesia. He had orated time and again on Germany's need for *lebensraum*—more and more territory to the east.

As for the people of those regions, he would either enslave them or kill them. But he couldn't have it all at once, so he signed that pact as a way of keeping Russia from going to war against him. If Stalin ever truly trusted Hitler, why he did so is a mystery.

But Stalin was just as devious. He knew that the Lithuanians wanted their former capital city, Vilna. He knew that Lithuanians resented the Poles for getting Vilna after World War I. And so, as part of a secret appendix to that pact, he agreed that the northern frontier of Lithuania would be part of the boundary between the German and Russian zones. Germany and Russia also recognized "the interests which Lithuania has in the Vilna region."[1]

Three weeks later the two dictators amended the pact, giving Russia a free hand to deal with Lithuania as it saw fit. On October 10, the Russians and Lithuania's foreign minister, Juozas Urbsys, signed an agreement under which "the U.S.S.R. transfers to Lithuania the city of Vilna and the Vilna district, which will become an integral part of the state of Lithuania. . . ."[2]

The Lithuanians were overjoyed. They had Vilna back after almost 150 years. It had once been their capital before Empress Catherine the Great of Russia gained control.

Like Hitler, Stalin never intended to keep his word and let Lithuania remain independent. But those agreements in 1939 served a purpose. In temporarily granting Lithuanians power, he unleashed their hatred and bloodlust. The targets of that hatred were Poles and Jews. Later on, after his puppets had done much of the dirty work, Russia would move in. It was not the first time or the last time that Stalin would operate in that way.

In the first weeks of the war, tens of thousands of people fled from the advancing German army. Although none of us had any idea what the Nazis would ultimately do, every Jew knew that German rule would mean extreme hardship. By that time we had heard of their repressive laws against Jews in Germany; of the cruelty toward Jews in Austria once Germany took it over; and of the trashing of Jewish businesses and synagogues all across the country in the 1938 pogrom that they called Kristallnacht. But even the most sober and best-informed Jews, like my father and his friends and associates, never believed that a German conquest would lead to organized extermination.

The German army did not arrive in Vilna for almost two years after the war's outbreak. But our lives changed for the worse immediately.

The Russians invaded Poland from the east while the Germans attacked from the west. When the first Russian soldiers arrived in Vilna in September 1939, Jewish residents were happy and relieved. At least it would not be the Nazis in charge. But that hopeful feeling about the Russians didn't last long.

Some Lithuanians who were anti-Communists and Jew-haters fled west to make common cause with the Nazis as the Lithuanian Activist Front, the LAF. The Lithuanians' feelings for the Jews they'd left behind were quite clear. The LAF published a manifesto in March of 1941, shortly before the Germans attacked Russia. It stated, "Local Communists and other traitors in Lithuania must be detained at once.... (The traitors will be pardoned only if they provide certain proof that every one of them has liquidated at least one Jew.)"[3]

Jewish refugees from cities like Warsaw in the western sector started to arrive by car, by train, and on foot. Many of them had walked for weeks. They were starving. People began to hoard food and water. Food prices rose. The Jewish community, led by the highly respected Dr. Jakob Wygodzki, opened its arms and doors to the refugees.

Dr. Wygodzki was a distant relative of the man whom I eventually would marry. He had been the Jewish community's head and spokesman to the Germans as far back as World War I. That was a very different Germany, however, which occupied Vilna and fought against the Tsar's army.

Dr. Wygodzki and the other Jewish leaders, my father among them, opened up our schools, synagogues, libraries, and other public buildings for use as dormitories. It helped but it was not enough. The population in the Jewish neighborhood went from about sixty thousand to close to eighty thousand. Hundreds of people slept in the streets, in hallways and doorways and cellars and attics.

Medicine was in short supply. So was soap; according to the diary of Herman Kruk, a refugee from Warsaw, laundry was the city's largest enterprise, consuming a half ton of soap per month. I will have more to say about Mr. Kruk and his involvement with my cousins Abba and Michael Kovner in subsequent chapters.

I felt the impact of this new and wretched existence immediately. The crowded Jewish quarter of the city became a frightening, unsafe, and unclean place. I could no longer walk the streets, play in the parks, or go to visit with my friends. I also lost the first of many family members at that time. A typhus epidemic broke out and claimed the life of Mania Kovner, another of my cousins.

Mania was seventeen when the typhus killed her. The family did not tell her mother, my aunt Genia, about it because she was bedridden and very sick with kidney disease. I did not attend Mania's funeral, but I was told that one of her teachers came forward to the casket, put his head down, and wept for her.

The Lithuanians took control of the city on October 28. Russian troops pulled out. But before leaving, they arrested many intellectuals and political activists. Lithuanians, who had been fewer in number than the Jews or the Poles, were now in charge. They had resented the loss of their capital, which they called Vilnius, to Poland after World War I. It was exactly the kind of situation that the Russian devil Stalin loved to instigate. This was not the last time he would be able to pit groups and factions against one another, standing back and letting them fight to the death before he moved his forces back in.

Violence and chaos erupted. Three days of anti-Jewish rioting commenced. The Lithuanians and the Poles hated one another, but they both targeted Jews. Polish mobs thronged the streets yelling, "Down with the Lithuanians! Down with the Jews! Down with the Soviets!"[4]

One Jewish boy was killed in the rioting, and two hundred other Jews were injured. Anti-Semites blamed Jews for rising food prices and the disappearance of bread from bakery shelves. Someone spread a rumor that Jews had murdered a child and a priest. When rioters broke into Jewish shops and trashed them, Lithuanian policemen joined them, beating up the Jewish victims and arresting Jews who tried to defend themselves.

My father and Uncle Yisroel were able to go to their shop, take out the leather and some other goods, and bring them to our home. They hid the merchandise in the cellar.

Dr. Wygodzki's plea to the Lithuanian government to stop the rioting fell on deaf ears. He finally appealed to the Russian commander at

Novo Vileyka, some seventy miles away. Russian tanks rolled in, order was restored, and the Lithuanians blamed gangs of Polish and Jewish youths for the riots.

The Jewish community remained on edge and apprehensive, because riots targeting Jews on November 10 and 11 had become a tradition in Vilna. Back on November 10, 1931, a Polish youth had died after a quarrel between Jewish and Polish anti-Semitic mobs. Each year since then, Polish punks and thugs had assaulted Jewish people in the streets on those days. The authorities did respond effectively this time, however. The Lithuanian Minister of Interior met with all principals of the schools and warned them that police had been ordered to shoot on sight anyone who was disturbing the peace.

Meanwhile, Jewish refugees streamed into Vilna from both the East and the West. The Lithuanians closed the Vilna district borders in November. Zionist youth groups and professional smugglers then helped Jews sneak in. Many of those Jews were abandoned on the way after paying the smugglers. Others were shot by Lithuanian and Russian patrols or froze to death in the harsh winter of 1940, when temperatures often fell to forty degrees below zero.

As difficult as life became for us all, the eight months of Lithuanian rule was still a time of vigorous activity within the Jewish community. Dr. Wygodzki and the Central Refugee Committee coordinated relief efforts and received support from the American Joint Distribution Committee.

Zionist groups like Betar and the Polish Zionist Organization stepped up activities and established a Palestine Office in Vilna. About 550 Jews were able to leave the country for Palestine and other lands before the Russians took over. In June 1940 the Russians claimed that Lithuania had breached the agreements between the two countries. Immediately, they began the process of "Sovietization."

For me and my siblings, that meant an abrupt change in our school life. We stayed in school, but the language of instruction changed to Russian when their Ministry of Education took control of the schools. Because Vilna had once been part of Russia and my mother had spoken Russian growing up, we spoke Russian at home. I had no difficulty in understanding the teachers. I recall my friend Bella having difficulty with the new language and struggling more with her studies than I did.

The teaching of Hebrew, the Bible, and Jewish history ceased. All Jewish libraries were taken over by the government, and any books that did not support Russian ideology were banned. Russian music began blaring from loudspeakers on the city streets. The Russian officers also brought their women along. My mother once said, "They wear their nightgowns as evening dresses."

For my father and uncle, it was much worse. The Russians nationalized—meaning, they stole—all private businesses. There were 102 factories and workshops and 370 businesses taken away from their owners, who were "capitalists" in the minds of the Russians and therefore were considered enemies of the state. Of those 370 businesses, 265, including my father's, had belonged to Jews.

The Russians also evacuated Elektrit, the radio and lightbulb factory, to Minsk in Byelorussia. Elektrit had been a thriving business, producing radios for export as well as for the local population. It was an important part of Vilna's economy. My uncle Meyer Suchowski, my mother's second-to-youngest brother, worked there along with more than one thousand others. Elektrit became the Vyacheslav Molotov Radio Factory and was an important part of Russia's war effort.

When the Russians took the factory away, Uncle Meyer was moved to Minsk along with his wife, Musia, and son, Bernie. We were all very distressed at their departure. But it turned out to be a blessing. They all survived the war and eventually came to America.

The Jews who lost their livelihoods had to find work elsewhere. Some went to work for the Russians who had taken over their former businesses. Others worked for Russian government organizations and departments. My father and uncle, who knew the leather trade, became shoemakers.

The Russians also announced that foreign countries' diplomatic missions in Lithuania would be closed. A final wave of emigration took place before that went into effect in May 1941. About sixty-five hundred Jews who were refugees from German-occupied territories and who had entry visas for countries like Japan, Curacao, Surinam, and Palestine were able to leave Lithuania between March 1940 and May 1941. Many of them received transit visas for passage through Russian territory from the Japanese government. According to Yad Vashem[5], between twenty-one hundred and thirty-five hundred of those transit visas were issued by Japan's vice consul, Chiune Sugihara, against the orders of his superiors.

In June of 1941, just one week before Germany broke its nonaggression pact and attacked Russia, the Russians deported about twenty thousand people from Lithuania to various locations in Siberia. The deportees were accused of being anti-Soviet elements, which meant that they included business owners, intellectuals, journalists, professionals, and other potential leaders. There were about six thousand Jews among them.

On the eve of the German invasion, the Jewish population of Vilna was approximately seventy thousand. The Russian army, retreating from the forces of Hitler's Operation Barbarossa, abandoned their unfinished construction of a military fuel storage facility. At the forest of Ponary, about seven miles to the southwest of the city, they had dug six large pits, from five to eight feet deep and from twelve to thirty yards across. The Russians had planned to install metal tanks there. The place would shortly become, instead, one of the sites of mass slaughter of Jews.

Ponary was also known as Ponar or Panerai. At least eighty thousand, and possibly as many as one hundred thousand people, would be killed there by Lithuanians in collaboration with the Germans. The vast majority of those murdered were Jews. The name of Ponary rivals in infamy those of Babi Yar, Rumbula Forest, Katyn Forest, and the many death camps of the Nazis' Final Solution.

My First Years in Palestine

I am at left in this photo taken on the deck of the *Polonia* on
the way to Palestine, 1938.

AFTER GRADUATING IN 1936, I felt the full brunt of officially sanctioned discrimination against Jews. It probably ended up saving my life because it drove me out of Poland to Israel
a year before Germany attacked and started World War II. But at the
time, I didn't feel very fortunate.

I wanted to study chemistry at Stefan Batory University in Vilna. My father was in the textile business, and that business had good jobs in the paint departments. The color masters, or *farbemeisters,* as they were called, were either engineers or chemists. Most of them were Germans. I soon found out why.

Stefan Batory University did not accept me, but they did take a Polish girl whose math grades were unsatisfactory. I asked them for a written reason why, and they told me there were a lack of openings and a priority for students who graduated from Polish governmental schools.

Later on, I found out that in those years of 1935–39, there was a "numerus clausus"—a limited quota—for Jews entering a Polish University. For Jews who wanted to study engineering and medicine, it was "numerus nullus," or zero. No Jews could study science in Poland. They had to go abroad, to places like France, Czechoslovakia, and Belgium. Another choice was the University of Jerusalem or the Technion in Haifa, in the British Mandate of Palestine.

I loafed around for about two years, living with my parents and tutoring students in math and other subjects. That kept me in money and allowed me to go to parties, movies, and dances with my friends. It was a carefree life, but I was going nowhere.

When students who had studied at European universities came back to Poland, they couldn't find jobs in their chosen fields. It seemed, as well, that another war in Europe was on the horizon. The only way to break free of my stagnant and increasingly dangerous existence was to enroll in one of the Palestinian universities, and to leave Poland for an extended period or perhaps permanently.

My way out was through a Hebrew Tarbut high school in Bialystok. Zionist families sent their children there because it was a feeder school for students who wanted to go to university in Palestine. My parents agreed that I should enroll in the Tarbut school. I also joined La Matarah, "the Purpose," an organization that prepared young people for Aliyah, or emigration to Eretz Yisrael, the land of Israel. I applied to the Technion, the prestigious Hebrew College of Engineering in Haifa, and was accepted for the year 1938–39.

And so my life started to develop a real purpose and direction. I took courses in Hebrew and English and studied up on the political situation. But I didn't totally put aside my wilder youthful indulgences either. While I won't go into any explicit detail about it, I had my share of sexual escapades, one-night stands, and semi-steady girlfriends.

I also became very close with a girl named Razia Rizanska, who was three years younger than I. We spent a lot of time together, and she understood and agreed with my plans to go to Palestine. Breaking with her was hard. I told her that she should forget about me, and with that in mind I never wrote to her from Israel. I regretted that very much.

In September 1938, almost exactly one year before the war broke out, I left for Palestine with my friend Nissah Warrat. I'd known him since first grade. We went by train through Lwow to the Romanian port of Constanza on the Black Sea. There, on the steamship *Polonia*, we met three other La Matarah members from Bialystok: Antek Grodziennsky, Gedik Strychev, and Israel Levit.

I came close to ruining my chances to get a fresh start in life. The last night before we disembarked, I almost got arrested. I'd met a girl aboard ship, and she and I went to sleep together in an unoccupied place. Early in the morning the steward caught us. But luckily, perhaps because it was the last day, the authorities on board let it go.

Even before I became a university student, I became a soldier. On the voyage, members of the Haganah approached us all and swore us in. The Haganah was the Jewish paramilitary organization that grew in response to the Arab Revolt and riots during those years. They trained us in the use of firearms. Within a few weeks we were guarding Jewish buildings and synagogues against Arab terrorists in Haifa. I was part of the Technion Group in the Haganah's Seventh Division.

As members of the Haganah, we had a complex mission. We were illegal, in that we were not officially recognized by the British authorities. But sometimes we cooperated with the British in keeping the peace against Arab agitators. On the other hand, we often resisted the British. They had placed onerous restrictions on Jewish immigration to Palestine. The Haganah organized demonstrations against British rule and helped Jewish settlers sneak into the country by boat.

Nissah and I rented a room from a family named Batochnik at 5 Pevsner Street in downtown Haifa. It was in a safe neighborhood, close to the Technion's original location. Most of the inhabitants of downtown Haifa were Arabs. The Arab markets were close by, along with the Arab night entertainments that included belly dancing.

Haifa's Jews lived primarily on the lower slopes of Mount Carmel, in an area called the Hadar HaCarmel. The wealthier Jews, the British, and a few Arabs lived in Har HaCarmel, on the upper slopes of the mountain. Most of the Jews there were Yekkes of German descent who had fled to Palestine after Hitler came to power.

My Technion class numbered about one hundred students from Austria, Germany, Poland, and Palestine. I usually hung out with the ones from Poland. Our academic days were long, with lectures from eight in the morning to two, and laboratory work from four to seven. The work was pretty intense; it included math, physics, chemistry, descriptive geometry, technical mechanics, building materials, engineering parts, and engineering drawing.

I and my Polish friends had a tough time with engineering drawing and some of the other scientific courses. We hadn't been allowed to take many of those subjects in our gymnasia back in Poland. The Technion students who had graduated from the *realschules* in Austria and Germany had a definite advantage over us.

I soon got into a routine of studying, partying, and guarding Jewish properties in the Hadar along with my fellow Technion students in our Haganah unit. We worked in units of four; two of us would take a watch of two hours while the other two slept in the synagogue and were available for call if needed. The neighborhood was usually fairly quiet. Occasionally, Haganah Headquarters would send a non-student to work with us.

One time, a guy who worked as a mason and was a member of the Mapai labor movement came to relieve me for my ten at night to one shift. Around one we heard a shot. We woke up and found the guy at his post, bleeding from his left hand. He said that he'd been shot by an Arab outside the building, but from the burn marks on his hand I could tell that he had shot himself.

We called an ambulance to take him to the hospital. He recovered and never came back to our unit. A few years later, at a party, I met him again. He was in army uniform and had the rank of colonel in Air Force Supply. I asked him if he remembered me, and he denied it. But he seemed embarrassed, so I didn't pursue the matter further.

Another time, on my way down from the Hadar, I saw a Jewish man running. I approached him and asked why he was running. He saw my dark complexion against my white shirt and thought that I was an Arab carrying a gun. I can't blame him for that; I really did look like an Arab.

One evening while on duty, I saw a girl sitting in the window of a house, in an Arab neighborhood not far from the synagogue. I thought she was Arab, and I waved to her with a friendly smile. A few days later, I met her and she told me she was a Jewish Sephardi whose family happened to live in the Arab quarter. I asked her out but she refused. She said that her parents would not approve of her having an Ashkenazi boyfriend. Sephardis and Ashkenazis did not mix very much because of their origins in different parts of Europe. The Sephardis had left Spain and Portugal after the expulsion in 1492; Ashkenazis had their roots in northern and Eastern Europe, primarily Germany.

I did well in school, except for descriptive geometry. I had to repeat that subject in the second year. Back in Europe, things were getting much worse for my family and former neighbors in Bialystok. In August of 1939, Hitler and Stalin signed the Molotov-Ribbentrop Pact that divided Poland into two sectors. Bialystok was east of the dividing line and came under Russian rule. German troops pulled out of Bialystok, but not before they burned the synagogue and assaulted Jews on the streets.

When the Russians moved in, the people of Bialystok thought that life would at least become bearable again. That didn't happen. Stalin and his minions immediately began persecuting the wealthy, the middle-class business owners, and the intelligentsia.

My own family got caught up in the purges and terror, but at least they survived. My father was accused of being an "enemy of the people" and was exiled to Siberia. He had been the administrative director of a textile factory, working for a man named Leon Polack. Mr. Polack fled from the area before the Communists came in, leaving my father in charge.

Anybody of Polack's rank in society, anybody whose station commanded respect in the community, was a potential threat to Communist rule. With him gone, my father became the target. After a sham trial, they sentenced him to seven years of hard labor. He was shipped off to Igarka in northwestern Siberia to work in the salt mines.

My father used to write me once a week after I left Bialystok for Palestine. After the Russians moved in, his letters arrived less frequently—perhaps every two or three weeks. They were written very carefully, praising the Communist regime while containing hidden hints about what was really going on. After he was arrested, my mother used to write that he was not at home. I found out about his arrest from my grandmother.

I did get one letter from him, postmarked Minsk. It was very short, and said where he was going. It was probably mailed by a Russian Jew whom he'd befriended on the train.

A few months later, they came for my family. In the middle of the night, the Russian security police, the NKVD, knocked on my mother's door. They told her and my brother to get ready within a half hour and take whatever they needed for a long voyage. Why? Because they were the family of an "anti-communist" prisoner.

My mother left the house key with my father's younger brother Michael. After many days of travel by train, they arrived in Kazakhstan, deep in south-central Russia. There were many other Jewish and Polish families there, banished because they were enemies of the state.

Most of the Jews were the families of capitalists, the factory owners and business proprietors. Most of the Poles were teachers, professors, and senior government employees—the intelligentsia. By getting rid of the leaders and potential leaders of the society, Stalin then had a subject population that he could easily dominate and terrorize.

Having common oppressors—Russians and Germans—and a common fate with the Jews did very little to soften the anti-Semitic hatred that seemed to be in the blood of the Polish. Most of them refused to sleep in the same compartments with Jews, and they called the Jews all sorts of vile names.

When my mother and brother arrived in Kazakhstan, they were sent to a *sovkohz* near the city of Pavlodar. It was a socialist collective farm, almost like an Israeli kibbutz, that was owned by the state. They lived in a hut that the Russians called a *barak*. They lived a subsistence life, receiving food and meager clothing for their labors.

After a few months they were allowed to move to the city of Pavlodar, where they rented a small room. My brother found work as a bookkeeper. My mother bought and sold things in the market. One day my brother received a cow from the cooperative; it was a bonus for his good work. They used some of the cow's milk for themselves and sold the rest.

Life was bearable, under the circumstances. They knew where my father was but could not correspond with him. The Kazakh family with whom my mother and brother stayed was kind and helpful to them. That family had three sons in the Russian army, and they felt that if they were nice to the Jewish refugees, perhaps their sons would return from the war unhurt. And so it was. All three of them survived the carnage of the Eastern Front and made it safely home.

Vilna, 1941: the Nazis Invade

My father, third from right, and his brothers Yankel, Beryl, and Moshe

SUNDAY, JUNE 21, 1941, the first day of summer, was the first day of nearly six months of hell for my family and the Jews of Vilna. That is when the Holocaust truly began.

As I mentioned before, there were approximately seventy thousand Jews living in Vilna in June of 1941. By New Year's Day of 1942, mass shootings at Ponary had claimed more than fifty thousand Vilna Jews' lives. There were only around eighteen thousand of us remaining.

Germany broke its treaty with Russia and attacked across the Molotov-Ribbentrop Line that was approximately seventy miles to our west. Sirens sounded throughout the city at ten in the morning. Russian radio announced news of the attack at eleven, and bombs began falling on the city at noon.

Russian forces and many civilians, including Jews, fled eastward. The Russians' departure unleashed the boundless hatred of the Lithuanians. They no longer had to pretend that they were friends of the Russians, and they no longer had to keep from killing the people they despised—Russians, Poles, but especially Jews.

One German soldier's experience on the first morning of the invasion demonstrates the cooperation that the Germans could come to expect from the Lithuanians. Adam Grolsch was the radio operator with an armored unit that crossed the Memel River on the border between German-controlled territory and Lithuania. When Grolsch reached the far side of the river and entered a small town, he saw bodies hanging from the trees. A Lithuanian explained to him that they had already "taken care of things" by robbing and murdering all twenty Jews in town.

Grolsch later said, "They had exploited the situation. 'Hitler is against the Jews anyway. We'll kill them and we'll take all of their stuff.'"[1]

In Vilna, the bombing continued for two nights. We huddled in the basement and prayed that we would be spared. All we could do was wait for what would come next.

And what came next was mass extermination. The Nazis had already decided on it. They had begun to build their horrible extermination camps in Poland: Belzec, Chelmno, Sobibor, Treblinka, Majdanek, and the Birkenau killing grounds at Auschwitz. The building of all these evil places, where more than three million Jews would die in the gas chambers, began in 1941.

Hitler had told the men of his inner circle, sometime in 1941, of his "Final Solution" to the "Jewish Question." He also said that the extermination facilities in the East were not yet built. And so, construction would begin immediately. Until they were ready, Jews would be abused and starved in ghettos and executed by firing squads.

We knew none of that, of course. My parents, and almost everyone of their generation, believed they would be able to endure whatever cruelty and abuses that the Germans had in store. Jews had been persecuted by ruling classes for hundreds of years. We had endured the Russian pogroms. We could get through this, too, we all thought.

If my parents were actually fearful of death at the hands of the Nazis, they never showed that fear to me. They had surely heard reports of what the Nazis did to Jews even before the war started, such as the Kristallnacht pogrom in Germany and the abuses of Jews in Vienna in 1938. They must also have known, from the thousands of Jewish refugees who made it to Vilna after the attack on Poland in 1939, what the Nazis were doing to Polish Jews. But Germany was a cultured and civilized nation. That Germans hoped to kill all of the world's Jews was unthinkable to the Jewish adults of Vilna.

The young people of Vilna soon saw through the lies and deceptive tactics of the Nazis and their Lithuanian helpers. My cousin Abba Kovner was the first to proclaim it. "We must not go as sheep to the slaughter," he wrote on New Year's Eve of 1942. I will return to that part of the story later.

Russian forces and many civilians, including some Jews, fled eastward. Lithuanian soldiers who had been in the Russian army shot at the retreating Russians and began hunting down and killing Polish sympathizers. But it would not be long before the Lithuanians turned their murderous attention to the Jews.

The German army entered Vilna—in trucks, in tanks, on motorcycles. Within a few days of the Germans' arrival, they began to harass and intimidate the Jews. Lithuanian gangs roamed the streets, kidnapping Jewish men and bringing them to the Germans for forced labor. Sometimes they would attempt to seize groups of Jewish men who were on their way to work and bring them to the prison or to Ponary. But the Germans, needing the Jews' labor, would make the Lithuanians release them.

My father's younger brother, my uncle Moshe, was snatched off the street and killed. His wife Katia became very worried about him, but she believed he would come back eventually. He never did return.

Lithuanians also broke into Jewish homes at night, forcing everyone to come outside and then marching the men away. They would help themselves to whatever money and valuables they could find. Those Lithuanians were members of a group called the Ipatinga, which means "elite." They did the snatching and the kidnapping in Vilna and the murdering at Ponary.

Sometimes, the kidnapped Jewish men would return home. More often, they would not. Instead, the Germans and Lithuanians would throw them into Lukiszki prison. Few got out alive; occasionally, their families or friends were able to bribe someone—usually a German—to intervene and get them released. Lukiszki prison became the place where thousands of Jews were held before they were sent to their deaths at Ponary.

My father and brother and my uncle Yisroel were fortunate in those awful early days. They had work permits, and they seldom went out except to work. Their leather business had been closed down, but they were able to find employment in companies that had been taken over, first by Russians and then by Germans.

We lived on Niemiecka Street, a main avenue through the center of the Jewish quarter. On July 8, an order was posted that Jews could not appear on many of the larger streets including Niemiecka, Wielcka, Trocka, and Zawalna. If we lived on those streets, we could only walk as far as the closest corner and then walk down a side street.

We had to endure many other harassments and humiliations. We could not use the sidewalks. When we were walking on the streets, we had to walk in single file. We could not be out on the streets from six at night to six in the morning. Jews could no longer use public transport, public baths, hospitals, cinemas, theaters, coffee houses, and barbershops. Lithuanians also confiscated all radios owned by Jews.

Food became scarce. Long lines queued up outside the stores, and separate food shops for Jews were established. In some places, Jews could still shop with other people, but not until the hours between ten and noon. By that time, the stores had been open for five hours and most of the food was gone. Where there were lines at those shops, the Lithuanians broke them up—one line for Jews, one line for Aryans.

The German military commander also ordered all Jews, aged ten and over, to wear a white armband with a Star of David. Shortly afterward, they changed it to a yellow star. Those who were caught without the star faced severe penalty.

It was around that time that I escaped the first of my many brushes with death. I had gone outside and had forgotten to put on the star. A group of German soldiers saw me and brought me into an office. I was terrified. I cried and sobbed and was unable to speak and answer any of their questions. It was my blue eyes that saved me. Jews were not supposed to have blue eyes. Only Aryans did. At least, that was what one of the soldiers said. "Oh, let her go. She's got blue eyes. She's probably not even Jewish."

As they did in other conquered areas, the Nazis sent in squads of murderers called Einsatzgruppen. These squads were members of the Nazi Schutzstaffel, the SS. The one assigned to Vilna was Einsatzkommando 9. It arrived on July 2. Its commander, Alfred Filbert, told his men that their mission, ordered by Hitler, was to exterminate the Jews as well as key officials of the Russian regime and the Communist party.

Killing of Jews, as well as some Poles and Russians, began almost immediately. One of the first things Filbert did was to organize 150 men of the Lithuanian Ipatinga into a squad that would kill Jews at Ponary. They had SS men to oversee them, but they did the killing. Many more Lithuanians joined Nazi police units and carried out the kidnappings and murders in Vilna and in neighboring towns and villages.

There was an eyewitness to the murders at Ponary. Kazimierz Sakowicz, a Polish journalist who lived near the site, heard shots in the forest and began writing daily accounts of what he saw. He died of a gunshot wound in 1944, but his notes were eventually discovered and were finally published as *Ponary Diary* in 1999. I wish to quote a few of his early entries here. His first was on July 11, when he wrote,

> I discover that many Jews have been 'transported' to the forest. And suddenly they shoot them. This was the first day of executions. An oppressive, overwhelming impression. The shots quiet down after 8 in the evening; later, there are no volleys but individual shots. The number of Jews who passed through was 200. . . .
>
> By the second day, July 12, a Saturday, we knew what was going on, because at about 3 p.m. a large group of Jews was taken to the forest, about 300 people, mainly intelligentsia with suitcases, beautifully dressed, known for their good economic situation etc. An hour later the volleys began. Ten people were shot at a time. . . . Executions continue on the following days: July 13, 14, 15, 16, 17, 18, and 19, a Saturday.

The Shaulists [from Sauliu Sajunga, the Lithuanian Riflemen's association] do the shootings, striplings of 17 to 25 years. . . . Only the Shaulists do the shooting and guarding.[2]

Sakowicz also describes in horrifying detail what awaited the Jews at Ponary. The victims believed that they were being taken to work sites, so they often brought extra clothing, money, and other personal valuables. Once there, they were marched into the forest and stripped to their underwear. In groups of ten or twenty, they were made to stand at the edge of the pits and were shot in the back.

Their bodies were covered with sand. The Nazis took the best of the clothing and valuables and left the rest to the Lithuanians. Eventually, many items of clothing reappeared on the black market in Vilna. Executions went on until July of 1944 when the Russian army arrived back in Vilna.

In that month of July, in a span of 17 days, Sakowicz counted 4,675 Jews, almost all of them men, shot at Ponary. After being snatched off the streets or dragged from their homes, they were first sent to Lukiszki prison. Soon they would be bringing women and children to be killed, but they wanted the men first. Men would be more likely to rebel and resist if they found out what was really happening. Also, those left behind in Vilna continued to believe that the men had been taken away to work and would be coming back.

The Nazis also found a way to make themselves rich. They had demanded that a Judenrat, a Jewish council, be formed. The elderly Dr. Jakob Wygodzki, one of Vilna's most respected citizens, became its leader. On August 7, the Nazi deputy for Jewish affairs, Franz Murer, summoned the Judenrat and demanded a "contribution" of five million rubles. Murer was hated and feared by everyone. He was called The Mem, which stood for the first letter of his name and Malekhamoves, the Angel of Death.

Dr. Wygodzki urged the Judenrat to collect the money. They did succeed in delivering one and a half million rubles in money, gold, and jewels. Murer took it and disappeared. Shortly after that, on August 24, they threw Dr. Wygodzki into the prison. He was in poor health, and he died there a few days later, at the age of eighty-six.

That same day, August 24, a group of four hundred Jewish women gathered outside the offices of the Judenrat to demand that their husbands be brought back from their work assignments and other men sent in their place. The women were sent away without an answer. More than a month earlier, on July 10, a rumor of killings at Ponary reached the Judenrat members. They refused to believe it.

Moshe's wife Katia and daughter Golda

My mother and my aunt Genia were not among those four hundred women on that day because my father and my uncle Yisroel had not been taken; they had work permits. A permit, which was usually a brown slip of paper, gave its holder some measure of protection. Not always, however. Sometimes the Lithuanian snatchers would demand to see a man's permit, then would keep it and take the man away to the prison or to Ponary. Being found without a permit was a death sentence.

Death sentences for many more Jews soon followed. It began this way. In late August, Murer's superior Hans Hingst received an order to build a ghetto in Vilna. The Nazis had done this in several other cities already, usually by walling off the existing Jewish neighborhood. Hingst directed Murer to choose the place for the Vilna ghetto.

That man whom the Jews called the Angel of Death decided that our Jewish quarter would be the place. But he did something that the Nazis did nowhere else. He ordered that the Jews living in a selected district first be driven out of their homes and killed. Then the Jews that remained alive would be forced into the vacated homes before the walls went up.

The Nazis put this plan into motion with another deceptive tactic that became known as the Great Provocation. It happened on the afternoon of August 31. Two Lithuanians entered a house at the corner of Szklanna and Wielcka Streets. They fired shots out the window in the direction of a group of German soldiers. Then they ran out of the house shouting, "The Jews are shooting."

The Germans and Lithuanians broke back into the house, dragged out two Jewish men, beat them cruelly, and shot them. The next day, September 1, Hingst posted a notice that blamed the Jews and the entire Jewish community. It went on to state:

> All Jews, men and women, are forbidden to leave their homes from today at 3 o'clock in the afternoon until 10 o'clock in the morning. Exceptions will be made only for those Jews and Jewesses who have valid work passes. This order is for the security of the population and to protect the lives of the inhabitants. It is the duty of every honest citizen to cooperate in preserving quiet and order.[3]

My uncle, my father, and my brother all were at work and not at home when the raids—the Nazis called them *aktions*—happened over the next two days and nights. The first of those aktions took the lives of three more of my closest relatives—my aunt Genia and her two surviving daughters, Mila and Tzila. Their oldest sister, my cousin Mania, had died of typhus in the previous year. In the first aktion, Lithuanian guards and German soldiers broke into homes on Glezer, Gaon, Strashun, and Szawelska Streets, as well as one side of our street, Niemiecka. Uncle Yisroel and his family lived on Strashun.

When he came home from work that day, the house was empty. Aunt Genia had been sick in bed with kidney disease. She and my cousins Mila and Tzila had been taken to the prison. Uncle Yisroel found that out from his superior at work. The man promised he could get them out and demanded money for it. My uncle paid him every day for a week, but he never saw his wife and daughters again.

On the next night they raided more homes on Niemiecka as well as on Ozmianska, Jatkowa, Lidska, Ridnicka, and Szpitalna Streets. The Germans and Lithuanians first drove all of the evicted Jewish residents—most of them women and children—to Lukiszki prison. From there, they were marched or taken in trucks to Ponary. The Lithuanians first robbed the imprisoned Jews of their money and valuables.

Some—only a very few—of those Jews who were taken were freed by Germans who accepted bribes. Knowledge of that possibility surely was what made my uncle Yisroel pay his boss to get Aunt Genia, Mila, and Tzila freed. We never knew whether that man actually made the attempt, or whether he just saw a chance to prey on my uncle.

The Germans announced that they had executed 3,700 Jews as a reprisal for the Jewish shooting of the soldiers. There were 864 men,

2,019 women, and 817 children who died, shot by the Lithuanians and buried in the pits at Ponary. Many more would soon follow them.

Not all of the women that they shot and threw into the pits died at that time. Most of the Lithuanian shooters were drunk. They killed the men first. Late in the day they began shooting women. Six of the women were only wounded. They lay in the mass grave, naked and bleeding, until after dark. They then crawled out and went off through the forest. A peasant woman took them in, gave them clothing, and let them stay overnight.

Those women made it back to the city the next day. I saw one of them, running down the street, screaming, "They're killing us all." No one believed her. They thought she had gone mad. They took her to the hospital and treated her wounds.

It is hard to imagine, but many members of the Jewish community who remained alive at the time believed the Germans, that what had happened was a one-time punishment. The men also believed that having work permits would protect them. But that awful day was the start of the wholesale slaughtering of all the Jews. Work permits would not matter. The Einsatzkommando had its orders from Hitler: to make Lithuania *Judenfrei*—Jew-free. Their next step in carrying out their leader's orders was to drive us all into the ghetto.

On the evening of September 5, an order went out to everyone who owned horses and wagons to assemble in the lumber yard at six the next morning. This was to ensure that there were no carts or any other vehicles available for Jews being forced into the ghetto. We would only be able to take what we could carry.

The Lithuanian police spread out through the city and began pounding on doors at about six o'clock. They gave us thirty minutes to pack and leave. My mother's brother Chone helped us to make a hole in the wall and hide some small valuable items behind it. The rest of our nice household items we just had to leave behind—my mother's crystal and silverware, my father's violin, family photographs, our silver samovar. These too were valuable, not in themselves, but for the many fond family memories that were attached to them. I remember my mother locking the door behind us and saying that soon we would return.

Like the day that the Germans started bombing Vilna, September 6 was hot and oppressive. We dressed in as many layers of clothing as we could, including our winter coats. We carried a large bag in each hand. My mother carried my baby sister Sala, who was one year old.

Along the way, non-Jewish residents lined both sides of the streets. Some of them were sad, and a few were crying. But more of them were happy to see us go; they jeered and hooted, and some even drew a finger across their necks, as if slitting their throats. Some offered to buy clothing and other valuable items for a pittance.

There were actually two ghettos. Our street, Niemiecka, separated them. Because the houses of Niemiecka were boarded up and not included in either one, we were forced to leave. The larger ghetto became known as Ghetto Number One; it included Straszuna, Oszmianska, Jatkowa, Rudnicka, and Szpitalna Streets. The smaller one, which only lasted six weeks before everyone was killed, was Ghetto Number Two. It included Zydowska, Szklanna, and Szpitalna Streets.

It took all day and into the night for all of the Jews to get through the gates and checkpoints, which were manned by security guards and SS men. They had planned on sending a total of forty thousand Jews into the ghetto and six thousand more directly to Lukiszki prison. During the afternoon the Lithuanians decided that there were too many people lined up to get into Ghetto One. They diverted about two thousand more Jews away from the line at the Straszuna Street gate and to the prison. We were fortunate to have made it inside the ghetto walls before that change of plans. All of those sent to the prison were taken to Ponary and shot within a few days.

We were exhausted, hungry, and thirsty when we finally made it to Uncle Yisroel's house on Straszuna. Our family took one room, at the far end of a corridor near a back wall. We were fortunate that our room had a stove in it. Many other people crowded into the rest of the rooms.

I remember having a great sense of relief. We were all together. We had made it through the Nazis' retribution for the shooting incident. Other members of our extended family were nearby. There would be no more harassments and petty rules. There would be no more snatchings off the streets. All the men in the family had work permits. We could keep to ourselves and survive until the war was over.

How naïve we all were.

The Nazis lost no time in pushing ahead with their plans to make our corner of the world Judenfrei. As I mentioned previously, the Einsatzkommando 9, which was part of the SS, was responsible for that. If they had had total freedom to operate, they would have murdered us all within a year. But fortunately for some of Vilna's Jews, another factor that worked against the murderers soon loomed up.

Germany's forces, the Wehrmacht, drove deep into Russia, and the Russians retreated. But then they began to resist and to counterattack. The Germans, thinking that they would be as successful in Russia as they had been in Poland, had not equipped their soldiers with adequate shoes or winter clothing. Machines and vehicles began breaking down. Rains and cold weather began to set in.

The German military found itself in great need of slave labor to support its frontline troops. They needed tailors, seamstresses, shoemakers, leatherworkers, furriers, and mechanics. Vilna's Jews had both expertise and facilities. The mass killings continued until the end of 1941, but then the Jews who were still alive got a reprieve. The Nazis still were determined to kill us all eventually, but some would be spared so that they could support the war effort.

By the end of Sunday, September 7, there were about thirty thousand Jews in Ghetto One and ten thousand in Ghetto Two. The Nazis demanded that a Judenrat for each one be set up, along with a Jewish police force. They put Jacob Gens, a Lithuanian Jew, in charge of the Jewish police. Gens was soon to become an important figure in the ghetto.

One week later, the Nazis announced that people of Ghetto Two who held work permits, or who were craftsmen or artisans, would be moved to Ghetto One. Orphan children, sick people, and the elderly were sent from Ghetto One to Ghetto Two. Then, on September 15, they announced that those remaining in Ghetto One who did not have work permits were to move to Ghetto Two.

About three thousand Jews without permits responded to that summons and were led out of Ghetto One. Of these, only six hundred reached Ghetto Two. The rest were dragged to the prison and then massacred at Ponary. Murer, the Angel of Death, then commanded that all telephones be removed from the ghetto, all postal services ended, and barbed wire be added to all the walls around the ghetto. The Nazis then waited until the next opportunity to round up and kill as many Jews as possible—our holiest day of the year, Yom Kippur.

That day, October 1 of 1941, 5602 by the Jewish calendar, was one of many sad and bloody days for the Jews of Vilna. In the Yom Kippur Aktion, more than twenty-nine hundred people were seized, hauled away, and murdered at Ponary. It did not matter to the Nazis that many of the men they seized held valid work permits. They needed to report a large number of Jews killed.

The Grand Synagogue in Ghetto Two was crowded with worshippers that morning. The Germans and Lithuanians burst in and arrested eight hundred of the faithful, many of them wrapped in their prayer shawls. After taking their first victims to Lukiszki prison, the thugs returned to Ghetto Two and went house-to-house, seizing and dragging away nine hundred more.

In Ghetto One, meanwhile, the Nazis demanded that the Judenrat hand over one thousand Jews who were without passes. The Jewish police went through the ghetto announcing that those without passes had to come to the ghetto gate. When only a few did, the Germans and Lithuanians began breaking into houses and hauling out everybody they could find. Finally, twenty-two hundred people with passes came forward, with their families, believing assurances that the passes would save them. They were sadly mistaken. All of them were taken to the prison.

My father, brother, and uncle did not believe the lies about the passes. They stayed inside and hid. That Yom Kippur Aktion showed us that the work passes were almost useless. Some of the men seized that day—perhaps about a hundred—were released after their families paid bribes to Germans they knew. But twenty-nine hundred were murdered, and more would soon follow.

Three more aktions in October completed the destruction of Ghetto Two. When people write or talk about it, they call it "liquidation." That is such a harmless-sounding word. It was kidnapping, violence, and murder.

On the night of October 3, the Germans and Lithuanians raided homes and dragged out two thousand people. They first told the victims that they were going to another ghetto to work. But when the Jews saw that they were headed for the prison instead, they sat down and refused to move. That was the first organized resistance, and those who resisted paid with their lives. The Germans and Lithuanians began shooting. They killed 432 Jewish men, 1,115 Jewish women, and 436 Jewish children.

On the night of October 14, the Nazis seized three thousand more from Ghetto Two. One week later, they were back again and took the remaining twenty-five hundred residents directly to Ponary. Ghetto Two was no more. Ten thousand of our neighbors were killed within a span of two weeks.

There were still more aktions to come. They were called the Gele Schein Aktions because they involved a new scheme about yellow-colored work passes. The Nazis announced that all work certificates were canceled and that the holders had to re-register for work. The holder of a yellow *schein* could be protected along with a spouse and two children.

But there were only three thousand yellow passes issued. That showed that the Nazis intended to reduce the ghetto population to twelve thousand from the more than twenty thousand still living. My uncle Yisroel got a yellow schein, but my father and brother did not. They had to stay indoors. During the frequent house searches, they hid in a *melina*. That was the Jews' name for hiding places. Our melina was a furnace in the cellar of the building.

My uncle had already lost his wife and children. So we became his new family. Many of Vilna's Jews did this in order to get some kind of legal protection. He registered my mother as his wife Genia. I was his daughter Mila. My sister Lila was his daughter Tzila. I don't know how they managed to keep baby sister Sala safe. Perhaps she was too small to register, or perhaps she was put onto some other family's pass.

I remember vividly my mother's urgent instruction to me: "You are Mila Kovner. Mila Kovner. If anybody asks who you are, you are Mila

Kovner." Over and over she would say that to me. It worked. I never again referred to myself as Mera Tabachowitz while still in Vilna.

As it turned out, my uncle and those who had work permits were laboring in businesses that became critical for support of the German army. Many of their soldiers were frostbitten, and some froze to death, as the weather turned cold. Their leader had sent them into battle with lightweight clothing. They desperately needed fur coats, hats, collars, gloves, boot linings—anything that would keep them warm.

In mid-December, the Nazi government appealed to all of its civilian citizens in Germany to donate their fur clothing. In Vilna, the Jewish police came round to all homes and ordered everyone to bring their furs to the Judenrat. Anyone caught with a fur garment after that would be shot.

After they issued the yellow passes and after I became Mila Kovner, the Nazis conducted two more aktions. On October 24, when the men were out at work, they made house-to-house searches and apprehended six thousand more people who had no work passes. They all died at Ponary. My father and brother hid in the melina and were not discovered.

Two weeks later, the Germans ordered many of the Ghetto One residents to move to Ghetto Two while they searched the buildings of Ghetto One again. They found and killed about fifteen hundred more Jews. We were not among those ordered to move, and once again my father and brother were not discovered.

There was one more aktion in December when the Nazis seized four hundred more people and took them to their deaths at Ponary. It was called the Pink Pass Aktion. The Nazis had issued additional passes that were pink, then conducted another house-to-house search for people who had neither yellow nor pink documents.

We didn't know it at the time, but the first part of our ordeal in the ghetto was nearing an end. Germany's war on the Eastern Front had bogged down badly. On the Western Front, Britain did not surrender and had turned back the German Luftwaffe in the air war. America entered the war on the side of Britain and Russia. The SS was forced to temporarily scale back its slaughter of Jews. The German Wehrmacht and its need for Jewish labor won out over the SS and its race to make the world Judenfrei.

The aktions in Vilna, especially those in the month of October, had killed many skilled Jewish workers. The SS had gone too far. The following order came out from the Wehrmacht's chief quartermaster in mid-November:

> In the process of liquidation, Jewish skilled workers in armament factory and workshops, who cannot be replaced at present, are being taken away from the Wehrmacht.
>
> I unequivocally demand that the liquidation of Jews employed as skilled workers in the armament factories and workshops of the Wehrmacht be stopped as there is no possibility of replacing them by other local workers at the present time. . . .
>
> This Order also refers to Jewish skilled workers in factories which do not serve the Wehrmacht directly, but perform important tasks for the war economy.[4]

These developments gained a little more time for those of us who remained. Karl Jäger, head of the Einsatzgruppen in Lithuania, wrote in his report:

> I can state today that the goal of the solution on the Jewish problem in Lithuania has been reached by Einsatzkommando 3. There are no longer any Jews in Lithuania except the working Jews and their families. . . ." [After noting 34,500 Jews in three cities including Vilna, he continued] "I intended to kill off these working Jews and their families, too, but met with the strongest protest from

the civil administration (Reichskommisar) and from the Wehrmacht, and I received an order prohibiting murdering these Jews
and their families. . . . The working Jews and Jewesses left alive for
the time being are badly needed, and I presume that even when
winter is over this Jewish labor force will still be badly needed.[5]

So, as 1942 began, I and my immediate family were still together.
Where family love is present, God is present. Now we were living a
life of privation and constant fear, but we could face that life together.
All of the happy times of my childhood had been in the company of
family members. Those times were gone forever. But I still looked forward to a future—perhaps not with a carefree optimism, but at least
with hope.

CHAPTER 6: MARY

Vilna, the "Quiet Period," 1942–43

Cousin Yetta and husband Sachne Klumel. Yetta perished with
their children. Sachne survived, moved to Russia, and was
never seen again.

PEOPLE WHO TELL of the history of Vilna call the year
1942 and the early months of 1943 the Quiet Period. You
might read elsewhere that life "returned to normal" for those of us
who had survived the Nazis to that point.

This is wrong. It was not normal. For me, normal would have meant
walking the streets, playing in the parks with my school friends, cele-
brating our holidays at home with plentiful food, and, in grand style,

spending the summers with our large extended family along the river at Pospieszcki.

It is true that the large *aktionen* throughout the city stopped for that period. Because the Nazis needed our labor to support their war effort, they did not round up and murder hundreds of Jews at a time. But the killing at Ponary did not stop. Arrests and snatchings by Germans and by Lithuanians whom we called Chapunes (snatchers) continued, both in Vilna and throughout Lithuania.

It is also true that several of the things that you find in any civil society returned, at least in some form. These included a court of justice, libraries, newspapers, a theater, concerts, community kitchens, a hospital, child care centers, and an athletic field. The Jews of Vilna found some comfort and diversion from them, even as they worked hard every day and endured hunger, darkness, and cold each night.

There were also two schools in the ghetto, on Szawelska Street and on Straszuna Street. The ghetto's Department of Child Care set them up in September of 1941. I was one of approximately one thousand school-age children who attended. There had been about forty teachers in Vilna when the schools began, but when the Nazis began giving out work passes, only ten teachers got them. Later on, ten more teachers got protection permits from the police, but the majority of the teachers were kept from working.

I went to the school on Straszuna, which was close to our apartment. We attended from nine in the morning until two. We had very little in the way of supplies, books, or furniture. In the beginning, we did not have formal classes. Instead, the teachers just held discussions on various topics. Later on, they had classes in Yiddish, nature, arithmetic, hygiene, crafts, singing, drawing, and music.

That was my last formal education. It was not what anyone would consider normal. But I had always loved school and learning. So I made the most of it, despite the limited resources and the constant oppression and harassment we all endured.

And the Nazis found new ways to oppress us. There were endless rules, edicts, and directives that kept changing and that kept the Jews wrapped in doubt and in fear. They declared that no children could be born in the ghetto. In the cold January of 1942, they reduced the electricity coming into the ghetto. We could have electricity on only between six-thirty and nine in the morning, and after nine at night. Many people were so desperate for heat and fuel that they began to burn any wood that they could find—furniture, doors, floorboards, woodwork, and fences.

I lost eight more of my relatives in early 1942. The extreme cold of that winter took the lives of three of them, but we did not find out about it until spring. My first cousin Yetta, daughter of my uncle Shimon, who was my father's brother, had married Sachne Klumel, a well-to-do businessman. They lived with their two sons outside of Vilna, in a town named Vitze. Sachne had heard of the Lithuanians' snatchings of people in the Vilna streets, and he offered to take me into his home where he thought I would be safe. I and my parents did not think that would be wise.

The Nazis sent their Lithuanian kidnapping squads, and later their Einsatzgruppe killers, out to these smaller Jewish communities as well. Sachne was taken to work outside of the town. He asked one of his trusted customers to look after his wife and children, and he offered the man his possessions in return. He planned to return for them later, and they would escape together.

Soon after that, Yetta and her sons disappeared. Their bodies were buried by snow and were not discovered until the spring thaw. Sachne somehow survived the war. We believe he ended up in Russia and was able to start a new life. But our family never heard from him again.

The other five relatives were killed at Ponary. My father's brother Beryl (Boris) Tabachowitz lived with his wife and three children in the shtetl of Koltiniani, about fifty miles from Vilna. We know that they were swept up in one of the raids out in the countryside, because one day a man came calling on my father. The man had a shirt with Boris's name on it; he had discovered it while sorting the clothing that had been taken from the shooting victims.

The Nazis' methods and tactics divided our community into two factions—the "legal" Jews who held work permits, and the "illegal" Jews who did not have them.

The system of work permits made the Jews who lacked them into second-class citizens. They had to stay in their homes and hide in their melinas at a moment's notice. Being caught without a work permit was a sure ticket to the prison and then to Ponary.

The illegal Jews were not counted as persons when food rations were distributed. The legal Jews had to share their small allotments of food with them. As time went on, jealousies and resentments of those on the other side of the divide grew and festered. For many Vilna Jews, their own survival and that of their families became the only thing that mattered.

My family members had work permits. My uncle Yisroel had the yellow permit, which protected my mother, who was registered as his wife, and my sister Lila and me as his daughters. My father and brother also had permits. They went out of the ghetto to work every day. I don't know exactly what they did for work, but I do remember that my brother always carried his toolbox.

I also worked for a short time at an electric company called Elektrovina. When I was not working or in school, I could walk about the ghetto and meet up with friends. We also attended some performances at the ghetto theater.

The Nazis knew how to make the divisions within the Jewish community wider and to make resentments deeper. They got Jews to enforce their rules and to eventually make life-or-death decisions about other Jews. It was the Jewish police and the second Judenrat that did much of the dirty work for the Nazis during that so-called Quiet Period. Especially the Jewish police.

After the aktionen of late 1941, the members of the Judenräte of Ghettos One and Two were killed. The Nazis demanded that a second Judenrat be established. The members of that group were not like the first. They were not leaders like Dr. Wygodzki, who was respected and admired by all of Vilna's Jews. Rather, they were much more willing to carry out the Nazis' orders.

As I mentioned previously, the Nazis placed Jacob Gens, a Lithuanian Jew and a veteran of the army, in charge of the Jewish police. He built the police force, appointing many of his friends and allies. The members of the Judenrat were his superiors, but they feared him because he had connections to the Nazis. In July, the Nazis declared that the Judenrat was dissolved because it did not act fast enough. Gens was appointed the ruler of the ghetto.

There are those who believe that Gens was an evil man, that he had cast his lot with the Nazis and worked willingly on their behalf. There are others, myself included, who do not view him quite so harshly. Yes, he loved wielding his power and he did not tolerate challenges to it. He was mistrusted and feared. He was arrogant and condescending. On one occasion he attacked a Jewish doctor and whipped him for fifteen minutes because the man did not want to go out to work in the forest.

But as a Jew, Gens tried to show that he was one of us, too. He sent everyone in the ghetto his personal greeting for Rosh Hashanah of 1942. On the eve of Yom Kippur, he came to the Kol Nidre ceremony at the synagogue and wore a *tallis*, the Jewish prayer shawl. After the ceremony, he spoke to the congregation and began with the Kaddish, the prayer of mourning, for those who were gone. He also stated that we had gone through a hard year, that we should pray to God that next year would be better, and that we must be "hard, disciplined, and industrious."

It is impossible to be certain about how much he knew, and when he knew it, of the Nazis' real plans for the Jews. Gens was in a difficult situation. He often had no choice but to do what the Nazis ordered, particularly when they demanded that a certain number of Jews be handed over to them to be executed. There were times when he was able to get the number of victims reduced, or to have "unproductive" Jews—meaning the elderly, the sick, those unable to work, and those without work permits—taken away first.

Herman Kruk, whose diary *The Last Days of the Jerusalem of Lithuania* is the most complete source of information about Vilna during those sad times, had extensive dealings with Gens. Kruk's intense dislike for Gens is obvious from his writings. But Kruk's descriptions of Gens and how we Jews of Vilna came to feel about him and his police are mostly accurate.

Kruk describes the aftermath of a murder trial in June 1942. Six Jews were convicted and hanged. Gens delivered the following message. It showed his Nazi masters that he was willing to be ruthless in his dealing with us:

Police, Judenrat

Of 75 thousand Vilna Jews 16 [thousand] remain. These 16 must be good, honest, hard-working people. Anyone who is not will end up the same as those who were sentenced today. We will punish every such case and will kill with our own hands.

Today we carry out an execution of six Jewish murderers who killed Jews. The sentence will be carried out by the Jewish police, who protect the ghetto and will go on protecting it. The police will carry out the sentence as its duty.

We begin! [1]

Gens constantly preached "Work to Live." He believed that if the Jews of the ghetto could show that through their labor they were essential to the German war effort, then perhaps at least some of us could survive. But Gens was sadly mistaken. When the Nazis were ready to liquidate the ghetto and no longer needed him, they accused him of a made-up offense and shot him.

The Jewish police were widely disliked and came to be hated more and more as time went on. But we had no choice but to deal with them. Anyone who held a permit of any sort—a work permit, a pass to leave the ghetto, a permit to walk around the ghetto in the afternoon, or any other protective document—had to register with the Jewish police.

It was easy to see why many people thought that the Jewish police were willing collaborators with the Nazis. When the Germans put out their appeal for "voluntary" collections of fur for their soldiers on the Eastern Front, it was the Jewish police who came house-to-house to look for the fur garments. Once inside, they often helped themselves to other valuable items.

Many of the policemen were corrupt, using their power to enrich themselves. They would catch Jews and fine them for petty offenses such as having a light on after dark or for heating an electric teapot. Jews paid a fine for not having all corners of their Star of David patch sewn precisely on their clothing. If you were late for a meeting with the police, or if you were out on the street after seven at night, you paid a fine. The police would keep the money.

As of September 1942, according to Kruk's diary, about nine thousand people left the ghetto to go to work each day. On the outside, they often had access to additional food. The Jewish police would confiscate food that Jews returning to the ghetto from work were attempting to smuggle in. The police were always much better fed than the rest of us.

The Nazis wanted the Jews of the ghetto to be hungry, all the time. Smuggling food in was punishable by imprisonment or death. If SS men happened to be on duty at the ghetto gates, no one would dare try it. There were times when Franz Murer showed up at the gate and beat or shot a Jew on the spot for attempted food smuggling.

Kruk called Murer "the Haman of the ghetto," which is a reference to the evil, Jew-hating vizier in the book of Esther. Murer often berated the Jewish police for not being thorough enough or cruel enough. And there were those among the police who, deciding to impress him, obeyed him with a vengeance.

In one notorious incident, a captain of the gate guard named Levas seized a kilo of peas and a piece of bread from an elderly woman named Mrs. Trocka. He beat her so severely that he knocked out one of her eyes. Then he claimed that she had fallen and struck her eye on the door latch.

On another occasion, Gens brought Murer to inspect the athletic field. Murer entered the bathhouse next to the field, where many of the Jewish women happened to be bathing. Seeing so many of them naked, he announced that they were too fat and should be sent out of the ghetto to work.

Gens was present with Murer, and he just grinned and said nothing. But he did his own harassing as well. He announced that the women who left the ghettos to work were too elegantly attired, with modern hairdos, hats, and lipstick. He ordered the gate guards to detain those women, and he forbade the wearing of lipstick.

There were many other indignities and insults directed at the Jewish women. Several who had been intimate with German military men were arrested and jailed for the crime of *Rassenschande,* or racial shame.

Not all of the Jewish policemen took the smuggled food away from those entering the ghetto gate. Some of them would pretend to inspect people's clothing and pockets, and then allow them to slip by with the precious extra food. Others provided advance information about raids and surprise inspections for people without work passes.

This was life in the Quiet Period of the Vilna ghetto. Our family endured our hardships and humiliations. We had few changes of clothing. We only had what we were able to carry when they forced us out of our home, so we washed and wore the same clothes for nearly two years. But at least we were together as a family.

My mother was always optimistic, telling us that this will pass and we will be back in our home soon. And we hoped and prayed for Germany's defeat in the war. In his diary, Kruk wrote, "As a Jew counts the days of the Omer [after Passover], so we count the kilometers and every sort of movement of the Germans and . . . the Russians."[2]

There were encouraging signs. We heard that the Russian army had begun to push back, and that they were fifty kilometers from the border of Latvia in early January. In March, Russian planes dropped bombs on Vilna and dropped leaflets urging the population to hold out. Britain had beaten the German Luftwaffe in 1940 and did not make peace. America entered the war in December 1941. The Germans were defeated in Africa.

We had no way of knowing, however, that the turning of the tide of war against the Nazis had no effect on Germany's plans for the Jews. If anything, it made them pursue those plans even more fanatically.

Hitler and his henchmen had already decided that their Final Solution was to kill us all. They had begun constructing their killing camps in 1941—Belzec, Sobibor, Chelmno, Treblinka, Majdanek, Birkenau—where they would murder thousands of Jews every day in the gas chambers.

History books tell of the Wannsee Conference in January 1942. Adolf Eichmann delivered a report that enumerated where the Jews were, country by country. Reinhard Heydrich, second in command of the SS under Heinrich Himmler, reported that the SS was responsible for that Final Solution.

As I mentioned before, most of the Jews of Vilna did not believe that this would happen, that the Nazis truly intended to murder every last Jew in Europe. But one who did understand what they were all about was my relative, Abba Kovner. He was the first in Vilna to comprehend, and then to proclaim, that Vilna was not the only place where the Nazis would kill all the Jews. They planned to do it everywhere. The Jews must fight back.

My Kovner Relatives

Abba Kovner

T THIS POINT in my story, I want to tell you more about my relatives: Abba Kovner; his older brother, Gedalia (Genia); and his younger brother, Michael. Their lives touched mine directly only a few times in the awful months of 1942–43 leading up to the final liquidation of the Vilna ghetto. But their stories from that time—what they did to resist the Nazis, how two of them managed to survive, and more about my Kovner family—belong here with mine.

Abba Kovner

One night in December of 1941, some Jews who had sneaked out of the ghetto to forage for food in the forest came upon a teenage girl named Rosa. She was naked, covered with bruises and blood, and had been walking around for two days. She told them that she had seen the Jews of Vilna murdered in the forest at Ponary.

The Jews who found her brought her to Jacob Gens. He did not believe her story—that she had been transported to Ponary, stripped of her clothing, lined up on the edge of a pit with nine others, and shot from behind; that she had fallen into a heap of hundreds of bodies, waited until the guards left after dark, and climbed out and through the barbed wire fence. Believing she was insane and not wanting to spread panic, Gens told her to tell no one. He sent her to the hospital where, heavily sedated, she told her story to members of the Hashomer Hatzair—the Zionist-Socialist movement also known as the Young Guard—who worked there.

One of those young Jews was Vitka Kempner. A few nights later, her colleagues of the Young Guard sent her out of the city to a Catholic convent. Her mission was to find Abba Kovner, the group's leader, who was in hiding at that convent along with about twenty others, and to tell him that it was time for him to return to the ghetto.

Abba told the convent's superior, a remarkable and courageous woman whose religious name was Mother Bertranda, that he must leave immediately. On New Year's Eve of 1941 he wrote and issued his famed manifesto that began, "Let us not go as sheep to the slaughter."

Abba, who was a distant relative of mine, was the first Jew to state publicly and directly what many of the Jews of Lithuania had come to understand intuitively—the full scope of what the Nazis were doing. The brutality and murders were not happening just in Vilna. They intended to kill all Jewish people. There was no alternative but to fight back.

His family's roots can be traced back to 1648 in Kovno, Lithuania—hence the name Kovner. One of our most prominent ancestors was Rabbi Mordechai Eliezer Kovner, who in the 1860s earned the highest title attributable to a rabbinical scholar, the Vilna Gaon. Abba's father, Israel, was a cousin to my aunt Genia's husband. Around the beginning of the twentieth century, Israel Kovner moved to Sevastopol in the Crimea along with two brothers and a sister. Lithuania was then part of Tsarist Russia, and educational opportunities for Jews were severely limited.

Abba was born in Sevastopol in 1918. His branch of the Kovner family prospered in business. His uncle Shalom was an expert appraiser of antique jewelry, including that of the Russian Crown. But that prosperity did not last. His father was thrown in jail by the Russian secret police when Abba was four years old. After the Russian Revolution and civil war, private commerce was forbidden and the "bourgeoisie" had to pay heavy fines.

Israel's wife and siblings collected a large sum of money and got him released. But there was no future in Russia, either for business-people or for Jews, so they moved back to Lithuania and rebuilt their fortune. Israel became well known for his generosity, especially to students of the Tarbut Gymnasium, the elite Hebrew school. He died suddenly, of tuberculosis, in 1928. The family's fortunes went into decline and Abba's mother Rachel (Rosa) opened up a small restaurant to earn her living.

From age twelve to seventeen, Abba attended the Gymnasium and excelled as a student. He left that school in 1935 and took to studying on his own. Vilna, the Jerusalem of Europe and seat of Jewish learning and culture, was an ideal place for him. He spent many long days studying philosophy, history, and the Talmud in the Strashun Library near the Grand Synagogue. He also began writing poetry, and he became passionately involved with Hashomer Hatzair.

That Zionist-Socialist movement's Vilna chapter was founded in 1920. They stressed personal fulfillment through becoming a kibbutz member and the building of a socialist society in Eretz Israel. The group organized scouting trips and folk dancing, and it used them along with flags and symbols to enforce its norms of behavior and morality.

Historian Dina Porat writes of Hashomer Hatzair: "It formed cohesive groups that were emotionally close to a leader whose authority and personal example were decisive and who was at once a father figure and teacher imparting knowledge and ideological values."[1]

Abba, whose name means "father" in Hebrew, became that leader. When the Russians took over Vilna in 1940, after the brief period of Lithuanian rule, they began to destroy all parts of the society that were non-Communist. Abba and his colleagues knew that Hashomer Hatzair would be declared illegal, so they ceased their public activities and broke up into individual cells of five people. This was the beginning of the youth underground movement in Vilna. They continued to study Hebrew and tried to assist those who wished to emigrate to Palestine before the Russians closed the borders in March 1941.

Abba would survive the war and remain an inspiring, though controversial, figure in the new state of Israel. Vitka Kempner would be his lifelong companion. I would see both of them and Genia again, in Israel. Another cousin, Klara Bar, survived and entered my life again in Israel. My first cousin Ber Kovner, to whom I was much closer during my youth, had already emigrated to Palestine four years earlier.

But that all lay in a future that was a long way off for all of us. When the Nazis broke their treaty with Russia and invaded in July

1941, the SS and Lithuanians began snatching and kidnapping Jews immediately. Abba witnessed a brutal example of what was in store for Vilna's Jews at that time. Hiding in a stairwell during one of the aktionen, he saw a German soldier seize an infant from its mother's arms, swing it around, and dash its head against a wall.

In July of 1941, several of the Hashomer Hatzair members persuaded Abba to take refuge in the Dominican Convent of the Little Sisters, which was about four miles from Vilna. Two Catholic members of the Polish Scout Movement, Jadwiga Duziec and Irena Adamowicz, arranged the accommodations with Mother Bertranda. It was a returned favor; Hashomer Hatzair had found them a hiding place in Vilna when the Germans invaded.

In October, when the aktionen were raging in Vilna, Abba's mother, Rosa, and his brother Michael fled out to the convent along with Sala (Sulamit), the four-year-old daughter of Abba's brother Genia and his wife, Neuta. Rosa became the convent's cook. Abba, Michael, and the other men worked in the fields and with the animals. Michael and Abba slept in the cow shed. Mother Bertranda also used her connections in the local Catholic community to get documents and money for the Jews and to arrange for hiding places for their relatives in the city.

For close to six months, Abba and his colleagues stayed in the convent. The visit by Vitka Kempner, with news of the teenage girl Rosa and her survivor's account of Ponary, made his immediate return to the ghetto an urgent matter. But there were other reasons that his time there could not last. The Germans, aware that convents and monasteries had been sheltering Jews, had launched an anti-Catholic campaign. Mother Bertranda decided that she had to shut down her convent and disperse its inhabitants.

Still, she was reluctant to let the Jews that she was harboring go back to the ghetto. She accompanied them to the gate, but the guards recognized her and would not let her in. She did return once more, a few weeks later, saying that "God is in the ghetto." This time, rather than wearing her religious habit, she was dressed in ragged clothing that had the yellow Star of David sewn on it. She asked if she could stay with them. Abba once again persuaded her to go back to the convent.

But she left him a gift. Concealed beneath her clothing she had three hand grenades. Abba had previously asked her to use her connections to get guns and weapons, and she had always refused. The grenades were the first explosives in the arsenal that Abba knew he would need to equip those who would organize and fight in the resistance.

Mother Bertranda survived the war. She and her sisters continued to shelter Jews in their convent. It was disbanded at last in 1943. She spent some time in a labor camp, but was not killed by the Germans. After the war she left her religious order and lived under her Christian name, Anna Borkowska. She told her order's superior that she could not continue a life in service to a God who allowed human beings to be treated in the way she had witnessed.

On New Year's Eve, December 31, 1941, Abba called a meeting in the soup kitchen at 2 Strashun Street in the ghetto. Many young people from other Jewish groups in addition to Hashomer Hatzair were present. He urged them all to cast aside their hopes and illusions that the people who had been seized from the ghetto were in a different city or camp.

It was the first known time that anyone had dared to say that the roundups, imprisonments, and transports to Ponary that they witnessed were not local events. Rather, they were part of an organized program of extermination planned by Adolf Hitler and the Nazi leadership.

The following is the full text of Abba Kovner's manifesto, translated by historian Dina Porat:

Let us not go as lambs to the slaughter!

Jewish youth, do not believe the perpetrators. Of the 80,000 Jews of the "Jerusalem of Lithuania," only 20,000 have remained. We saw how
They tore us from our parents, brothers, and sisters.

Where are the men, hundreds of whom were kidnapped by the Lithuanian "Chapunes"?

Where are the naked women, and the children, driven away
On the horrible Provocation night?

Where are the Day of Atonement Jews?

Where are our brothers from the second ghetto?

All those forced out of the ghetto never returned.

All the roads of the Gestapo lead to Ponar, and Ponar is death!

Throw away illusions. Your children, husbands, and wives are all dead.
Ponar is not a camp—everyone was shot there.

Hitler has plotted to murder all of the Jews of Europe. The Jews of
Lithuania are doomed to be first in line.

Let us not go as lambs to the slaughter!

True, we are weak and helpless, but the only answer to the hater is resistance!

Brothers! Better to fall as free fighters than live at our murderers' mercy!

Resist! Resist to the last breath.

The 1st of January, 1942. Vilna, in the ghetto.[2]

Abba's speech and manifesto that evening fired up the young people and inspired them to prepare for an armed rebellion. But they were not ready. They needed weapons. They needed training. And they needed allies. So those who had work permits went on with their day jobs, while those who did not have permits stayed in hiding.

Late in January 1942, Abba received a note that read, "We should meet." It was from Isaac Wittenberg, the head of the local Communists. Though the Communists had been the Zionists' enemies, they were both the enemies of the Nazis. Wittenberg brought Joseph Glazman to the meeting. Glazman was the head of Betar, a right-wing Zionist organization. Glazman was then a member of the Vilna Jewish police.

The three men agreed to put aside their differences and join forces as the Fareinikteh Partinzaner Organizatzich (United Partisan Organization, or FPO). They decided that they would acquire weapons, train fighters, sabotage the German war effort, and spread the word of resistance to other Jewish ghettos. They took code names for themselves. Wittenberg was Leon; Glazman was Abraham; Abba was Uri.

Wittenberg, fifteen years older than Abba and more experienced at organizing, was named the FPO's first leader. Glazman and Abba were his deputies. They sent couriers with copies of Abba's manifesto to the Jews in the ghettos of Bialystok and Warsaw.

The Jews of both the Warsaw and Bialystok ghettos eventually fought back against the Nazis. Warsaw Jews resisted at a deportation call in January 1943, and then organized a ghetto-wide stand in a month of desperate fighting from April through May. Members of both Hashomer Hatzair and Betar were among the leaders. In Bialystok, resistance came in August of 1943. News about the Jews of Warsaw influenced the increasingly repressive measures taken by both Gens and the Nazis in Vilna in the months before they liquidated the ghetto.

The histories of the desperate battles in Warsaw and Bialystok are well told elsewhere and are not required in my story. But I wish to make two points about them.

First, I recall the prejudice directed against me and other Holocaust survivors once we made it to Eretz Israel and started to build our new lives. Much of that prejudice, even from fellow Jews, came from ignorance. They looked down upon us because they believed that we had done nothing to resist the Nazis, that we should have fought back.

Within a year or two, that attitude began to change as the truth came out. But the change came slowly, and the lingering prejudice was hurtful and hard for me to deal with. Those who disdained us had neither any idea of the agonizing choices we faced, nor an understanding of the overwhelming odds against us. I will return to this topic of confronting that prejudice when I tell you about beginning my second life in the land of Israel. But the Jews did resist. The history should be clear about it.

Second, an organized uprising like the one in the Warsaw Ghetto was the goal of Abba Kovner and the FPO. Abba's strong and unmistakable warning about the Nazis' true intentions undoubtedly helped to motivate the Jews of Warsaw to organize and fight. That did not happen in Vilna.

News about the Jews of Warsaw influenced the increasingly repressive measures taken by both Gens and the Nazis in Vilna in the months before they liquidated the ghetto. But even though they were not able to arouse enough of the Jews of Vilna to mount a full-scale uprising, the FPO did have some successes during the last months of the Vilna ghetto's existence. Some FPO members, including Abba, escaped to the forest and lived to fight on.

Training the FPO fighters was one of Abba's primary duties. He instructed them in how to make homemade bombs and in how to fire the guns that the FPO was able to steal from the Germans or buy from underground organizations on the outside. Both his older brother, Genia, and his younger brother, Michael, were FPO members.

Some of the most effective FPO fighters were the young women. They also served as messengers and couriers, because they were less conspicuous than men. Because they were not circumcised, they also were not as easily identified as Jews as were the men.

I was seventeen at the time. Abba came to our room in the ghetto one day and asked me to join the FPO. He mentioned the forest. He probably wanted me to be one of his messengers, but I don't recall what else he said about what he had in mind for me. But I did not want to leave my family behind. I declined.

That messenger duty was perilous. In October 1942, a Jewish policeman told Abba of the Nazis' plans for an aktion in Ozmiana, a shtetl about thirty miles from Vilna. He sent a girl named Liza Magun to warn them. She walked through the forest, met with Jews on the streets, and urged them to flee with her. Only a few of them believed her.

Liza returned to the town and pleaded with its leaders. When she was there, the German Security Police and Jewish police arrived. They rounded up 406 of the town ghetto's 4,000 Jews, transported them four kilometers into the forest, and shot them. Liza was never heard from again. To honor her memory, the FPO made its emergency command, the summons to prepare for battle, "Liza is calling."

The most dramatic of the FPO's acts of sabotage came one evening in July of 1942. Abba once again chose a woman for the mission: the same Vitka Kempner who had summoned him back to the ghetto.

Using instructions from an old Russian military manual, Abba built a bomb. He sent Vitka out of the ghetto to plant it where it could wreck one of the Germans' military trains. Vitka had been scouting along the train tracks for two weeks before she found the perfect spot: a trestle across a gorge twelve miles from Vilna.

The train, carrying troops and supplies to the Russian front, tripped the bomb's detonator and set off the blast. The engine toppled into the gorge. Vitka and her companions, two boys and a girl, threw homemade grenades at the soldiers before retreating into the forest. The Germans did not pursue them, but they fired pistols and a machine gun in their direction and killed the other girl. Vitka buried her in the forest.

The explosion was far enough from the city so that the Germans blamed Polish partisans and did not suspect the Jews. Wittenberg learned though his sources that over two hundred German soldiers had been killed. It was the first successful act of sabotage in Occupied Europe. They sent the SS into the nearest Polish town and killed sixty peasants.

Through the fall and into the winter of 1943, the city was relatively quiet. The German military needed the slave labor of the Jews who had work permits. Word began to filter in about more Russian gains and German losses on the Eastern Front. It seemed to many that the "Work to Live" preachings of Gens might actually be correct, and that as long as the Jews of Vilna could be productive workers, they would be safe.

Abba and the FPO leaders never believed that. They continued to recruit fighters and to smuggle in guns and explosives, hiding them in cellars and using the city's network of sewers for storage and as passageways. But it was getting harder for Abba to convince his fellow Jews that it was only a matter of time before the Germans liquidated the ghetto and killed them all. The majority of them preferred to work and wait for the Russian army to arrive, rather than to rise up and face almost certain death.

Jacob Gens knew of the FPO's existence and that its members had been acquiring guns. He did not attempt to break it up or to arrest any of its leaders, as long as the city remained quiet and work for the German Wehrmacht proceeded.

The tranquility did not last. Out to the east and unknown to us at the time, the three extermination camps at Belzec, Sobibor, and Treblinka, were already in full operation, each day killing up to fifteen thousand Jews, who were shipped in by train from ghettos in Poland. In Warsaw, the rebellion lasted a month, but it ended in May with the ghetto's total destruction.

Joseph Glazman, one of the three FPO leaders and still a member of the Jewish police, refused a Gens order to go with the police and help to liquidate a ghetto in one of the small rural towns. Glazman believed, correctly as it turned out, that there would be more killings, as there had been at Ozmiana. Gens tried to have him arrested in the ghetto, but FPO members attacked the Lithuanian guards and freed him. Gens summoned Abba and Isaac Wittenberg and demanded that they turn Glazman over to him. He could not be seen as losing control, or the Nazis would replace him.

After a tense negotiation, Abba and Wittenberg agreed to turn Glazman over. Gens told them that he actually agreed with some of their sentiments, but that he did not want to give the Germans any excuse to kill them. He promised that Glazman would be allowed to return after two weeks at a labor camp in Rzesza, about ten miles away. Gens kept that promise and a crisis was averted temporarily.

But soon came that crisis, the Wittenberg Affair. It would be the final proof to Abba that his wish for the Jews of Vilna to rise up en masse and fight would not come true.

The German Gestapo had heard of a Communist leader nicknamed the Lion. That was Wittenberg, the FPO leader with code name Leon. The Gestapo arrested a young Communist named Kozlowski and tortured him until he broke and gave them Wittenberg's name. The Germans demanded that Gens deliver Wittenberg to them.

Gens summoned Wittenberg, Abba, and Glazman to a midnight meeting. German SS soldiers burst in and arrested Wittenberg. Gens told Abba and Glazman that if he had not betrayed them as he did, the entire ghetto would be burned down. But that was not the end. An FPO scout in the street had seen the SS soldiers approaching. He whispered into many ghetto doorways and windows, "Liza is calling."

By the time the two SS men were marching Wittenberg through the ghetto street, Jews were waiting for them. They attacked the soldiers and freed Wittenberg. Vitka Kempner dressed him in a peasant dress, wrapped a scarf around his head, penciled his eyebrows and lipsticked his lips. They walked through crowds of Jews angry about the escape, and got away. Even Abba and Glazman did not know where Vitka hid him.

The next morning, Germans surrounded the ghetto with tanks, trucks, and machine guns. Gens summoned Abba and demanded Wittenberg. If he was not turned in, alive, for questioning, the Germans would destroy the ghetto. Abba refused.

That evening Gens took his case to the people. He sent his Jewish police throughout the ghetto, shouting that the ghetto was in danger and to assemble in the yard of the Jewish council. All the leaders of Vilna Jewry came. Gens told them that the Germans only wanted one

Communist. He warned them that the stubbornness of a few people in the underground was endangering the entire ghetto.

Abba met one final time with rabbis and other elders of the community. He pleaded with them to stand and fight, but they insisted that Gens should be trusted. They believed that handing Wittenberg over would save the remaining Jews of Vilna. Out in the streets, a mob of Jews of all ages began to riot, egged on by a group of Jewish gangsters called Di Shtarke, the strong ones, that Gens sometimes used to do his dirty work.

Knowing that he was beaten, Abba asked Vitka Kempner to take him to Wittenberg.

The three FPO leaders knew that the majority of Vilna's Jews were against them. Wittenberg agreed to surrender himself to Gens, so that the Gestapo would again be assured that Gens was working with them. Wittenberg gave Abba his gun and appointed him FPO leader.

Gens put Wittenberg into a cell for the night. He also gave him a capsule of prussic acid to hide in his ear and take if the anticipated interrogation was too brutal. But that interrogation never happened. Wittenberg swallowed the prussic acid and was found dead the next morning.

Things moved very quickly after that. Abba knew that there would be no Warsaw-type uprising. He also knew that it was only a matter of time before the Nazis would kill all of Vilna's remaining Jews. He decided to begin sending his fighters to the forest, in small groups at first, but about two hundred in all. He would stay in the ghetto until the end along with Vitka Kempner and Ruzhka Korczak, another of his best female fighters.

The first group to depart was called the Leon Group, named in honor of Wittenberg. There were twenty-one members including

Joseph Glazman and Abba's younger brother, Michael. They both died, killed by Polish peasants.

On September 23 came the order from Heinrich Himmler, the head of Hitler's SS, to liquidate the Vilna ghetto. By that time, only about thirty of Abba's fighters remained. He had been planning to slip away into the forest as the others had done. But German and Estonian troops had surrounded the ghetto. There seemed to be no way out.

Then Abba remembered the sewer network. He consulted his sewer expert, Shmuel Kaplinsky, who told him that an escape by sewer would be possible. It would be tight in spots and dangerous if it rained too hard.

The entrance to the sewer was in the cellar of a building. Only trained fighters with guns were allowed into the tunnels. Abba was the last one to enter and the last one to emerge, seven hours later, in a yard behind the German Security Police headquarters. From there, they made it to the forest, and Abba Kovner's time of leading the Jews of the Vilna ghetto resistance ended.

That night, it rained hard. Had they waited, they all would have drowned.

Before he left, Abba bade farewell to his mother in her ghetto apartment. He explained his decision, that only trained soldiers with a strong chance of surviving would be allowed into the sewers. Her last words to him were, "What will become of me?"[3]

Michael Kovner

The historian Rich Cohen describes Michael Kovner as "Abba's shy, dark-eyed kid brother." Michael was born in the shtetl of Ozmiana, where his family first settled after returning to Lithuania from Russia.

Perhaps Michael was shy, but he was as fiercely dedicated to Zionism and to the Jewish people as Abba was. During the difficult early days of Russian rule in Vilna, Abba initially decided that the Vilna branch of Hashomer Hatzair would have to disband. The local commissar had demanded a list of its members as a condition of letting it continue to operate. Abba's decision to decline that demand and to disband was prudent, because arrests would certainly come next.

Michael and many of the young were saddened by that move and furious with Abba. Michael even called him a traitor, and the two did not speak for several weeks. Finally, Abba relented and mended fences. He asked Michael and a few others to find out whether the Hashomer Hatzair members continued to meet in secret.

When he found that they did, Abba decided he had to organize the underground. They would meet in cells of five people, in private homes and in places outside the city. They continued to study Hebrew and to encourage emigration to Eretz Israel. This underground grew to between two hundred fifty and three hundred young people.

There was another Jewish underground as well. Called the Second Struggle Group or Yechiel's Struggle Group, after its leader Yechiel Scheinbaum, it was more loosely organized and less disciplined than Hashomer Hatzair. The groups were rivals, especially when it came to procuring arms. They collaborated reluctantly in the last months of the ghetto's existence, but relations were never warm between them.

Abba remained the leader of Hashomer Hatzair and of FPO after Wittenberg's death. But it may never have happened without Michael's determination to confront his older brother.

Michael returned to the ghetto from the convent along with Abba. He brought back Sala, the daughter of their brother, Genia, who had been hiding there with them. Michael lived with Genia; his wife, Neuta; and his mother, Rosa.

Michael, along with Ruzhka Korczak from the FPO, was recruited into the so-called Paper Brigade by its head, Herman Kruk. The assignment was one of the best in Vilna. It was in an office, outside the ghetto, at YIVO, the Yiddish Scientific and Cultural Institute that was founded in 1925. It was an ideal spot from which to contribute to the FPO's sabotage efforts. Michael proved to be very good at that.

Kruk is the diarist who wrote the lengthy and detailed *Last Days of the Jerusalem of Lithuania.* He had been asked by the Judenrat to organize the ghetto library. Then one day in February of 1942, three Nazis showed up and gave Kruk a task: to find and turn over to them the best books from the several libraries of Vilna.

Those Nazis, Hans Muller, Gerhard Wolff, and Alexander Himpel, were from the Einsatzstab Reichsleiter Rosenberg, or ERR. Headed by Hitler's old friend from Munich, Alfred Rosenberg, the ERR was the agency that oversaw the plunder of art and other Jewish cultural treasures. In Vilna and in other places around Eastern Europe, they put a Nazi who was a former Catholic priest, Johannes Pohl, in charge.

Pohl ran what he called the Institute for Investigation of the Jewish Question. His slogan was *Judenforschung ohne Juden,* or Judaism without Jews. But he knew little about Judaism. He had to rely on Kruk and his team of Jews, the Paper Brigade, to tell him what was valuable and important.

The brigade members did their best to save some irreplaceable documents and books. They set up melinas, or hiding places, for these items. Some of them included original works by Sholem Aleichem, manuscripts by Tolstoy, drawings by Marc Chagall, the diary of Zionism founder Theodor Herzl, and the daily records of the Great Synagogue that dated back to 1635.

They also watched in sorrow as thousands of books were sold for scrap paper, and parchment from Torah scrolls became linings and insoles for German military boots. Pohl made money on the side from this plunder. One of his biggest payoffs was his sale of the printing plates of the Romm Press edition of the Vilna Talmud. He got thirty-nine marks per ton from the German military for the eighty tons of lead. The Germans melted the plates down to make bullets.

Michael worked on the first floor at YIVO. He examined and catalogued Judaica books. Ruzhka Korczak worked in the Pedagogical Department on the second floor. Among the documents and books that arrived at YIVO from around the city included shipments from the days when Vilna was still a city of the Russian empire.

At lunchtimes, when their supervisors were out and no other workers were around, Michael and Ruzhka picked the lock on the room that housed the Soviet books. They were looking for munitions manuals. After many break-ins, they found a set of small books with "Library for Military Commanders, Published by the Defense Commissariat" on the cover.

Michael and Ruzhka smuggled those books into the ghetto. Abba used their bomb-making instructions to build the land mine that Vitka Kempner planted on July 8. He also learned how to make grenades and how to clean and use guns.

Michael was also involved in the dangerous activity of buying guns and smuggling them into the ghetto. The Paper Brigade and the FPO collaborated in this matter, and Michael was a central figure. The FPO had many of its people, not just Glazman, working for the Jewish police. When the brigade wanted to smuggle precious objects back into the ghetto, it would inform the FPO. Then the FPO would arrange for its people to be on duty at the gate and to pretend to search the returning Paper Brigade members for forbidden items.

The FPO's biggest storage facility for arms was in a bunker at 6 Shavel Street, more than sixty feet underground and accessible only through the sewers. The FPO let the Paper Brigade store some of its goods there. In return, the brigade set up a hiding place for its machine guns in the ghetto library. It was in a compartment behind a bookshelf with copies of Josephus's *Jewish Wars*.

The FPO bought arms through an arrangement involving Schmerke Kaczerginski, a member of the FPO; Julian Janakauskas, a Lithuanian friend of FPO head Isaac Wittenberg; and Moshe Brause, an FPO member who worked for the Jewish police. Brause bought the guns, grenades, and bullets from Janakauskas and gave him money to pay for them.

The weapons were expensive—more than fifteen hundred German marks each. Michael Kovner and Ruzhka Korczak were the source of much of those funds. They would smuggle precious items into the ghetto from YIVO—silver kiddush cups, Torah pointers, and other ritual items made of gold and silver. The FPO would then melt those items down and use the gold and silver for their black-market arms purchases.

Michael and Ruzhka also were the ones who checked in the incoming weapons, made sure they worked, and evaluated their worth. Most of the early gun purchases were pistols, however, and the FPO needed heavier arms like rifles and machine guns. So Schmerke asked Janakauskas if he could get some. Janakauskas came through, but almost at the cost of the lives of Michael and his colleagues.

Several days later, Janakauskas showed up at YIVO carrying a viola case. In it was "a viola that shoots," as he put it—a machine gun. It was near the end of lunch hour, so the FPO members needed to work fast. They decided to dismantle the gun and hide the separate parts.

Michael and Ruzhka would then smuggle the parts into the ghetto and reassemble the gun.

Right after lunch, some Germans arrived unexpectedly to check on how the work on Pohl's project was proceeding. The barrel of the machine gun had not yet been hidden away and was laying in open view under three paintings in the art room. The visitors were in the process of viewing all the paintings in the room and were getting close to the gun barrel when Rachela Krinsky, another FPO member, realized what was happening.

Krinsky called out to the senior German officer, "Mr. Chief. I've found an important manuscript."

It turned out to be a document from a Polish uprising in 1830. But it was enough. After examining it, the Germans left the room. Michael and Ruzhka smuggled the gun into the ghetto, one part at a time. The FPO had another important weapon, and Michael still had his life— for at least a little while longer.

Two days after the death of Isaac Wittenberg by suicide, on July 19, the Paper Brigade knew that their work was coming to an end and that the final liquidation of the Vilna ghetto was imminent. Kruk was told to prepare a final report for his Nazi bosses, summarizing the work of the previous eighteen months. The Nazis sealed off the ghetto on August 1 and allowed no more workers to leave each day.

Michael had left a few days before, on July 27, with twenty other members of the Leon Group. They were disguised as a party of wood-cutters. They were to walk fifty miles to the forest of Narocz. There, they were to meet up with a group of partisans commanded by a Russian named Markov. He had sent notes to Abba and the Vilna underground, urging them to come out and join the fight.

In the evening of the first day, after they crossed a railroad bridge, they were ambushed by a party of German soldiers. The Germans killed nine of them. They took the dead men's identity papers, returned to the ghetto, arrested all of their families, and killed them at Ponary.

Michael and Joseph Glazman escaped, along with Schmerke Kaczerginski, and made it to Narocz. But there they encountered only hostility from Markov and his unit, the Voroshilov Brigade. He would let only a few of the Jews join up and become fighters. The rest he assigned to be cooks, tailors, and cobblers. He also took away their guns and demanded that they donate their valuable items like watches and leather coats to his Fatherland.

The next month, the Germans surrounded the Voroshilov Brigade and attacked. Markov and his men scattered and abandoned the Jews of Vilna, firing their guns in their direction to prevent them from following.

Michael and Glazman were in a small group of Jews that set out through the country, stealing food and guns from houses and trying to live off the land. Polish peasants attacked them in an open field on October 8, after the wheat had been harvested. The Germans had promised the peasants a kilo of sugar for every dead Jew.

All but one of them died there, gunned down in the stubble of the wheat field. One girl escaped. Eventually, she met up with Abba and told him the story of Michael's death.

Later on, according to historian Dina Porat,

"Little Michtzik, little Michtzik, fallen on the road," Kovner eulogized. "The pain comes not from his being my brother," but from his being talented and virtuous, and it was he who should have stayed alive. "Little Michtzik, little Michtzik, there was no one like him."[4]

Gedalia (Genia) Kovner

Genia and Neuta Kovner

Author's Note: This section is in the words of Genia Kovner, Abba's older brother. Genia was born in Feyodosia, a port city in the Crimea. According to Dina Porat, Genia "took after his mother, who was a bustling, sharp-tongued, short-tempered woman, the ruler of the household."[5]

When Abba, Michael, and their mother, Rosa, were hiding out in the Carmelite convent in 1941, Genia and his wife, Neuta, stayed in the ghetto. They would come out to visit occasionally to see their four-year-old daughter, Sala.

Genia was part of the FPO under Abba. What role he had is unknown. Michael, the younger brother, had a closer relationship to

Abba than Genia did. Mary was reunited with Genia and Neuta when they made it to Palestine after the war.

The following is a nearly complete transcript of a conversation among Genia (G), Neuta (N), and Mary's son, Avi (A). It was transcribed and translated from the original Yiddish by Mary's daughter, Charlene. It begins abruptly, and it is unclear where "there" refers to, in Neuta's opening words.

There has been very little editing of this transcript.

N: We were sitting there. We were all together. I brought some money where his [Genia's] mother and the child were.

A: And with your daughter, what happened?

N: They took her to Ponary with his mother.

G: They killed her. They took her.

N: They killed our child.

A: They took from your hands?

N: They took the child from my hands. They hit me in the head or the face. I don't remember. We were all together in the jail [the Gestapo jail]. One hundred and twenty people.

G: When we were imprisoned in the jail, we were taken to the fields to work. When I came back, they [my mother and daughter] were gone. They took them when we were in the fields. We didn't always go back to the jail.

N: I was there. They took her when I was there. The German asked whose child was this. I said mine and the German said I was lying. They took her from my hands.

G: My mother was taken earlier. I don't know. Went to deliver something, but I'm not sure what happened. I could not save her. I was told that she was in the Gestapo jail.

A: My mom was in the ghetto and then taken to concentration camps in three places. Did they take people from the ghetto either to work or they were killed?

G: There were people leaving daily, fifty, one hundred people brought to the trains, and at night would be returned back until they were eventually killed.

G: I helped build the bunkers at Ponary. When workers were finished, they would be killed. Workers were brought from the Gestapo jail and the Germans wanted the evidence erased. So, they had us remove the dead bodies and burn them. Bunkers were built, with beds, etc., and workers stayed until work was finished and then they were killed.

I escaped sooner, as I knew not to go back to work. I hid, because I was warned I would be killed.

We were hiding in the crawl space under a building with about ten other people. We were there for days. One of the men finally couldn't take it anymore. He decided to leave. Everyone appealed to him not to, but he went anyway. The Germans caught him and were able to force him to reveal the hiding place.

A couple of Germans came to the hideout and got us all out at gunpoint from the crawl space. They lined us up along the side of the building and began questioning us. I was near the back of the group. When I saw that one of the Germans was distracted, talking with someone and checking his papers, I knew that was my chance. I grabbed Neuta's arm and dragged her behind the building. They didn't see us. From there we ran as fast as we could, past a few more buildings and into an adjacent wood. Nobody followed us.

It was just an instant gut reaction that took only a few seconds. But it saved our lives. That was not the only time. There were some other occasions where we had to make a split-second decision. Go to the left or go to the right? One meant life. The other meant death. Our survival was pure luck. Everyone who survived at that time and place was incredibly lucky.

But I want to tell you something. Survivors of the Holocaust (Shoah). Metzulay HaShoah. No one saved me. They had guns and tanks. I did not. I saved myself.

Your mother did not have to deal with the Germans like we did. She had other experiences, such as the camps.

I did not come [to Israel] with my brother, Abba. He came a few days before. He came a different way, smuggled in past the English. He sat in prison in Egypt for a while. I came with the Haganah legally, through France.

Melina, bunker . . . it was different. Depends where you were.

In Ponary the bodies were burned. Put on wood planks and set fire. Just bones were dug out but Germans wanted all evidence destroyed, erased. Ashes were spread among the fields. More than seventy thousand just from Vilna. From the whole surrounding area, one hundred and fifty thousand may have died there.

Camps in Poland? You could see at concentration camps the warehouses full of eyeglasses, shoes, and documents piled up high to the ceiling. I saw it after the war before I came to Israel. I never went back to Poland. I came to Palestine without shirt or pants, just what I was wearing, shorts and an undershirt.

At the train station a Russian took what I was carrying and everything in my pockets. I came with nothing. No one to talk to or help me. Not like today, where you get help to settle, with an apartment, food, and clothing. Neuta came and got very sick. I had no money, no clothes, not even a fork, nothing.

Today what I have is what I worked for, forty-five years of work, and Neuta also worked. We didn't even have bread. No help from anyone. We came legally with Haganah, by boat at night. We were brought to a nearby kibbutz to sleep the night. There they gave us pajamas and next morning they asked where we would like to go and they would take us. But we had nowhere to go, so they took us to a kibbutz in the Galilee.

On the way they stopped in Haifa and bought me khaki pants and shirt. We wanted to work for ourselves, be on our own, not on a kibbutz. They asked us again where we wanted to go. Tel Aviv, we said. They said OK, so they gave us British identity papers. It was all British police, British workers that handled and processed us and brought us to Tel Aviv. They gave us a little money, and we said we could pay it back once we started working.

We had no apartment. By force we entered a garage and let ourselves in and set up house there. We were called *plisha* in Hebrew— squatters. We had no contract and the owner couldn't do anything. We started with no one to help us or to talk to.

Neuta was sick; she stayed in bed for months. She miscarried and couldn't bear more children because of her previous illness, tuberculosis [*shachevet* in Hebrew]. She got sick originally in Romania, very sick. It took two or three months until she got better, but ultimately she could not get pregnant because of it.

I had no interest to go back to visit Poland. Maybe to Vilna. But it was now all Lithuanians. I don't speak the language and they are anti-Semites anyway. We were busy making a living, money. We visited there after the war.

Everyone that comes out of the Holocaust has a story. Mary suffered much too. Mary's story is different. She worked hard, but she couldn't run from one place to another. They suffered and they knew the end would not be good for them. Hungry and no food and you could not escape. If you did try and escape, they would shoot and kill you. We fled from place to place. I wouldn't have let them shoot me standing, only if I'm on the run.

N: Remember you got beat up in Ponar?

G: Yes.

N: Why? Say why.

G: When I turned the stove on and it didn't work, the German guard beat me. But no broken bones.

When in the ghetto, a German soldier that worked on the train came to buy something in the factory where I worked. He came with ten other people. I could tell he was just a German soldier, not from the Gestapo. I told him I have things at my home and if he came with me, I would give him something. I wanted to transfer some belongings to the ghetto.

In the middle of the day, with a military car, he came with me to my house where I had a locked room. I had items like leather goods, pocketbooks that I could sell in the ghetto to make money. All kinds of things to sell. I gave him a leather pocketbook. Just one.

He agreed to do it a second time, but someone found out about it, broke into the house, and took everything. The German took a chance. We knew it would mean our demise if caught, but he took a chance. He could have been punished or killed. But he still helped us. When I told the story, no one would believe me, that a German would help me in that way.

The Gestapo came and took 120 of us and put us in jail with children. Unbelievable conditions. How we survived there, without air. It was difficult to breathe. We were there two or three weeks. The jail of the Gestapo was terrible.

A big part of the group was taken and killed, brought to Ponar. Part of us they took to work in camp, for those who had a skill. We would sew and make uniforms for the soldiers on the front. They took ten men including me, not Neuta. They didn't believe she could sew or that she was my wife. She stayed behind.

This is another long story. At another *lager*, or camp, we worked on coats, [*parvot* in Hebrew]. When that camp was disbanded after a week, I decided to escape with Neuta. We escaped, but was very dangerous. We were successful reaching the *goya* [gentile]. She was a friend of Abba from the university and she helped us. She kept us for a month until the Partisans came and picked us up. We lived the rest of the war with them. It is a long story. I explained it to . . . [tape unclear here]

It was all very dangerous. When we escaped from the last factory, we jumped from a second floor. Crossed the fence. They shot at us. It was at night and we were lucky to be successful. Slept and stayed all night. We could not move during the day. We were in a bathroom in the city, a public toilet, until the morning. There were other people coming and going. We were hiding in a stall, moved between stalls, as people came in and out.

In the morning we left to go to the goya's house. Abba arranged that she keep us until he could come and get us. I had her address, so I knew where to go. We were there about a month. It was in a nearby city. Abba sent two female partisans, associated with Russian soldiers, to pick us up. They came into the city. Every meter we walked was a life-threatening danger. I had a Jewish face, so it was difficult to get around. The Germans wouldn't have recognized us so much, but we were scared of the Lithuanians. They were anti-Semites. The travel from the house to the partisans was the most difficult. We stayed with the partisans until liberation.

*

This concludes my stories of Abba, Michael, and Genia Kovner in Vilna. I will next return to my own story in the final days of the Vilna ghetto.

I began this chapter with Abba Kovner's manifesto, so I will end it with the lyrics of a song: "Never Say that You Have Reached the Final Road." In Yiddish, the title is "Zog nit keynmol az du geyst dem letstn veg."

I remember this song from 1943, when it was composed by Hirsh Glik. I remember singing it to myself when I was in the concentration camps. Glik was one of the young fighters of the Vilna underground. He was inspired to write it by the news of the Warsaw Ghetto uprising. He gave the lyrics to Joseph Glazman at the labor camp in Rzesza. Glazman brought the lyrics back to the ghetto when he returned. They were set to the music of an existing Russian marching song, and it became the anthem of all Jewish partisans and resistance fighters. It is sung to this day in Holocaust commemoration ceremonies.

> Never say that you are walking the final road,
>
> Though leaden skies obscure blue days;
>
> The hour we have been longing for will still come,
>
> Our steps will drum—we are here!
>
> From green palm-land to distant land of snow,
>
> We arrive with our pain, with our sorrow,

And where a spurt of our blood has fallen,

There will sprout our strength, our courage.

The morning sun will tinge our today with gold,

And yesterday will vanish with the enemy,

But if the sun and the dawn are delayed—

Like a watchword this song will go from generation to generation.

This song is written with blood and not with lead,

It's not a song about a bird that is free,

A people, between falling walls,

Sang this song with pistols in their hands.

So never say that you are walking the final road

Though leaden skies obscure blue days.

The hour we have been longing for will still come—

Our steps will drum—we are here![6]

Vilna, 1943, Final Months & Liquidation

My father's registration at Klooga, a labor camp in Estonia

THE WORST DAY of my life was September 24, 1943. The Nazis liquidated the Vilna ghetto. They tore my family members away from me and sent them all to their deaths. They spared me and some others for slave labor. I was alone in the world. God abandoned me that day. So I turned my back on Him. For a long time.

In this chapter I return to my own story and the events leading up to that day. Some of them have already been mentioned in the stories of my Kovner relatives—Abba, Genia, and Michael.

Such a deceptively innocent word: "liquidation." It sounds almost like a financial transaction, an exchange of goods, of value converted into some other form. So much of what the Nazis did was disguised in deceptive terms like that: "special handling," "resettlement," even "Final Solution." For my family and most of my Jewish neighbors, "liquidation" meant a death sentence.

Liquidation of the ghetto, and then execution at Ponary, was what Abba Kovner had warned Vilna's Jews about. He tried to get them to organize and fight, as the Warsaw Jews had done. Liquidation was what most of the Jews of Vilna feared might happen, but hoped would not, if they just did what Jacob Gens preached: "Work to Live."

Right up almost to the end, that hope seemed like a realistic one: to survive by being productive and supplying needed materials for Germany's war effort until the Russians and their allies in the West could liberate us. And there were positive signs. The Germans suffered massive losses at Stalingrad. The Russians were advancing from the East. The Americans and British had prevailed in Africa and had landed in Italy.

The German military, the Wehrmacht, and the civilian government in charge of Lithuania, were satisfied with the workers of Vilna. Hinrich Lohse, the Reichskommissar für das Ostland, sent a secret report to the central German authorities for April-May of 1943. It stated that the ghetto workshops in Vilna and Kovno had expanded their production of items like uniforms, cooking utensils, and shoes, and that the demand for Jewish labor was increasing.

No one in the ghetto ever saw that secret report. If they had, they might have been encouraged. But in truth, it did not matter. So far as we Jews were concerned, the civilian government and the Wehrmacht were not in charge of our fate. The SS was.

As of April 1943, according to the ghetto historian Yitzhak Arad, there were 10,115 workmen in the ghetto community. Of these, approximately 3,000 worked inside the ghetto. The rest went to work on the outside every day, in factories supporting the German military or in labor camps where they felled lumber and dug peat.

My father and brother, Chaim, had the yellow work passes, the *scheinen*. They would leave the ghetto every day, carrying their tool boxes, and return in the evening. My uncle Yisroel had a more coveted job; he lived and worked at Kailis, a large facility outside the ghetto.

The word *kailis* is Lithuanian for "fur." All of Vilna's fur businesses had been consolidated and moved to the former Elektrit factory, where another of my uncles, Meyer Suchowski, had worked before the Russians moved the factory to Minsk.

Fur coats, hats, and other warm garments were a critical need of the ill-prepared German forces on the Eastern Front. About one thousand Jews lived and worked at Kailis, making and repairing those garments. Their working conditions were better than almost anywhere else in Vilna, and the rest of Vilna's Jews resented them.

My uncle was hired to work there by a woman he knew. She had owned one of those fur businesses. That woman had told him that the ghetto was going to be liquidated, and that he could save himself by going to work for her and living outside the ghetto. I don't remember the woman's name, but I do recall that my mother disliked her intensely. While my mother was happy that my uncle had improved his chances for not being sent to Ponary, she was angry that he worked for this particular woman and that he stayed apart from us and the ghetto.

But while the Wehrmacht and the civil administration of what the Germans called Ostland favored keeping Jews alive and working, the SS had the exact opposite priority. Their task was to make the world Judenrein (also known as Judenfrei) or Jew-free. The Final Solution was the job of the SS, as the Wannsee Conference in January 1942 had made clear. Vilna's turn would come. The SS would prevail over the Wehrmacht. It became more important for the Nazis to kill Jews than to win their war of conquest.

After the many aktionen of 1941, the SS in Ostland had to stop its mass murders and bide its time. The Nazis started sending thousands of Jews per day from Polish ghettos to their deaths in the killing camps in the East beginning in April 1942.

Throughout 1943, and even in the so-called Quiet Period of 1942, there were ominous signs that "work to live" would not be a lasting protection for the Jews of Vilna.

The Old People's Aktion of July 17, 1942, was the first such sign. It was just five days after the Nazis had put Gens in complete control of the ghetto. The Jewish police went from house to house and arrested elderly people and chronic invalids. They first shipped the old people in wagons to Pospieszki, the former resort town where I and my family had spent many happy summer vacations.

Less than two weeks later, the SS and Lithuanians returned with trucks to Pospieszki. They forced all eighty-four elderly Jews into trucks, drove them to Ponary, and shot them. Gens claimed that he had no connection with the purge. He had twenty people imprisoned for a night for spreading rumors of future aktionen. He also said that the Nazis had wanted several hundred, and that he was able to reduce their demand to one hundred.

This aktion, a purge of the elderly, did not cause a great deal of anger or concern among the Jews of the Vilna ghetto. As Yitzhak Arad wrote, "The surrender to the Germans of the elderly and ill did not evoke bitter criticism; most of the Jews in the ghetto resigned themselves to the act, and perhaps even approved of Gens's policy and the method of its implementation."[1]

If that observation by Arad is true, it shows that the Nazis' methods of setting Jews against one another were working. The "legal" Jews, the ones with the work permits and who were actually working, were not sorry that other Jews were taken away and killed. The workers were just relieved that it was not they who were targeted—this time.

The killing of the 406 elderly Jews at Ozmiana was another dire sign. I told you about it earlier when I mentioned the heroic Liza Magun, who tried in vain to warn the townspeople. But I did not explain how that incident was different from previous aktions and mass killings. At Ozmiana, the Jewish police were the ones who selected those who were to be killed. Jewish policemen were present when the executions took place.

Shortly before that incident in October of 1942, the Nazis had told Gens that he must organize the ghettos in the smaller outlying communities around Vilna. Gens and his deputy, the Jewish police chief Salk Dessler, had known what was in store for the people of Ozmiana. They did not tell the rest of the policemen what would happen until the aktion commenced.

Gens later explained, once again, that he had had no choice but to do what he did. The Nazi SS man in charge of the security police, Martin Weiss, had initially demanded that fifteen hundred Jews be killed in the aktion, and that women and children be included. Gens bribed him with some gold rubles and got him to agree to kill six hundred of the elderly and infirm who could not work.

The Nazis knew that having the Jewish police be visible to the Jewish victims at Ozmiana and in the earlier Old People's Aktion would be less alarming to the people than having gangs of Lithuanian snatchers and SS men do all the dirty work. This helped them to prevent organized resistance, agitation, and flight from the ghetto, because the people could be made to believe that the operation was limited in scope.

But it also meant that Gens, the Jewish police, and the Judenrat were more closely implicated in the Nazis' plans than before. This was another way to divide the community and to sow fear and doubt. The Jewish police made it worse by bringing back sacks of jewelry and money from Ozmiana. Herman Kruk's diary states that the police marched back into the ghetto "as in a victory parade."[2]

After Ozmiana, the ghetto buzzed with rumors that more aktions and killings were planned. Kruk's account echoes the earlier observation by Arad when he wrote that "the mood in the ghetto is still terrified . . . the tragedy is that the . . . public mostly approves of Gens's attitude. . . . The Jewish police made money, and that certainly was allowed in order to corrupt them. It is quite possible that a similar Aktion will be performed again, and then the Jewish policemen themselves will volunteer."[3]

In the early months of 1943, the Jews of the Vilna ghetto continued to work and to hope for Germany's defeat. Fewer and fewer people believed Gens's assurances that "Work to Live" would keep us safe and that the Nazis had no plans to kill us. In fact, as Vilna's Jews heard rumors and reports of German military defeats on the Eastern and Western Fronts, the more we feared for our own lives. What would stop the Nazis from coming for us first, before the Russians even got here?

The head of the Gestapo in Vilna, Rolf Neugebauer, told Gens that "If we win the war, we will give the Jews a corner of the world somewhere and they shall live there. But if we lose, the Jews will be annihilated."[4] More and more ghetto residents built melinas, hiding places, in their homes and stocked them with what provisions they could find. Many took to sleeping in their melinas at night. The police and the SS would frequently conduct surprise inspections, looking for the melinas and for hidden weapons.

In our building on Strashun Street, the primary melina was a large furnace. My father and Chaim would hide there whenever we heard rumors of a police raid. They were in more danger of being snatched than my mother and my sister were, because the Germans again began seizing groups of men for labor camps. On January 17, one hundred men were taken in a snatching and brought to work outside the city.

Events both within and outside of Vilna made our lives ever more desperate as time went on in 1943. In the Warsaw Ghetto, Jews began shooting at Germans in January. As deportations to the death camps in the East continued, the Warsaw Ghetto broke out in a full-scale revolt in April. German military defeats on the Eastern Front emboldened the partisans in the forests and rural areas to the east of Vilna. The Germans brought Lithuanians into their army and sent them to the most dangerous areas of the front. Many of those Lithuanians fled or deserted.

In mid-February, we heard reports of mass deportations from the Bialystok Ghetto. Earlier, in late November, the Jews of Grodno had been sent to their deaths and the city was Judenrein, as the Nazis wanted. The rumors of impending death for Vilna Jews became so rampant that Gens called a meeting of all ghetto staff in the Ghetto Theater.

Gens tried to calm people's fears by saying he had been assured by the district commissar, the Gestapo, and the SS that they didn't know what was happening in Bialystok. He repeated the old line that the Jews of Vilna must remain calm and work. He may have still believed that, but few of us, if any, believed him. But there was nothing we could do but keep working and hoping.

In March, at the same time that the reports of Bialystok and Vilna atrocities began circulating in Vilna, the Nazis again cancelled everyone's yellow scheinen, the work passes. They replaced the passes with numbered identity cards that had to be worn on a chain around the neck. My father, brother, and uncle all had them. But no one over the age of sixty got one.

Gens tried again to calm everyone with an editorial in the ghetto newspaper, *Geto Yedies*, of March 21. He wrote that the German administration had previously forbidden Jews to live near the Belorussian frontier to the west, and that

> On this basis the evacuation of Jews began from the small ghettos situated in "Vilna-Land": Swieciany, Oshmyany, Mikhailishki, and Sol. Some would be transferred to the Vilna ghetto and others to various labor camps. It should be emphasized that the transfer of these Jews is implemented with the help of, and under supervision of, the Jewish police of our ghetto. . . .

> Nothing has changed in the situation of our ghetto, and no danger threatens it. Consequently we advise—Do not lacerate your nerves with unfounded guesses. We must again demonstrate that everyone continues with his work, remain quiet and calm.[4]

It was all a monstrous lie. On April 4–5, the Nazis murdered four thousand of those Jews from Vilna-Land at Ponary. Soviet partisans had become especially active in that area. The Nazis wanted to get the Jews away from there and then kill them. But they needed a ruse to ease the Jews' fears.

The presence of Gens and the Jewish police, instead of Gestapo or SS, deceived the people into cooperating. Gens and his men separated out approximately twenty-five hundred skilled workers for the Vilna ghetto and physically fit men for the labor camps. The remaining four thousand Jews were told they would be sent to the ghetto at Kovno.

All of them, more than six thousand, were loaded into railroad freight cars that were locked from the outside and that had barbed wire over their small windows. They stopped first at Vilna and uncoupled the cars with skilled workers. Around midnight of April the train started off, purportedly to Kovno. Instead, it went straight to Ponary.

The Lithuanians who were waiting for the train arrested Gens and his Jewish police and brought them back to the ghetto. The Lithuanians then waited until morning and unlocked the freight cars. Many of the Jews realized what was happening and tried to run. Only a handful escaped, made their way back to the Vilna ghetto, and told their story.

A second train with more victims was brought in after the first ones were annihilated. Four thousand people died, gunned down at the pits and in the surrounding fields by Lithuanians.

The following day, the Nazis even stopped trying to keep the killing grounds of Ponary a secret. Martin Weiss, the SS man overseeing the ghetto, demanded that twenty-five Jewish policemen go with him to Ponary to bury the several hundred dead who were shot trying to escape.

Weiss actually gave those policemen a tour of Ponary after their work was done. He showed them which mass graves held bodies from all the previous aktions—the Great Provocation, the yellow pass aktion, the pink pass aktion. The Jewish police came back to the ghetto that evening. That was the first time that the Germans had allowed any Jews to see what had happened at Ponary, and then to return to the ghetto.

The Jewish policemen's stories of what they saw, as well as the accounts of the few dozen survivors who escaped back to the ghetto, removed any doubts of the Nazis' plans for us. They had played Gens for a fool. His assurances meant nothing.

In June, the Nazis installed Bruno Kittel, a brutal and sadistic SS man, as officer-in-charge of Jewish affairs of the Security Police. He immediately ordered the liquidation of three labor camps—Biala Vaka, Kena, and Bezdany—and the murder of their Jewish workers. Some of these Jews had been transferred just two months previously, after they had been taken from Swieciany, Oshmyany, Mikhailishki, and Sol.

At Biala Vaka, Kittel had sixty-seven people lined up and shot. At Kena and Bezdany, he summoned all the workers into buildings and told them it was their duty to work. Outside, his police and Lithuanians cordoned off the buildings and locked them from the outside. After Kittel emerged, they opened fire with their guns and threw in grenades, killing everyone.

In the following months and throughout the summer, the people's fear grew and grew. More and more melinas were built wherever the Jews of the ghetto could construct them. Gens no longer ignored the ghetto underground, the FPO, led by the Communist Isaac Wittenberg, Joseph Glazman, and my relative Abba Kovner. He knew that they were acquiring guns, and he began to crack down.

Throughout the summer, break-ins and searches for guns and melinas by the Jewish police became regular occurrences in Vilna. The brief imprisonment of Glazman, the Wittenberg affair, and Abba Kovner's last futile attempt to get the ghetto to rise up in rebellion, all took place in mid-July. About half of his armed FPO fighters left the ghetto for the forest, while another two hundred or so remained. I have described those events in detail in my chapter about Abba.

On August 6, a large force of German and Estonian solders seized more than a thousand of the Jewish men who were working outside the ghetto. They forced the men into a train and shipped them to a labor camp in Estonia. Their forced labor included mining shale oil, making concrete, and cutting timber in the forests. Their working conditions were brutally hard.

Everyone believed that the captured men had been taken away to be killed, and that the end of the ghetto was at hand. But a few days later, letters came back from them, requesting warm clothing and stating that they were still alive. Some of their relatives, as well as ghetto residents who did not have work permits, volunteered to go and join them.

But still the Germans demanded more workers, and the snatchings continued when not enough Jewish men volunteered to go. Estonians joined in the kidnappings along with German soldiers, grabbing people off the streets and dragging them from their houses. Gens finally persuaded the Germans and the Estonians to leave the ghetto, but it was only because he promised to find the workers that they demanded.

Gens believed that by avoiding a battle between the resistance fighters and the military, he could preserve the ghetto and save at least some of its Jews until the Russians arrived. He recruited an additional two hundred Jewish men and made them auxiliary policemen.

So it was the Jewish police and their informers who then began to search the ghetto and kidnap Jews to be sent to Estonia. Some Jews, hoping to save themselves, informed on others and betrayed them. Many of the Jewish police and recently recruited auxiliary police took large bribes from those they seized, promising to keep the Jews who paid them safe. Those promises were meaningless. In those last days of the ghetto, the intensity of hatred of Jew for Jew was at its peak. The Nazis' scheme to divide their victims against one another had worked.

Some of those betraying Jews paid the ultimate price at the hands of other Jews. Vitka Kempner, who fought alongside Abba Kovner and eventually became his wife, later stated:

> I was running around the ghetto and saw Lotek Zaltwasser ac-companied by police officers open a melina full of crying chil-dren and screaming mothers, and drag the men out. I caught him by the arm and yelled, 'Lotek, in the name of God, what are you doing, have you gone mad!' He had once been my brother's friend and even a member of the underground. And he betrayed and abandoned us and went over to Gens. After we went into the for-est I returned, found him in hiding and brought him back with me so he might be executed, and I am proud of having done it.[5]

My father and brother had escaped that first snatching for laborers in Estonia. They stopped reporting to work. To avoid the snatchers during those last days of the ghetto, they spent much of their time in our building's melina. The Jewish police and their betraying accom-plices managed to kidnap and send away another six hundred men.

That six hundred was still not enough. So the Germans came back into the ghetto. An informer had told them that there was a large melina at 15 Strashun Street. That was true, and it was right next to our building. My parents had been tipped off that the raid was com-ing. My brother, father, and two uncles hid in the cellar.

My mother told me to leave, to take my little sister Lila to the far end of the ghetto. She said don't come back until I tell you. She stayed in the house, in our room on the first floor, with my baby sister Sala. I took Lila's hand and crossed the intersection of Zmudzka and Strashun Streets, then all the way to the end of Oszmianska Street. The ghetto wall was just after the intersection of Oszmianska and Jatkowa Street.

I stopped there and waited for my mother's signal to return. I remember turning around at one point and seeing my mother waving to me. I didn't know why it was so important for me to get away from the house. But I soon found out.

The Germans ordered everyone to come out of 15 Strashun and show their passes. When no one did, they tossed bombs into the cellar. Then they did the same at 12 Strashun. Both buildings were partly destroyed. I don't know how many men they killed that day, but there were many who died. My father and brother, miraculously, survived.

Several of the armed FPO fighters had been stationed at 12 Strashun. One of them, Yechiel Scheinbaum, opened fire and was killed by a German gunner. A few of the other fighters threw hand grenades. But that was the extent of the armed resistance. Ruzhka Korczak, who was one of Abba Kovner's top lieutenants, ordered the rest of the fighters to retreat. It was a wise decision that saved lives, probably including my own. The Germans did not advance further, stopped their shooting, and left the ghetto.

A Jewish police officer who knew me took my hand and led me back. I picked my way through the rubble of the ruined cellar. Some of the walls of the buildings were still standing, but the cellars were a heap of stones, charred wood, and twisted metal. There was blood everywhere. The blood of the dead and wounded covered my shoes and legs.

Then I saw my father. His arm was just visible in the rubble. He was badly hurt, but he was alive. Next to him was Chaim. He too was alive. He told me that his tool box, filled with shoemaker's gear, had saved him. A wall had collapsed right next to him. It tore the tool box from his hand but just missed him. He was buried in the rubble but almost uninjured.

We took my father to the ghetto hospital. He was dazed and had many cuts, but he recovered and walked with a limp. We brought him back to our half-destroyed house and waited. It was all we could do.

One of my uncles was also buried in the rubble. He survived but was so shocked that he was unable to talk about it afterwards.

The Germans did not return to the ghetto. Gens and his Jewish police and informers kept up their kidnappings and took two thousand more people for forced labor camps in Estonia. That reduced the ghetto population to about nine thousand. Still, they fell short of the number of people that the Germans demanded.

There was one more tense standoff with the resistance, this time in the courtyard at 6 Straszuna Street. Kovner and the remaining FPO fighters were inside, armed with guns, grenades, and their machine gun. Gens came with Germans and Lithuanians and demanded that they come out. They did not respond, and no one fired a shot. Gens and the soldiers withdrew. That may have been planned by both sides. They knew a pitched battle would be suicidal and would have killed everyone in the ghetto.

We all realized that the end was near on September 14. The Germans decided that they no longer needed Gens. They took him to the ghetto prison yard, where Rolf Neugebauer, the head of the security police, shot him. They said that he had failed to find enough Jewish men for forced labor. They also accused him of communicating secretly with the Resistance, which was probably true.

Gens had been warned of what was coming, but he refused to flee. Whether we loved him or hated him, he was the leader of the ghetto. He had kept it functioning. He had believed to the last that his "Work to Live" approach would keep at least some of its people alive. Now he was gone. And ten days later came September 24, the worst day of my life.

After Gens was killed, the Nazis appointed his chief of Jewish police, Salk Dessler, to Gens's old job. Dessler stole a satchel of diamonds and gold rubles from the Judenrat safe and disappeared.

Several others who were able to flee also did so. The ghetto had no official leadership, but that hardly mattered any more.

The SS was in charge and our fate had already been decided. Back on June 21, 1943, Heinrich Himmler, the head of the SS, issued the following order:

> I order that all Jews remaining in ghettos in the Ostland area have to be closed in concentration camps . . . a concentration camp must be erected in the vicinity of Riga, to which must be transferred all the manufacturing of clothing and equipment that the Wehrmacht is now doing outside . . . the greatest possible part of the male Jews shall be brought to the concentration camp in the oilshale area for the mining of oilshale. . . . Non-essential inhabitants of the Jewish ghettos are to be evacuated to the East.[6]

Oilshale mining meant the camps in Estonia. "The East" meant the death camps of Treblinka, Sobibor, Majdanek, Belzec, Chelmno, and Auschwitz.

The Germans sealed off the ghetto entrances on September 15, and no one could go out to go to work. They stopped sending food rations in, and black-market prices soared. A loaf of bread, bought from Lithuanian smugglers, cost us 250 rubles, or 25 marks.

My parents initially decided that we would not answer any summons or roundup. We had made another melina in our building that no one on the outside knew about. My father and brother dragged a large cabinet that extended from the floor to the ceiling across the door that connected a bedroom to our back bedroom. They also cut a hole in the back of the cabinet so that we could crawl out when no one was around. We would hide there and take our chances.

Several hundred Jews in the ghetto also went into hiding. Most of them, but not all, were eventually discovered or betrayed and taken to Ponary. Two who did survive in this way were Abba Kovner's brother

Genia and his wife, Neuta. They were hidden by a Gentile friend of Abba's until the Russians arrived.

The night before September 23, a force of German and Ukrainian soldiers surrounded the ghetto. That morning the SS sadist Bruno Kittel announced, in the courtyard of the Judenrat building, that the ghetto was being liquidated. He gave the residents until two o'clock to pack their belongings—only what could be carried by hand—and to assemble at the ghetto gate.

Kittel also warned the Jews that the Germans would return to the ghetto after the liquidation, shut off the water and electrical supplies, blow up the buildings, and shoot anyone who came out of hiding.

We still were not going to go, even though our chances of our surviving in that melina were slim. But we never put the plan into action. Just as the roundups started, my sister Lila crawled out from behind the cabinet to look for a toy. She stepped out the door of the apartment, which happened to be open. She was grabbed on the street, along with other Jews, and marched away. We couldn't leave her to face her fate alone. We decided to join the rest of our neighbors, and we found her with some of our friends.

At two, hundreds of soldiers, German and Lithuanian, marched into the ghetto. They lined up on both sides of every street, brandishing their rifles and machine guns. Kittel, Martin Weiss, and other SS thugs counted us all as we stepped through the ghetto gate.

Fierce growling dogs snarled at anyone who stepped out of line. Many of the exhausted Jews could not carry all of their luggage and dropped it along the way. Local people, Lithuanians and Poles, snatched up those belongings and jeered at us from the sidewalks. I remember looking up at one point and seeing the dead body of a baby hanging from a tree.

The Nazis performed their first selection of "essential personnel" as the throng wended its way down Subocz Street to an assembly point near Rossa Square. Kittel sat at a piano he had set up in the square, pounding on the keys and leering as his men decided who would live and who would die.

Ignoring our pleas and cries of anguish and swinging their rifle butts and truncheons, the Nazis separated the men from the women, children, and elderly. They drove the men into a swampy valley off 20 Subocz Street and the women and children into the courtyard and graveyard of a monastery that overlooked Rossa Square. I never saw my father and brother after that.

In the men's valley the Nazis made another selection. But first, to further intimidate the men and to banish all thoughts of escape, they built four gallows and hanged members of the FPO who had been captured as they tried to flee to the forest. Bright strobe lights blinded the men and jazz music blared over loudspeakers.

The SS and the Lithuanians were having a good time for themselves, tormenting us all and snatching away the last of the worldly goods we had brought with us.

The younger and able-bodied men were packed into railway cars and sent to the camps in Estonia. I learned, many years later, that my father and brother were among them. The others were shot at Ponary or sent to a death camp—either Sobibor or Majdanek.

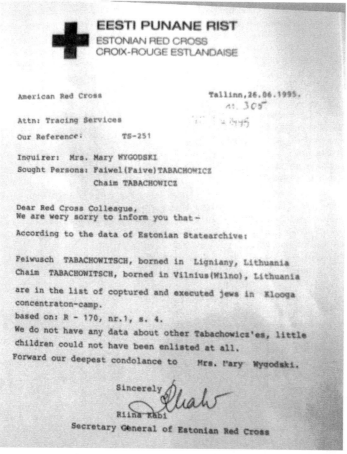

EESTI PUNANE RIST
ESTONIAN RED CROSS
CROIX-ROUGE ESTLANDAISE

American Red Cross   Tallinn,26.06.1995.

Attn: Tracing Services

Our Reference: TS-251

Inquirer: Mrs. Mary WYGODSKI
Sought Persons: Faiwel(Faive)TABACHOWICZ
                Chaim TABACHOWICZ

Dear Red Cross Colleague,
We are wery sorry to inform you that-

According to the data of Estonian Statearchive:

Feiwusch TABACHOWITSCH, borned in Ligniany, Lithuania
Chaim TABACHOWITSCH, borned in Vilnius(Wilno), Lithuania

are in the list of coptured and executed jews in Klooga
concentraton-camp.
based on: R - 170, nr.1, s. 4.
We do not have any data about other Tabachowicz'es, little
children could not have been enlisted at all.
Forward our deepest condolance to Mrs. Mary Wygodski.

                Sincerely

                Riina Kabi
        Secretary General of Estonian Red Cross

1995 Letter from Estonian Red Cross, confirming the deaths of
my father and brother at Klooga.

The sun set. It started to rain. They made us wait all night in that courtyard, surrounded by barbed wire and by gun-toting Lithuanians. Then the morning of September 24 arrived. It was the women's turn. Two lines, separated by a barbed-wire barrier. They tore Lila's hand from mine and pushed her, my mother, and Sala to the left.

They shoved me to the right. I tried to go left and stay with them. "You're young, you can work," somebody growled. A Lithuanian guard grabbed me and smashed me with his rifle butt. I fainted right there.

Later that evening of that worst day of my life, they shoved me into a railroad boxcar. I was bound for Kaiserwald in Latvia. I would labor for Hitler's Third Reich. My mother and sisters would not. They were nonessential personnel. They were bound for death in the East.

"Be strong." My mother's final words to me. For the rest of my long life on earth, I have tried to heed her advice.

Kaiserwald

With Dora and Bella in 1945, after liberation

A T THE BEGINNING of the last chapter, I said that God had abandoned me. I stopped believing in Him. Let me explain further.

We were Orthodox Jews. We were observant and respectful of our laws and customs. But we were not "strict," as many people conceive the Orthodox to be. I did not find God in the rites and ceremonies of our synagogue. Nor did my parents. Rather, I felt the presence of God in the bosom of my family. I'm sure that they did too.

For instance, Orthodox Jews do not smoke. I've already told you that my father liked to smoke. He would sneak many a cigarette, even on Shabbat. I knew of it, and wouldn't tell my mother. That cigarette was our little secret. We had many other secrets, just between the two of us. And in that little part of our world, that special closeness between father and eldest daughter, God was present. Even though my father was breaking one of the rules of our religion. Our love was stronger than some law conceived by men.

God was there with my mother too. I would follow her about the house—though keeping my distance in the realm of her kitchen—and bask in the wonder of her worldly wisdom and her confident authority as she dispensed that wisdom to everyone in the immediate family. She could have had a direct line of communication to God, as far as I was concerned. When I imagined growing up and having children of my own, I wanted to be the same kind of mother to them that she was to me.

And when our extended family convened at our large apartment or at the summer dacha, whether on Shabbat or for any other holidays on our religion's calendar, at the celebrations that my mother planned and presided over, God was there with us.

In the dark of that grimy wooden boxcar, my family was gone from me. And so, too, as far as I was concerned, was God. He had left me. Life was no longer worth living.

They threw me into the car along with dozens of others, all screaming or crying or cursing the Nazis, the Lithuanians, and their fate. I stumbled and landed right on top of the girl who had sat beside me for so many years in school, Bella Klok. We looked around and saw Dora Fisher, my friend Tanya's younger sister, curled up in the corner of the car. Before the door slid shut and was locked from the outside, the two of us scrambled over to Dora. And there we stayed, until journey's end.

In the cemetery adjacent to Rossa Square, at the selection that separated those who would live from those who would die, Bella had been chosen to die. Small of stature and a year younger than I, she was initially in the wrong line along with her mother. Her father had already been murdered in one of the Vilna aktions. Bella's mother realized what was happening. She boosted her daughter up and over the barbed wire barrier that separated the two lines.

Either no guard saw, or no guard cared, amidst all the anguished bedlam. What Mrs. Klok did at that moment was extraordinary. Most of the mothers begged to stay with their children. But Bella's mother chose to be separated from her daughter, in the hope that Bella would be spared. Her hope was rewarded, though she never knew. Mrs. Klok died with my mother, my sisters, and all the others in that line that went to the left, either in the pits of Ponary or the gas chambers at Sobibor or Majdanek.

I wanted to die too. Only later did I come to realize that I still had family around me, and that death was not to be my escape. Bella and Dora were the first members of a new family that would surround and sustain and love me. There would be others—former neighbors, new friends, and even blood relatives—further along on my life's journey.

In those first awful hours and days, however, hope for such relief and redemption was the furthest thing from my mind. We three huddled there, sharing some physical warmth and, more importantly, at least some emotional and familial bond. And another spark kindled in me as well. At the age of eighteen I was the oldest, so I became a kind of mother to Dora and Bella. They weren't my own children, of course, but I felt that I had to assume some kind of responsibility for them. I didn't think it; I simply felt it. Maybe that was my first small step in building a new family.

Riga, Latvia, is only about two hundred miles north of Vilna. But I have no idea how long—perhaps three or four days—it took that train to get there. I have no memory of how long the train stood on the siding before it started to move. The boxcars, probably fifteen to twenty of them crammed with Jewish people, had no food, no water, not even a bucket for anyone to use as a toilet. Somewhere between fifteen hundred and two thousand of us were considered fit to be spared, if only for a little while, so we could labor in support of Hitler's war machine.

Our destination had once been host to a thriving Jewish community. The Nazi military swept into Latvia in July of 1941. They immediately began rounding up Jews and confined them to a small ghetto in Riga. In two days, November 30 and December 8, the Nazis and Latvian collaborators force-marched the great majority of those Jews twelve miles to a sandy, forested area named Rumbula.

At Rumbula, the Jews were forced to remove all their clothes and lie in ditches, where they were shot in the back. Other victims then followed, and fell dead on top of them. In all, twenty-five thousand Jews died in those two days. It was nearly identical to the slaughter at Babi Yar in the Ukraine, where more than thirty-three thousand Jews were murdered one month before.

Only a few thousand Jews, mostly able-bodied men who had been spared for labor, were still in Latvia when we were sent there to work. There had been no concentration camp there at all until March 1943. Heinrich Himmler, the SS leader, had visited the area and sent about five hundred Jews from the Sachsenhausen concentration camp in Germany to build it in Mežaparks, a small suburb of Riga that had been a seaside resort.

By the time of our arrival at the end of September 1943, the extermination camps in Eastern Poland had been gassing up to fifteen thousand Jews per day for almost eighteen months. That massive, coordinated wave of killing was named Operation Reinhard by the Nazis. Those camps would soon cease operating, and in the following year the murders by gas at Auschwitz would increase dramatically. But

Kaiserwald was different. It was an *arbeitslager*, a work camp of relatively modest size and hastily constructed. Though the Nazis wanted us all dead eventually, they still needed some of us to work.

But even before they put us to work, they stripped us—of our clothing, but more importantly of our dignity. In those first few days, many Jews despaired and killed themselves. We were pulled out of the train and marched through the streets of the town. Local people stood along the streets to jeer and gawk at us; only a very few showed signs of empathy.

When we got to the camp, they marched us into a building where we were made to strip naked. It was beyond humiliating, being inspected and looked over by angry, hostile women and men as we proceeded from the entrance on one end to the exit on the other. They cut our hair and gave us scruffy striped dresses, trousers, and smocks. Some of the dresses had large white circles painted on the back, targets for any armed guards who thought a prisoner was trying to run away.

For some reason, probably because the raggedy camp clothes they gave us were not adequate for winter, they let us keep our coats and boots. I had a fine leather coat that my father had made especially for me. My mother had sewn a gold ruble into the shoulder lining. She said that it may save me. I lost that ruble because they took the coat away from me eventually. My father had also made my leather boots. I don't know why they let me keep my boots, but they did. Footwear that fit was a luxury in concentration camps. They also did not tattoo us—another small favor.

Kaiserwald had just eight prisoner barracks—four for men, four for women, surrounded and separated by barbed wire. There were about two thousand of us in the main camp. Jewish prisoners kept arriving through the fall and winter. The Nazis built sixteen satellite camps, and by March 1944 there were more than eleven thousand Jewish captives in and around Riga.

Though Kaiserwald and the surrounding satellites were work camps and not killing camps, the selections still continued. Anyone who fell sick or was deemed unable to work hard was liable to be hauled away and shot. They also killed prisoners in gas vans, which were trucks with enclosed rear compartments. They would load people into the rear, lock the doors, and start the engine. The exhaust gas, routed into the enclosed rear compartment, quickly killed those inside. Then the truck would drive away with the bodies, which were dumped in mass graves.

Doctors, as well as prison guards, were also part of those selections. We never knew when a doctor would show up at the barracks, decide that someone was too weak to keep working, and have her taken away. One night, one of the girls in my building delivered a baby. It was a healthy child. I could hear it cry, though I did not see it myself. The other girls in the building all knew that if the doctor or a guard discovered the mother with the baby, they would both be murdered. They made the awful decision to choke the baby to death. The guards never knew.

As the camp population swelled when more and more prisoners arrived, the older or weaker people became expendable. It was important to look strong and healthy, and even to keep your clothing looking as neat as possible.

On one occasion, the camp workforce expanded when several hundred Hungarian Jewish women arrived on a transport from Auschwitz. Though few of us spoke their native language, we could communicate in Hebrew or Yiddish. From those women we learned for the first time the true extent of the Nazis' plans to exterminate all Jews by bringing them together and killing them in gas chambers.

No, Ponary was not the only place where Jews were being slaughtered in great numbers. It was happening everywhere. Abba Kovner's dire warnings, which had fallen mostly on deaf ears in Vilna, were true. They planned to kill us all.

The guards and the SS also had their sadistic fun in treating us as cruelly as possible. We got up at four in the morning for roll call and stood at attention for many hours before starting work, even in the subzero cold of winter. If the roll-call lines were not straight, they would beat individual prisoners or shoot them.

The one daily meal consisted of a piece of bread and a thin soup. Sometimes the soup was sour, contaminated in some way, and it gave us cramps and diarrhea. We had only cold water for bathing, and of course no soap. They kept our heads shaved. Bella, Dora, and I shared a single bunk, under one thin blanket and on a heap of dirty straw.

Our slave labor at the Kaiserwald camp complex supported several German companies that made both consumer goods and heavy industrial products as well as military supplies. The biggest of the companies was Allgemeine Elektrizitats-Gesellschaft, a manufacturer of electrical products.

My work consisted of collecting, loading, and unloading metal cans, which were eventually sent to ammunition factories. We worked outside, even in the long and cold subarctic winter. My bare hands often stuck to the cans. Sometimes, a guard would let us come inside just long enough to sew gloves for ourselves out of old burlap sacks. Fortunately, I knew how to sew.

I almost didn't make it to that miserable winter, however. It was early in October when we arrived and they put us to work. Despair still possessed me. I decided to kill myself.

One day that October they sent a work party that included me out of the camp. We were not far from the river Dvina. A dock jutted out onto the river. I deliberately cut my hand, showed it to the guard, and asked if I could go down to the river to wash it off. He let me go.

I ran out to the end of the dock. I couldn't see the bottom; the water was deep enough. I jumped.

I sank, head first, and gradually started to lose consciousness. But as I descended, and as death approached, I saw my family. I saw their faces, all smiling. I saw them holding up their hands, palms toward me. They were not beckoning me to join them. They wanted me to go back.

Up above, on dry land, the guard yelled to two men who were working nearby. He ordered them to jump in and get me. And they did. They took hold of my boots and pulled me to the surface. Those two were chimney sweeps from Vilna. I didn't know their names, but I recognized them. They had thought my fall into the water was an accident. But that is not what the guard thought. He knew.

"You don't decide when you die. We do," he said.

That was my near-death experience. That was one of many times when, as my son, Avi, is fond of saying, I escaped dying as the coin came up "heads" for me. And as I look back on it now, I see that there was a higher power that was keeping me alive. I did not feel that, at the time. I did not all of a sudden believe that God was again back in my life and watching over me. I still wanted to die.

Not long after that, the Germans were lining up victims to load into the gas vans. I was in the line, and I was ready to go. Someone—I can't remember who, but it had to be one of the people I'd met in the camp—pushed me out of line. I didn't resist or protest. At that stage I was apathetic and hopeless.

It wasn't that I was determined to die. I just didn't care either way, and that higher power came along and impelled someone to push me in the direction of the living. No guard saw me move away. Once more, I was spared. "Heads" again.

A few weeks after that, I had a glimmer of hope for escape flare up in front of me. I ignored it.

A man who lived in Riga, not a Nazi, who worked in the camp offered me a way out. He said that he had a large family in the city, and that I could come and live with them. He said that my blue eyes would allow me to pass for a Gentile.

I turned him down. At that point, I was still listless and not thinking of anything like a future. Looking back after these many long years, I believe that I had moved a little beyond the depths of despair. But I was not ready to make any bold moves either.

Something else was happening too. I had other people around me. As bad as Kaiserwald was, and as poorly as they treated us, we still had opportunities to make connections with other people. In that camp, I came to know other people whose love was important to me. They gave me a reason to feel that life might be worth living after all.

I've mentioned my almost motherly concern for Bella and Dora. That was one aspect. They needed me.

There was also Edith, or Edita Gutreich (Goodrich), who became a lifelong friend. She was from Vilna. I never knew her before Kaiserwald because we had gone to different schools. She and her mother became my good friends at the camp. Edith worked in a factory where they made electrical cables. Her mother sorted clothing. They both slept at the factory.

Edith

One night, Edith's mother did not return to their sleeping quarters. She had been taken away in a selection and was killed. Edith tells her story in her own words in another chapter of this book, so I will not repeat it all here. But there is one other thing about Edith: because of her job she had more connections with non-Jewish workers, and therefore to the outside world, than I and the other girls did.

Edith heard reports and rumors about the course of the war. She relayed them to us and gave us reason to hope. That was the second most popular subject whenever we had a chance to talk. The first? Food. We were always hungry.

Edith also had at least one experience where she thought she was going to die. The camp commandant summoned her to his office. A letter had come to her at the camp from a friend who had been taken away to work in Estonia. The commandant had the letter. Edith thought she was going to be punished with death.

Instead, he gave her the letter and said that he hoped it never happened again. Even though he was the commandant of a concentration camp, the man had at least a spark of decency. Edith thought that it was because he had a Latvian girlfriend.

Then there was Eva Misrah and her wonderful mother, Lily. They were from Riga. They had somehow escaped the mass killing of the Latvian Jews two years earlier, and they had been living in the Riga ghetto. Lily Misrah was from a wealthy family that made Wolfschmidt Vodka. More than a century before, the Misrahs had supplied their vodka—called *ochischenoje stolovoje vino* (rectified table wine)—to Tsars Nicholas I and Alexander III.

Eva also became a good friend to me. Lily was like a mother to all of us, but perhaps especially to me. She, more than anyone, was the reason that I put aside my desire to die and determined that I would do my best to survive.

At night, when our work was done, we would often gather together and listen to Lily sing lullabies and other sweet songs in Russian. Of the five languages I speak, I have always believed that Russian is the most melodic and picturesque. Just closing my eyes and hearing her brought back some love and beauty in the wretched surrounding of the concentration camp.

Later on, at Stutthof, Lily literally saved my life and those of Bella and Dora. Lily and Eva also made it to Israel after the war, as I did. Lily wanted to adopt me then, but I thought I was too old for it. But I am getting ahead of myself. I do think that the first time she saved my life was in Kaiserwald. She was my angel, in the true sense of the word. "Angel" means "messenger." Lily was the messenger from that higher power that insisted I must live.

I was in Kaiserwald for nearly a year, from September 1943 to August 1944. The tide of war was running strongly against the Germans by that time. At long last, the Americans, British, and Canadians had landed in Europe and opened up the Western Front. But that was far away, and mostly unknown to us. What was more important was happening just a few miles to the east of us. The massive Red Army was on the march, and Germany was in retreat.

We could hear guns in the distance. The Russians did not cross the border into Latvia until August 6, but the Germans started to evacuate Jewish prisoners in July. I and my girlfriends were all deemed fit to keep working, and we were among the first ones to go. By boat. In the lower hold of a stinking, rolling, pitching, unseaworthy vessel. But we got there. Our destination was Stutthof, on the Baltic coast not far from the city of Danzig in Poland.

Evacuations to Stutthof, by rail or by boat, continued through September. But those who were evacuated were lucky. Even as the German military was suffering crushing defeats, the SS and its collaborators kept up the murder of Jews. In Kaiserwald, they executed every remaining Jew over the age of thirty and under the age of eighteen. The Red Army liberated the nearly empty camp on October 13.

Stutthof

Eva Misrah

STUTTHOF WAS THE first concentration camp that the Germans constructed outside of Germany. My girlfriends and I were there for only about six weeks. But in that time, the Germans selected me to die twice, and twice I was spared by one of their guards. One of them was conscientious about doing his job. The other was careless and insouciant about his. Two more times, the coin landed on "heads" for me.

The fishing village of Sztutowo, some twenty miles east of the free city of Danzig (now Gdansk) and a mile from the coast of the Baltic

Sea, was the place the Germans chose for this camp. They built it in 1939, right after they invaded Poland. It was not originally an extermination camp, but it became a place of death by the time I got there in September of 1944.

The camp's initial purpose was to imprison and abuse Polish citizens from Danzig. Later on, opponents of the Germans from countries like Russia, Lithuania, Latvia, and Estonia, as well as some Gypsies, arrived in Stutthof. Even as the mass murdering of Jews went on in many other camps and at out-of-the-way places like Rumbula and Babi Yar, Stutthof had stayed rather small.

That changed quickly. In the spring of 1944, there were only seventy-five hundred prisoners at Stutthof. By the end of the summer, there were more than sixty thousand of us. The Red Army was on the march from the East. As the Germans fled, they either killed their Jewish captives or sent them to places like Stutthof. Transports began arriving from Auschwitz, Bialystok, Kovno, and Königsberg as well as from Riga.

We were part of the first group of some ten thousand Jews that the Nazis evacuated by ship from Riga between August and October 1944. The voyage of about three hundred fifty nautical miles to Danzig took several days, probably five or six. It was impossible to tell for sure. They crammed us below decks without food, water, or fresh air. We were covered with sweat, vomit, and excrement. Many of the Jews died along the way, either from starvation or from despair. Bella, Dora, Eva, Lily, and I clung to one another, and none of us gave up hope.

After we staggered out of the hold of the ship in the port of Danzig, the Germans loaded us onto barges and floated us up a tributary of the Vistula River to the camp. It was in a forested, marshy area that would have made any escape effort very difficult. The outskirts of the camp looked almost welcoming, with clean, neat houses and orderly streets. That was deceptive: it was where the camp commandant and the high-ranking officers lived with their families.

We were herded through the camp's main gate—called "The Gate of Death" with its Arbeit Macht Frei sign affixed—and the first building we saw had flowers draped over its balcony railing. Music from an orchestra played in the background. But any sense that things would be normal quickly disappeared. We went up a narrow street that had many dead bodies sprawled and stacked along each side. A man was loading some of them into a hand-drawn cart. We saw the smoke rising from the crematory ovens. We smelled burning flesh. The Germans selected some of our group for immediate death by gassing or shooting.

The large influx of Jews to Stutthof gave the Germans a ready supply of slave labor. Although it was not an arbeitslager like Kaiserwald, Stutthof quickly became one; the Germans set up a network of 105 forced-labor camps in the area. Thousands of prisoners died from starvation and overwork as they dug ditches, quarried stones, cleared trees from the land, and built roads, fortifications, and airfields.

There was also a hastily constructed factory that made airplanes for the Luftwaffe. Another made parts for submarines. The Germans still needed Jews to work in their armament industry. That need for labor ultimately saved our lives, but our labor would not be in a Stutthof subcamp.

Even with their failing military campaigns and their dire need for factory workers for their armed forces, the Germans did not slow down their killing of Jews. In the middle of the summer of 1944, Stutthof commander Max Pauli received an order from his superiors at the SS: no Jew was to be left alive in Stutthof by the end of the year.

The place had not been built for mass exterminations. They had a small building that had been used for delousing clothing; typhus epidemics from the plagues of lice throughout the camp made delousing a necessity. The Germans started using that building as a gas chamber in the fall of 1944, employing the same Zyklon-B gas that was used at Auschwitz.

We were not put to work in Stutthof. We were not even registered. That meant that we were marked for death, as soon as the Germans could get to us.

With no work to do and no daily roll call, we sat around waiting for something to happen. The awful smell of death was everywhere. That is what I recall most vividly about that horrible place: the acrid, offensive stench of burning and decomposing bodies.

Oddly enough, the food was a little better than we had at Kaiserwald. They gave us a daily ration of soup that had vegetable peels and scraps—turnip, cabbage, and carrot—mixed in. Those scraps often sank to the bottom. I was usually able to get a few scraps and peelings each day. That small bit of nourishment might have been just enough to keep me alive—and by that time I was determined to live.

We had no water in which to wash ourselves, so every day and every night was a battle to rid ourselves of lice. Jews who died from typhus or starvation lay in the overcrowded barracks or on the ground outside. Men picked them up and carted them away in wheelbarrows to be burned in the small crematories or on piles of wood on the camp's outskirts.

Sadistic German guards and their Ukrainian helpers rounded prisoners up, marched them off to ditches, stripped off their clothes, and shot them. We could hear the gunfire off in the distance. A gallows with eight nooses stood in the camp's central square. Prisoners were beaten and hanged for no reason. Sometimes we were forced to watch.

Stutthof was reputed to be the site for another infamous, vile—and never punished—deed of the Holocaust: the manufacture of soap from the body fat of murdered Jews. An SS man named Rudolf Spanner, who owned a small soap factory in Danzig, was said to have invented the process of making what he called "Reines Judische Fett"—pure Jewish fat.

Hundreds of Jews were believed to have been executed for Spanner to produce his soap. He survived the war and was never arrested or prosecuted. But some historians and scholars of the Holocaust, including those at Yad Vashem in Jerusalem, have stated that the facts of this story about soap manufacture have never been proven, and that it must be considered a rumor.

Even if that story of the soap was a myth, it does not lessen the horrors of Stutthof. The selections for killing were constant and random. They first targeted the prisoners who were weak, elderly, or pregnant. Doctors, pretending to be caring for sick people, gave lethal injections of phenol. At other times, they would simply shoot them in the back of the head.

Because the gas chamber was small, the Germans rigged up a railway car to serve as another place to kill by gas. They dressed guards as railway conductors and loaded victims in, telling them that they would be transported to another camp. That ruse was believable, because prisoners from Stutthof were frequently shipped out to work or to be killed elsewhere.

Bella, Dora, Eva, Lily, and I all avoided being swept up in one of those random selections. But one day, my number came up. A soldier grabbed me and told me to stand in a line. He said I was to take a shower. That, too, was believable; there had been showers in the camp. I was looking forward to taking a shower.

The line was a long one, and at first I didn't see where it headed. It moved slowly, and I came at last to a small brick building. An SS guard stood at the door. I was about to step through the door when he told me to halt. No more than 150 could enter. He had been counting carefully; I was number 151.

That building was the former delousing chamber. It was now a killing room. Everybody who entered before me died.

The guard walked away without another word. So did I and everyone behind me.

I don't remember feeling any great relief at the time. I was actually disappointed that I hadn't gotten to shower. I resumed my daily routine of avoiding confrontations with guards and simply staying alive. I didn't find out until later that everyone who had entered that door before me had been murdered. And it wasn't until many months afterwards, when I was safe in the land of Israel, that the full horror of what had almost happened to me came flooding back in nightmarish dreams.

October came. The Russian army was drawing closer. The Germans began evacuating prisoners from Stutthof. The first ones to go were the stronger ones who still could be useful as slave laborers. There was one more selection before they loaded up the westbound train. I was not chosen to go. Bella and I were shoved over to a group on the left. We had lost sight of Dora. We were all going to die.

Lily and Eva were at some distance, on the right. Their group was to be spared, sent away to yet another labor camp. Lily caught sight of me. She stepped up to a guard and handed him a small gold coin. She pointed to me. The guard looked at me, and motioned for me to go over to the other side.

Lily Misrah, Eva's Mother

At first I didn't move. I couldn't leave Bella. I couldn't leave Dora. But then Dora came running up. We all three of us joined hands and ran to the side of the living. The guard was annoyed. But he wasn't so dedicated to his job that he would make the effort to stop us. There was more confusion and chaos in that selection than there was order and discipline. There were no real lines, but rather a milling and jostling crowd where the saved and the damned were barely separated. I slipped across that separation and was spared again.

We were lucky to be picked to leave early from Stutthof. The misery and dying continued and intensified. A third typhus epidemic broke out late in the fall. It was so severe that they quarantined the entire camp for two weeks. There were fifty thousand prisoners remaining when the final evacuations began in 1945. Five thousand were marched to the coast and machine-gunned to death on a cliff overlooking the sea. Many thousands more were marched toward the east in the brutal winter cold, then turned back when they encountered Russian forces. Most of them froze to death.

A total of twenty-five thousand Jews died in those final evacuations. When the Russian army arrived at the camp itself in May of 1945, they found only about one hundred Jews, who had managed to hide during the evacuations.

Shortly after my latest close brush with death, they loaded us into railroad boxcars. Our destination was Magdeburg, three hundred fifty miles to the west. One of many satellite labor camps of Buchenwald, Magdeburg was a place of heavy industry, of smoking chimneys, of fiery furnaces.

I would work there for another half year. But I would also dance there.

Magdeburg

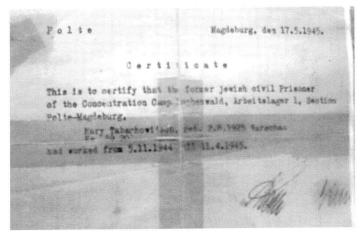

Certificate showing my time in Polte-Magdeburg, a subcamp
of Buchenwald, from May 11, 1944 to November 4, 1945. It
indicates that Warsaw is my birthplace.

*I*HAD NEVER BEEN to Germany and I had never heard of a
city named Magdeburg, situated at a bend on the Elbe River
seven hundred miles from my childhood home in Vilna. Perhaps it
was a good thing I had not known its sorrowful history. Magdeburg
had also been a place of mass murder amid the hell of war, much like
Ponary became during the days of Napoleon.

In a single day during the Thirty Years' War, November 30, 1631,
the troops of Duke Maximilian's Catholic League burned Magdeburg
to the ground and slaughtered twenty-five thousand of its thirty thou-

sand inhabitants. Frenzied soldiers looted, raped, and tortured at will, unchecked by their commanders. The devastation of 1631 was so great that a new word entered the German language: Magdeburgisieren (or "magdeburgization"), a term that signified total destruction, rape, and pillaging.

Later, in a letter, the Holy Roman Empire's field marshal, Count Gottfried Heinrich Graf zu Pappenheim, wrote, "I believe that over twenty thousand souls were lost. It is certain that no more terrible work and divine punishment has been seen since the Destruction of Jerusalem. All of our soldiers became rich. God with us."[1]

That day almost foretold the Final Solution of the Holocaust. It was not only the cruelty and mass murder that would reappear a little more than three centuries later. So, too, would claims of divine support and justification. Echoing exactly the words of Pappenheim, many of the Nazis' military medals, insignias, and citations were emblazoned with the words Gott mit Uns.

I would soon witness mass destruction of a different sort—bombing by the British and Americans that began on January 16, 1945. It leveled the entire city center and crippled three major factories. But that spectacle of destruction made me dance for joy.

My 350-mile journey from Stutthof in another crowded boxcar without food, water, or sanitary facilities, took just two days. My girlfriends and I were immediately put to work in the Polte-Werke ordnance factory. It was the largest ammunition factory in Germany. Thirty thousand slave laborers worked there—prisoners of war from Russia, Spain, and Italy as well as Jewish women from concentration camps like Ravensbrück and Auschwitz. There were also some American and British POWs, most of whom had been shot down in bombing raids. The factory's main product was artillery shells, enormous explosive projectiles that were thirty inches long and used in coastal defenses.

Magdeburg was one of eighty-eight satellite camps of Buchenwald, which was about one hundred miles to the south. An identification paper, issued by the United States forces after I was liberated, indicated that I was a "jewish [*sic*] civil prisoner of the concentration camp Buchenwald, Arbeitslager 1, Section Polte-Magdeburg."

So I was once again in a work camp, an arbeitslager, like Kaiserwald. It was not an extermination camp. But death was still ever-present. They made us work twelve-hour shifts in hot, dirty, noisy surroundings. The work itself was dangerous; there was never any training on how to use the massive production machinery, never any thought to industrial safety. Serious, often fatal, accidents were common. Polte-Werke had the highest mortality rate of all satellite camps of Buchenwald.

The only thing that mattered to the Germans, even as their inevitable military defeat approached, was to keep producing the shells for their guns. The factory and the camp also had their share of cruel and sadistic guards and supervisors. They made us stand at attention for long periods before and after work. If anyone stumbled or faltered, they were beaten up or whipped. Prisoners who became too weak to work or were injured were shipped back to concentration camps and murdered there.

Twice more during the six months I was at Magdeburg, I had close brushes with death and escaped—the coin flip came up "heads" for me again. The first of these was early during my time there. Eva and I had been sent to the part of the factory where they baked the shells. We had to load the shells onto carts after they came out of the ovens.

It was hot in there, but the worst part was the toxic fumes. At the end of the day we could hardly breathe. Later on we learned that the men who had initially done that work had all died from breathing the air. That is why the Germans then tried women for the job. Within just a few days, we knew that we would die as well. So we decided to plead for relief.

Eva and I went to the supervisor. I did the talking. I told him that we would die if we had to stay there. I begged him to release us for other work somewhere else. We were lucky—again. The man wasn't a typical, hateful Nazi. He listened. And he had at least a spark of decency within him, because he agreed to get someone else.

It was at Magdeburg that hope for the future truly came back to me. At Kaiserwald, I had not cared whether or not I lived, and had even attempted suicide. At Stutthof, with nothing to do but wait around with the stench of death everywhere, I was numb to everything. But at Magdeburg, I saw little hints of human warmth. I even felt the first faint stirrings of love and affection, both for and from people who happened to be men, beyond the tight circle of girlfriends who had been my personal life preserver up to that time.

An example of this warmth, one not directed at me, was a young German guard in the department where Eva and I worked after we escaped from the furnace room. He was not a member of the SS, but an ordinary soldier in the Wehrmacht. He became rather fond of Eva. He said to her, "You don't know me. You never saw me or spoke to me. But you may have my lunch every day." And he would leave her a delicious sandwich in a corner of the room, which was another large hall where there was constant bustle and confusion.

Eva would bring the sandwich back to the barracks, share half of it with her mother, and give the other half to Dora, Bella, and me. The bread and cheese were heavenly, such a difference from the meager rations of thin, sour soup that they gave us each day. That kind gesture by the anonymous German soldier did not keep us from starving. But it did give us even more hope that there was a better world waiting for us out there. We never knew his name. I hope that young man was able to survive the war and build a life for himself.

I also had a chance to give one of my fellow prisoners a cherished memory about food. On a few occasions, they put me to work in the kitchen. That was a coveted assignment; we had direct access to more food than the others. One day I sneaked an onion out and brought it to the barracks. I peeled it, layer by layer, and gave a piece to everyone around me.

Many years later, I was in a doctor's waiting room in New York City. A woman asked my name. When I told her, she said that she thought she had recognized me from the camp. She thanked me again for the piece of onion.

Then there were the Russian prisoners. When we first saw them over the fence, it was a huge relief. We finally knew that we were in a labor camp and not an extermination camp. Throughout the war in the East, the Germans had treated captured Russian soldiers with the most extreme brutality, starving them to death, working them until they dropped, and executing them. At least two million Russian soldiers died in captivity.

In fact, the first people to die in the gas chambers at Auschwitz were Russian prisoners of war, not Jews. About six hundred of them were selected for the first use of the infamous Zyklon-B. The original plan for Birkenau, the extermination camp at Auschwitz, was to be a slave labor facility for captured Russian soldiers. But so few of them remained alive in 1942 that Himmler and the SS began sending Jews there instead.

We didn't know that history at the time. But something told us that these young men, like us, now had to be kept alive. That was more reason for hope. After our work was done for the day, we could go to the far end of our camp and talk with them across the barbed-wire barrier. They were just like us—doing their best to stay alive and looking forward to better days. I found it easy to establish a rapport with them because I spoke Russian.

There was a handsome Russian boy named Boris. He would come to the fence and share some of his soup with me. There was never enough food for any of us, so he must have liked me.

Then there was Morris Kliot. We called him Booby. He was from Riga, and was a friend of Bella's boyfriend Max Funkelstein. Bella had met Max in Kaiserwald; that was the beginning of their life together. Max and Booby also survived the selections and made it out of both Kaiserwald and Stutthof.

Booby's job took him outside the confines of the camp. One evening after work he called me over and pulled a flower out of his sock. He had picked the flower when he was out with the work crew. "It's for your birthday," he told me, "whenever that is."

I liked Booby. I liked Boris. It was the first time in my life that boys paid any attention to me. It was wonderful. I was flattered. But even though I was inexperienced in love and romance, I knew that it would not be right to get serious with anyone. In fact, I would not be ready to establish a loving relationship for some time to come after the war ended. But I will save that part of my story for later.

Bella Klok

Bella did not feel that way. In Magdeburg, Bella would often sneak out of our barracks at night to be with Max. Dora and I, back on our straw mattress, worried greatly about her. If she were caught, it might have meant death for her.

We seldom heard real news about the progress of the war or about how long it would take for the Americans or the Russians to reach us. We did know that Germany was losing, and that it was only a matter of time. But there was always the possibility that the Germans would kill us, or herd us out on a death march, before fleeing. If they decided to hold out and fight to the death, we could be caught in the crossfire. Anything was possible.

We had been evacuated from Kaiserwald because the Russian army was closing in. We never saw them but we could hear the explosions and gunfire off in the distance. At Magdeburg, it was dramatically different. On January 16, 1945, the Allied bombers arrived.

In endless waves, they came from their bases on the east coast of England. The Americans arrived at noon. The British came later, at night. They wiped out 90 percent of the buildings in the city center and destroyed about 60 percent of the rest of the city. We watched it from our barracks, just a few miles away. It was glorious. The flames turned night into day. We sang. We danced. We hugged. We knew the end was nearer than ever.

The planes targeted and crippled three strategically important industrial complexes: the Krupp-Gruson-Werk, which built tanks, guns, and shells; the Junkerswerk, which made aircraft engines; and Brabag, which made synthetic gasoline. They did not bomb the section of the city where our barracks was located.

The bombers returned many times between January and April. In Magdeburg, and in several other places where the Germans incarcerated their prisoners for labor, the barracks were not far from residential areas. The local German families, mostly women and children, would come to the camp on those nights and huddle close to the fence. They thought, rightly as it turned out, that our camp would not be a bombing target.

Later, when the war was over, many of these same people would maintain that they had no idea about the camps or about what went on inside them. That is hard to believe, but it is also hard for me to hate them. I would have tried to save myself in exactly the same way, had I been in their position.

How should I describe my last days in Magdeburg? There is a famous expression for such situations: "the fog of war." In all the chaos and confusion, no one knows what to expect. No one knows whether it's better to hide and wait, to flee and hope we encounter friends, to obey orders or ignore them. Survival or death depended more and more on chance and luck. What should we do?

The only thing that was certain was that the Americans were approaching from the west and the Russians were approaching from the east. We were all caught in an ever-shrinking circle. The guards—many of them, but not all—paid less attention to us. But there were still Jew-hating SS fanatics among them. And the German commander, Lieutenant General Regener, stubbornly refused to surrender. His tactics brought death to several thousand more Jews who were right at the threshold of survival.

A few days before Polte-Werke ceased operating, the Germans executed a young Russian woman after accusing her of sabotaging a machine that produced ammunition. She was left hanging on the gallows for all prisoners to see.

We decided to hide. One day in early April, Bella ran up to me in the camp. She said that Max and Booby had fixed up a melina, a hiding place, in the ceiling of a barracks on the Russian side of the camp. We ran to that barracks and climbed in. Many other prisoners were there. We waited.

Nothing happened for a few days. It is hard to remember just how much time passed by. Then one of the men got restless and decided to go outside to look around. We begged him not to, but he left.

The Germans were still prowling around. They spotted him and followed him back to the hiding spot. They let him climb the ladder and close the hatch. Then they shouted "*Raus!*" ("Come out.") When no one responded, one of the soldiers shot a bullet through the ceiling. It wounded Max in the leg. We were caught, and we all came out to face the Germans who were brandishing their guns at us. I thought we would all be shot.

Max Funkelstein, Bella's husband

They had other plans for us. We were going on a forced march. To where, I didn't know. It could have been any of several destinations that they had in mind for us. They gave us bags of food, better food and more food than we'd been used to. They must have had a long march planned, and they probably wanted most of us to stay alive so we could be used as hostages.

All of the possible destinations would likely have meant death. One group of one thousand prisoners who had been herded out of Dora-Mittelbau to the south arrived in the small town of Gardelegen, just north of Magdeburg. They were massacred by SS men and local Nazi fanatics on April 13. The town was surrounded by American troops. The Germans herded them all into a barn, set it on fire, and machine-gunned anyone who tried to escape. The Americans did not get into the town until April 15.

On the same day as the Gardelegen atrocity, April 13, the Germans deported as many women prisoners as they could round up from Magdeburg to two other concentration camps: Ravensbrück, one hundred sixty miles north, and Sachsenhausen, one hundred miles to the northeast. Many of them died along the way; only about six hundred women from Magdeburg, I and my friends among them, survived.

We lined up, and the march started. I don't know if it was headed for Ravensbrück, Sachsenhausen, or somewhere else. But wherever the Germans intended for the march to go, their plans were thwarted. The fighting was still going on because the German commander wouldn't surrender, and the city came under an intense artillery barrage by both the American and the Russian forces.

Approximately three thousand prisoners who had started off were herded into the Neue Welt athletic stadium to wait out the bombardment. The stadium was suddenly overcrowded, and two grenades exploded. Panicked prisoners began to flee or tried to take cover. The SS men turned them back with machine gun fire, killing many. After the artillery bombardment stopped, the SS resumed the death marches of the prisoners who had survived the shootings.

In the noise and confusion, my girlfriends had gotten a little ahead of me. The Germans selected ten Jewish prisoners to remain in the camp, knowing that the end was near. One of the Jewish prisoners whom I knew slightly pulled me out of the line and pushed me into the cellar of a building. I screamed and tried to escape because I didn't want to be separated from Bella and Dora.

I was beside myself with panic and didn't stop crying. I could have ruined it for everyone else in the cellar, had we been discovered. Finally they shut me up in a small closet. I eventually fell asleep. Hours later I crawled out and rejoined the rest of them in the main part of the cellar.

Unbeknownst to me, some Jewish prisoners had made a deal with a few of the German guards. They agreed to try to save the Germans by vouching for them as decent people once the Americans took over. And when I was kept from joining that march, it probably saved my life. This was the final time that the coin came up "heads" for me.

We waited in the cellar while the sounds of battle echoed in the streets above us. We lost track of time. It could have been several hours; it may have been days. We couldn't tell if it was day or night.

When it finally fell silent, we didn't dare open the door. At long last, there was a knock. Everybody froze, and said nothing.

From the other side of the door we heard, in English, "You can come out now."

The door opened. There stood an American soldier with the sun shining behind him. I stepped out and saw a huge truck full of more Americans. They were from the 30th Infantry Division, which had come ashore in France on D-Day and fought their way across Europe. One of them was throwing cigarettes to us.

I picked up one bad habit that day. Smoking. It took years for me to break it.

One of the men on that truck was Lieutenant Frank Towers. I didn't speak with him that day, but I did connect with him more than seventy years later when we were both living in Florida. It was shortly before he died, in 2016, at the age of ninety-nine. Frank Towers was the division's liaison officer. After the war he got in touch with more than two hundred of the Jews he had helped to liberate, including me.

Frank Towers has written and spoken beautifully and sympathetically about the Jews and other prisoners he encountered and befriended. He had been with the American troop that had freed twenty-five hundred Jewish prisoners from a stalled train near Magdeburg on April 13. The SS guards had been ordered to drown all of those Jews in the Elbe if the train couldn't make it to its destination, the concentration camp Theresienstadt in Czechoslovakia. It was another planned atrocity, one that the timely arrival of the Americans prevented.

Lt. Towers orchestrated the hasty evacuation of those Jews to a former German air base in Hillersleben, about twenty miles to the west of Magdeburg. The Americans took over the barracks and set up a hospital after raiding local stores for medical supplies.

My first thoughts after emerging from the cellar, as I stood there in the bright sunlight, surrounded by American soldiers and puffing on my first cigarette, turned to my girlfriends. I couldn't help fearing the worst.

There was nowhere to go, so I returned to the camp. The first person from my group that I saw was Max. He was limping from his leg wound, but was otherwise unhurt. We looked around for a while, then gave up. We thought the girls had left the area, or worse. And I was drained emotionally, and covered with dirt and dust. I had a sudden urge to take a shower, a real shower.

Then I heard someone calling, "Merczia! Merczia!" It was Bella. Dora was with her. They had gone a little farther with the marching crowd and were headed for the stadium when a German family beckoned them to come into their house. They slipped out of line and the guards didn't stop them.

As for that family's true motive, we never found out. They might have felt sympathy for the prisoners. They might have feared the American conquerors. But it didn't matter. I had Bella and Dora back with me.

Edith Gutreich had a similar perilous experience. She had avoided the march by going with her foreman from work, a German civilian. He first sent Edith into the basement of a building. Later, he returned on a bicycle. Edith and some others held onto a rope tied to that bicycle, and the man took them through the streets to his family's house. They passed right through gangs of Hitler Youth, who were still patrolling the streets with guns. She eventually got back to the original camp too.

We stayed in that camp while the fighting continued. Artillery barrages and bombings kept up for another week. The cowardly General Regener never did surrender. He fled the city at two in the morning on April 18. On the 20th, he made a radio address from twenty miles away, congratulating his troops on their defense of the city and praising Adolf Hitler.

By that time, his leaderless troops had given up and surrendered, both alone and in small groups. Many of the Germans in the area wanted to surrender to the Americans rather than to the Russians. They expected, quite correctly, that they would be treated better by the Americans, who finally captured the city on April 18.

It is necessary to know the mindset of the American military in order to understand how and why my girlfriends and I were spirited out of danger as soon as it was possible. In a 2005 essay titled "Magdeburg Revisited," Frank Towers described the last days of the fighting and the Germans' refusal to surrender. He then went on:

> Many of these prisoners had gone for days without water, food or sanitary facilities, and they were weakened by exhaustion, sickness, hunger, and disease.

> After all of the joyous greetings following their liberation, there was a problem: What to do with all of these people, who then numbered well over 4,500. It was an immediate necessity to get them out of this area, as the final push of the battle and an air bombardment was about to take place the next day.

> At this same time, the Russian Army was preparing to move across our front, on the east bank of the Elbe River, enroute to Berlin, only 80 miles (about 130 km), away. Not knowing the precise attitude of the Russians towards these Displaced Persons, and particularly the Jews, it was thought best to remove them far

to our rear and away from the front lines. If they had made an attempt to cross the river and head eastward towards their own home country, we did not know how they would be treated by the Russians.

As rapidly as possible, all available 1 ½ and 2 ½ ton trucks were assembled and loaded up with these liberated prisoners.

At this time we were aware of a German Luftwaffe air base near the town of Helmstedt, not too far east of Brunswick, which we had just recently captured. There was a large number of barracks there which had recently been vacated by the German Luftwaffe personnel, and it was decided by the Military Government Section, to move them there. At this point they could receive medical examinations and assistance, as well as some available clothing, such as it was, and a feeding program was started, conducted by the local German citizens of the town, much against their will. The German citizens "were ordered" to obtain whatever supplies they could gather, and start to prepare meals for these former captives.[2]

I'm grateful to Frank Towers, those American troops, and their commander, General Leland Hobbs. Even then they could see, through the fog of war, the real character of their supposed allies, the Russians. They took it upon themselves to shield us from the Germans during those final days of fighting. But they also saved many of us from the clutches of Josef Stalin and his murderous regime. They could have left us there to fend for ourselves, as Magdeburg was turned over to the Russians and became a border city on the Iron Curtain. But they didn't do that.

We remained a few days in the Magdeburg area after the fighting ceased. We stayed in some vacated, fully furnished German families' houses. We slept in real beds and ate real food. Then they took us to Hillersleben. My second life was about to begin.

CHAPTER 12: MORT

Palestine, 1941–45

With other members of the Haganah

Y JUNE OF 1941, Hitler had pretended to be Stalin's ally long enough. Germany invaded Russia in Operation Barbarossa. Over a two-thousand-mile front, they drove the Red Army back, captured vast tracts of territory, and took hundreds of thousands of prisoners. The Germans were brutal captors, killing or starving most of the Russian prisoners they took, or working them to death in concentration camps like Auschwitz.

Though the Russians fell back swiftly into their almost limitless hinterland, they didn't collapse as Poland had. Poland had a Communist-leaning government in exile at that time. My father, as a Polish citizen, was released from the Igarka camp as a gesture of good will to that government. It took him a month to get to Pavlodar by train. But he made it there and lived with my mother and brother until the end of the war.

After their early military victories against the Russians, the Germans overran Bialystok. The killing of Jews began immediately, in June of 1941. The Germans burned down the Great Synagogue with about one thousand Jews inside. They then went on a shooting rampage through the streets of the Jewish neighborhood, killing about five thousand people.

As they did in many conquered cities, the Germans first drove the Jews into a ghetto and put them to work in support of the war effort. When mass deportations to the killing camps of Auschwitz, Majdanek, and Treblinka began in August of 1943, Bialystok's Jews revolted in much the same way that the Warsaw Ghetto Jews did.

The Germans, aided by thugs called Trawniki men, brutally put down the revolt. The Trawniki were recruited from Eastern European nations like Ukraine, Latvia, Estonia, and Hungary to do the dirty work of killing Jews. They were eager to save their own skins in service to the Nazis. Most of them, in all likelihood, felt the same way towards Jews as the Nazis did.

In the end, at least sixty thousand Jews from Bialystok died. Only a few hundred survived. After the war I searched for news of my relatives but learned very little.

Those who perished included my father's two brothers, Abram and Michael. I did hear a rumor that Michael, who was a good athlete, had jumped from the train on the way to Treblinka and was shot by SS guards. Some of those who jumped, and landed close to the rails, made their escapes because the guards did not get clear shots at them. Michael was one of the unlucky ones.

My mother's sisters, Shaina and Adelle, and brother, Myron, along with all of their family members, also died in the Holocaust. The only other relative who escaped was Jamikel Finkelstein (Jack Fink). After the Russians moved into Bialystok in 1939 and arrested my father, my mother urged Jack to leave. He agreed, knowing that there was no future in Communist Russia.

Jack was able to go to Grodno and obtain a visa for travel to China. He ended up in Shanghai, which had been open to European refugees due to the extraterritorial nature of the foreign trade concessions there.

Germany pressed its ally Japan to take some action against Shanghai's Jews. They were moved to a ghetto in the city in 1941, but they were not persecuted as they would have been in Germany. The Japanese kept the Jews and other foreigners who were trapped there in isolation, and they all were able to hold out until the end of the war. Jack eventually came to the United States, where his father lived and was an American citizen.

Having a visa saved Jack's life, but it did not help his brother Aron. Their father, in America, sent Aron an American visa after the war broke out. The Germans did not honor the visa. The Germans shot him and his sister Mary in Pietrasze, near Bialystok, after they liquidated the ghetto.

I was in my second year at the Technion when the war broke out in Europe. For me, life became harder. The money I had received regularly from my parents stopped coming. We had to give up our room on Pevsner and move into a Technion student dormitory downtown. That was an empty apartment building, given to the Technion to help the students affected by the war in Europe. Haganah duties, my studies, and occasional get-togethers and parties kept me busy. My aunt Henie in Chile and my uncle Jack Vernon in New York sent money that helped me get by.

The British were at war with Hitler, so we had to be on their side. But the British government had also issued its White Paper of 1939, a document that severely restricted Jewish immigration into the British Mandate of Palestine. The Arabs were pleased with that and their rioting ceased, but they remained pro-Nazi. Their leader was Haj Amin al Husseni, the grand mufti of Jerusalem and uncle of the notorious Palestinian terrorist Yasser Arafat. Husseni fled to Germany in 1941 and embraced the Nazis' mission of killing Jews. He later helped organize a Muslim brigade that killed most of the Jews in Bosnia. He never paid a price for his crimes. He returned to the Middle East after the war and, until his death in 1974, continued to foment terrorism and to preach hatred of Jews.

I was a student-soldier in a society that was both ally and enemy of the British. As David Ben-Gurion said in 1939, "We must help the [British] army as if there were no White Paper, and we must fight the White Paper as if there were no war."[1]

Some Jews volunteered for service in the British armed forces. They fought in a regiment known as the Buffs and in the Auxiliary Forces. Later on, they fought in the Jewish Brigade. About thirty thousand Jews from the British Mandate took up arms alongside the British during World War II.

I wasn't one of them. While I did help the British eventually, as a member of the Jewish police force, I took part in the protests and demonstrations against the White Paper. Those demonstrations took place throughout the country, and sometimes they got out of hand.

One time the Students' Group at the Technion decided to occupy the post office and courts in downtown Haifa. We marched down from the Technion and were stopped at the entrance of the building we intended to occupy. A skirmish began. Then stones started flying. Things got ugly, and a British policeman was injured.

The British imposed a curfew. We decided to break that curfew and hold demonstrations in the Hadar HaCarmel, the Jewish quarter of the city. Area Command put me in charge of the Technion group. They reinforced us with members of the squad from the nearby Hebrew Reali School. Our command post was in the main Technion building.

Shortly before we were to break the military cordon and go into action, our building was surrounded by British soldiers, police, and detectives. The soldiers came into the main Technion hall and began interrogating our boys, who were sitting around and pretending to be completely absorbed in their studies. They all gave the same story— that they had been unable to get out and reach home before the curfew began.

The British weren't convinced. They apprehended a group of us, students from both the Technion and the Reali School, and loaded us onto military trucks. They brought us to an ancient prison in lower Haifa and blocked us up in a large cell with criminals, communists, and some others who might have been police spies. The only convenience they allowed us was a big pot in the center of the room for urination.

Despite the presence of people who could have been planted among us to extract information, I was able to pass around instructions that we should all stick together and say nothing that had not been agreed upon among everyone.

During that first evening, we earned the respect of the other prisoners in a very odd manner. There were some Arabs in the cell with us. One of them fancied himself to be very strong, and he challenged us to have any of our members wrestle him.

Zarodinsky, a Reali School student whose nickname was Zaro, accepted his challenge. I appointed a referee for the match, but I was afraid that the big Arab guy would wipe the floor with Zaro. To our surprise, Zaro caught him in a half-nelson, lifted him bodily into the air, tossed him to the ground, and pinned him there. From that moment on, that vanquished wrestler and his buddies looked on us with something approaching awe.

The next morning the Jewish Agency brought us some sandwiches. The criminals among us had a great time. They were happy to get the sandwiches and to keep us company. The next day we were released, thanks to the Haganah, which was represented by the Jewish Agency. We weren't charged with a crime. One of the group was Chaim Laskov, an eighth-grader from the Reali School, who later became chief of staff of the Israeli Army.

When we got back to the Technion, we found that during the night a bunch of British policemen in civilian clothing had broken into the dormitory and beaten up students in retaliation for their friend who'd been hit by the stone. Some of the Technion students required hospitalization.

On guard duty at Bet-Lehem internment camp

Life in Palestine was getting more and more difficult. Whatever news from Bialystok reached us was discouraging. A few of us decided to do something that would help. My friend Nissah volunteered for the British Army Driver Corps. They put him through some brief training and sent him to Egypt. I decided to join the police.

The police force was under British officers and command. Its mission was to provide in-country security. Many of the police members had been in the Haganah. Still, the British trusted us more than they trusted the Arabs, because the Arabs favored the Germans in the war.

I went to the Palestinian Railway Detachment of the police force (PPRD) and got in despite my being 165 centimeters tall, one centimeter short of the minimum. They assigned me to Waldheim, a German perimeter settlement where middle-aged or elderly German farmers lived. Germans had been in Palestine since 1870 after Kaiser Wilhelm I had visited the country. There were four such German settlements, or colonies, in Palestine.

After the war broke out, the British allowed those Germans to stay and tend their farms with the help of Arabs. But they were interned in settlements behind barbed wire, with the Railway Police providing security. There were about sixty of us, living in military tents, and working security for Waldheim and another nearby settlement called Bet-Lehem.

They issued each of us a British rifle and twenty rounds of ammunition. We manned watch towers and did escort or surveillance duty on Germans who worked in the fields. The shifts we worked were usually three in a row, beginning at eleven at night and ending at one the next afternoon. We then had thirty-six hours off.

Every shift started with a roll call and inspection of arms. You had to be shaved and dressed in shirt and shorts. Most importantly, you had to have shoes that were as shiny as a mirror. The NCO at each roll call checked everybody's face, uniform, and shoes. If it was dark, he used a flashlight. It seemed ridiculous at times, but that was life in the British colonial forces.

We got paid six Palestinian pounds per month. Payday was a big production, with a military parade before the chief officer of the force. He would hand each of us our pay envelope, and we would salute him.

I couldn't continue with my studies at the Technion during those times. Waldheim was too far from Haifa, and there was only one train a day. I and a friend, Yona Sokolowsky, rented my old room at Pevsner 5 in Haifa, and we stayed over there on free days whenever we could. I wanted to get back to Haifa and the Technion.

It took me almost two years to do that. The police transferred me from Waldheim to Bet-Lehem, where I spent a year and a half. While at Bet-Lehem, I went to a Jewish Agency representative, a guy named Gostrowsky, and asked about a transfer to Haifa. Gostrowsky was a brother of General Yaakov Dori, who was the chief of staff of the Haganah. Gostrowsky turned me down abruptly, saying it was my duty to stay where I was.

That was too much for me to take. I wanted to be an engineer, not a policeman. So the next time that the British commanding officer, a Mr. Wright, came to Bet-Lehem, I made an appointment to see him. I laid out my case for a transfer. When he heard what I wanted to do with my life, he immediately approved and sent me back to Haifa.

So I was able to resume as a third-year Technion student. But I also had to work full time for the police. My job was to patrol along the Mediterranean Coast for German submarines, spies, and saboteurs. Even though it was particularly hard work at night, I tried to work the night shift whenever I could so that I could attend classes during the day. Each patrol unit consisted of two men; the patrols were spaced about a mile apart.

That duty lasted about six months. I had very little time for sleep. I often arrived at school with my rifle and bandolier. I frequently dozed off after a lesson or two; I just tried to stay alert and retain as much as possible. Over the course of that third year, I attended perhaps 50 percent of the lectures, and I studied mainly before the exams. It was my worst year in school but I did manage to pass all of the exams, mostly with Cs.

My police work also brought its hazards. One time, when I was assigned guard duty on a train coming into Palestine from Cairo, an Arab drug runner was on board the train. I realized what he was up to and confronted him. He took off, dashing from train car to train car.

As he got near to the end of the last car, he turned and fired his pistol at me. He missed and hit a light bulb behind me. I returned fire and got him in the leg. That was enough to disable and subdue him until we could arrest him and confiscate the hashish that he was carrying.

I did catch a lucky break after six months. They brought me into the station and put me in charge of the arms distribution, phone calls, messages, and the station log. I got that job because I knew English. My superiors were a British sergeant major named Williamson and a Jewish sergeant named Joel Shribman.

I was able to study a bit more during the evenings, when I was the actual boss of the station. Three students—Eli Chafetz, Chaim Tabshunski, and I—shared the duties and divided the shifts up so we could study. We did a good job of it, and our superiors allowed us to assign places of duty when they were not available. I gave the best jobs, inside the buildings rather than out on the beach, to other students so that they could study too. That made me a few enemies among the other policemen.

That third year at the Technion was a very hard one, both for me personally and for the Jewish people of Palestine. I broke up with my girlfriend Miriam and had a difficult time in finding another love interest. Miriam was from Bratislava, Czechoslovakia. She was intelligent and good-looking. We became romantically involved during the summer, but it didn't last because of my own immaturity and self-centeredness.

Miriam was a sickly girl. She developed ulcers, and I was not there for her to provide the loving care that she needed. I didn't appreciate her enough. That killed our relationship, and I later regretted it. For a while I took up with Irka, whom I'd met on one of the beaches. She seemed rather distant and confused about what she wanted from life. Our relationship didn't last very long at all.

Irka and her parents had been lucky to escape from Warsaw during the first month of the war. Her father had been a leader of the Jewish community back home, and in Palestine he became the head of the Jewish-Polish Mutual Help Association. I sent some packages of clothing through his organization to my parents in Kazakhstan. Most of them ended up being stolen by Russians. Bialystok's Association knew better about what to send abroad and how to send it, so I started to use them instead.

The military situation was precarious and fraught with danger for us. The Germans in North Africa had made it almost as far as Alexandria in Egypt. If they had broken through and taken Cairo and the Suez Canal, their next target would have been the British Mandate of Palestine. They would have had sympathetic Arabs on their side. The British, assuming they chose to stay and fight, would have been encircled.

We did not know it at the time, but the German armed force would have been followed into Palestine by an Einsatzgruppe, the band of SS thugs whose mandate was to kill Jews. In any case, my friends and I were not going to stick around if the Germans took Egypt. A small group of us, including Jona Sokolowsky, Zelig Solvetchik, Jack Gutstein, Stasick Erenwal, and I, developed a plan to move north through Syria, Iraq, and Iran, and eventually to Russia. We already had arms and ammunition from our work in the police force.

Fortunately, we didn't have to put that plan into action. None of the horrors of German conquest came to Palestine, because the British under General Montgomery defeated the German Africa Corps at El Alamein.

I actually had seen some of the troop preparations for that El Alamein battle and got to see what Cairo was all about as well. When I was in the PPRD, I accompanied an Arab paymaster to Cairo on a trip to pay the policemen working along the Palestine-Egypt Railway. We stopped at Kantara, on the border of Egypt. At that time the Egyptians did not let anyone into the country unless they were in the British army. I wanted to get to Cairo, so I decided to bluff my way in.

I went to the Egyptian policeman directing traffic. When he asked for a pass, I pulled out a red piece of paper that had some addresses on it. He waved me through and I boarded the train for Cairo after checking my gun with the local stationmaster.

The paymaster I'd been traveling with advised me to stay in a hotel called Churchill's House. When I got to the train station in Cairo, I told the porter to take me there. We walked for ten minutes until he pointed out a "house." It was a brothel. I laughed and told him that wasn't what I was looking for. After another fifteen-minute walk, we got to Churchill's House.

Fortunately, they had a room available. I was exhausted and went right to bed. The next day I went out to explore Cairo. The city was full of soldiers, moving to and from the front that was about one hundred fifty miles away. On almost every corner of the crowded street I heard solicitations for sex: "young boys" and "young girls." Boys would also approach you and offer to introduce you to their sisters.

During my three days there I visited the Museum of Antiquities, which was named for King Farouk. I also went to Heliopolis, the pyramids, and the Sphinx. One night I saw belly dancing; the queen belly dancer was about four-hundred pounds in weight and hardly moved at all. The crowd loved her and applauded wildly. In Arab countries, heavy women are considered attractive and are greatly admired.

On the trip back via Kantara I ran into my friend Nissah Warrat. He had joined the British army, and he was coming home on leave from Tobruk in North Africa. It was good to meet up again, however briefly, after not seeing each other for two years.

During that year of 1943 I was stricken with amoeba-dysentery. I had several waves of the disease; I would recover, and then have a relapse. It was probably caused by poor food and the climate.

During one of my bouts with the disease, they sent me to a resort for ten days to rest and recuperate. When I was there I became very friendly with a beautiful young woman from Canada. Her name was Neehama. Her husband was in the Persian Gulf, working for an oil-drilling company. She was devoted to him, but she'd had to come to the resort because she was lonely and depressed and needed rest. We liked to walk and talk together, and before we left she gave me her address and telephone number. We never became intimate; I was a gentleman with her and did not want to go beyond hugging and kissing. Our affair lasted until I left for Tel Aviv the following year.

On the whole, 1943 was a difficult and sad year for me. Sometimes, when I was alone on night duty at the station with a gun at my disposal, I wondered whether life was worth living. I quickly discarded thoughts of suicide, because of course life is worth living; I was not an optimist, but I wasn't a pessimist either. For me, things were black and white.

There is an old Arab saying, "Yom Asal, Yom Basal." It means, "One day is like sugar. The next day is like an onion." That is what it was like for me.

Finally, in 1944, things got much better. After three years on the police force, I resigned with a good-conduct certificate. Through a school friend named Moshe, I got a job as a security officer for a local oil company named Matacheff. The job entailed both day and night-time security for the plant as well as firefighting if needed.

I bluffed my way into the job by telling him that I had been a volunteer firefighter back in Poland. Before my interview I learned about all the uses of firefighting equipment, and they hired me. The owners were "white" Russians, and the local general manager was Arabic. The job itself was easy—twenty-four hours on and then twenty-four hours off. The only busy times were during pumping operations at night.

The pay was much better—eight pounds a week rather than six. I could study while I was at work, and my Technion grades improved dramatically. Moshe and I covered for each other when we needed time off or study time.

The war began to turn in the Allies' favor that year, and the letters from my parents and brother in Kazakhstan became more optimistic. It was hard for them out there in Central Asia, but at least they were alive. All of our Jewish friends and extended family who had stayed in Bialystok perished in the Holocaust.

I also found a new girlfriend—Chama, from the Neve Sha'anan neighborhood of Haifa. She was nice and caring, but still rather strange. Her life was devoted to music. She was an excellent piano player. We didn't have a common language, though, and when she left for Jerusalem to study piano at the Conservatory, that was the end of our relationship.

I graduated from the Technion with a four-year degree in Electrical Engineering, Electro Mechanical Department. My professor of Turbo Machinery was Hanan Ilberg, who managed a department at the Standards Institute of Israel. He was a demanding professor, but I got along well with him. He was impressed with my project, the design of a water turbine known as a Pelton Wheel. That worked out for me very well a bit later on.

The favorable turn of the war against Germany meant that the front lines were moving farther away from the Mediterranean. There was less need for security at the oil company, so my job was eliminated. But my studies weren't yet completed. It would take another six months of studies and completion of a project to earn my diploma and get the degree of Diplome-Engineer.

So back I went to the Palestinian Railway Police. I re-enlisted, got almost the same job responsibilities as before, and prepared for the exams. Groups of two or three of us would spend a lot of time going over test questions from previous years.

That approach worked. I passed my tests, completed my project, got my diploma certificate, and received the degree of INGENIER (EE). Immediately, I resigned from the police force. My superiors were furious with me for that, but I didn't care if I had burned those bridges. I wasn't going to pursue that type of career again.

Palestine, 1945–47

A beach date in Tel Aviv

HE YEAR WAS 1945. The war in Europe finally ended. I and my fellow students had been spared, but the Holocaust left a permanent mark on all of us. My parents and brother were alive, but most of my uncles, aunts, and cousins were gone. So were many good friends. My contact with the land of my birth simply ceased to exist.

My parents and brother were free to leave Russia, and the first thing they did was to go back to Bialystok. Nobody they knew was still alive. Approximately fifty thousand Jews from Bialystok had been killed by the Nazis. But they told the Russians that they were originally from Warsaw, not Bialystok. Had they been truthful about their former home, Chaim probably would have been conscripted into the Communist army, because Bialystok became part of Russia after the war.

As refugees, they were sent first to Szczesin on the Baltic Sea. They were given a house that had been vacated by a German family. But they had to get out of Poland and into occupied Germany, away from the Russians, to increase their chances for immigration to other countries. The Polish government, unlike those of other lands that had come under the sway of the Russians, at that point still did not prevent Jews from leaving.

It would have been unwise for any Jews to try to settle back in Poland anyway. Polish anti-Semitism never died out. Jews who had survived the war and who tried to return home to places like Bialystok were not welcome. Violence was common, both against Jews directly and throughout the country as the Communists moved in with their security police. Eastern Europe remained a miserable place to live in the aftermath of the war.

My parents and brother made it across the border to a United Nations Relief and Rehabilitation Administration (UNRRA) camp in Germany. I and other family members abroad went to work to get them immigration papers. I applied for their admission to Palestine. We abandoned that option because my brother, being of military age, would not be allowed into the country by the British. My parents, perhaps, would get in after a waiting period, but not he.

My uncle Jack Vernon, in New York, tried to get them into the United States. The U.S. still made it difficult to get in; they waited and hoped. My aunt Heine, in Chile, also applied for papers for them, and Chile responded favorably. They traveled via France. My mother contracted pneumonia in Paris and almost died. It took them almost a full year to get to Chile, but they finally made it in 1947.

For me, it was time to start my career as an engineer, to widen my circle of friends, and to continue doing my part for my community and my new country. Where should I work, and where should I live?

My first inclination was to search for an engineering job in Haifa. But Professor Ilberg, my mentor in Turbo Machinery at the Technion, asked if I would like to come to Tel Aviv and work for him at the Standards Institute of Israel. I jumped at the chance to do so. The Standards Institute was a big organization, an ideal place to launch a career.

And so I became an electrical engineer in Professor Ilberg's Mechanical and Electrical Department. My supervisor was Josef Karlebach, a member of the famous Karlebach family of rabbis and scholars from Germany. I performed electrical and mechanical testing of materials and electrical equipment. I also was responsible for technical writing and certification, research programs, safety inspections, and quality control. The wide range of duties and responsibilities was superb for my professional development.

I took the job for another reason too: my personal and social life. Tel Aviv was a dynamic city, full of young people, opportunities, and entertainment. Haifa worked, Jerusalem prayed, but Tel Aviv was the city of fun and future. It was the place for me.

After several short-term stays in rented rooms, I found a room with a breakfast arrangement with a family named "S" at Maccabi Street 10. I was making new friends at the Technion, going to parties—and getting involved with women.

The first of those females was Mrs. S, the owner of the apartment house. She was after me right from the start, and I immediately had a fling with her. I later regretted that one. Then along came Mrs. G, a very sexy and good-looking female with whom I had a torrid but short-lived affair. Competition between her and Mrs. S made it rather difficult, and both of the relationships ended for me.

The next woman in my life was Alima—blonde, beautiful, ten years younger than I, and probably still in love with her high school sweetheart. They had just broken up. Her parents didn't object to me or to our frequent dates. Her father was a chemical engineer; her mother was a pharmacist. Alima fitted in well with my circle of friends, many of whom adored her.

After a few months, however, she told me that she wanted to get back with that high school sweetheart. I didn't object, and my relationship with her cooled. Then all of a sudden she started dating Leiv, who was one of my friends. A few weeks later they announced their engagement and a wedding date.

I felt doubly used and abused by that turn of events. I knew she didn't love Leiv. She had never paid him any attention when we were dating. But Leiv's family was one of the wealthiest in Israel. She was after his money. That gambit with her high school sweetheart was a double-cross too. At least I felt that way.

The two of them got married. I stopped talking to Leiv and wouldn't reconcile with him despite my friends' efforts to bring us back together. I moved again and lived with my friend Gedik at an apartment owned by a Mrs. Kaufman, whom I'd known in Haifa. Mrs. Kaufman's son Moshe had been in school with me and was a good friend.

Living there, from 1946–48, in an exclusive area of Tel Aviv, brought me a little more balance and sensibility. I worked, partied occasionally, and went to the beach a lot. I also had one more relationship—this time with an older, more serious woman—before I finally met Mary, the real love of my life.

That older woman was Gizelle, an actress who had recently emigrated from Bulgaria. Her husband was a stage director. Their marriage was a cold and distant one, and they lived separate lives. She did like good company and fun, though, and we enjoyed being together. After I met my future wife, Gizelle and I parted as friends. I was pleased that we were able to separate in a mature manner. I was starting to grow up.

It is not as if I was totally absorbed in work and socializing. In post-war British Mandate Palestine, it was not possible for anyone to be entirely self-centered. Everyday life was challenging because the political situation was becoming more and more contentious. Radical change of one kind or another was inevitable. We had to be prepared, and I was.

We tried to bring in as many Jews as possible from Europe—either Holocaust survivors or refugees. The British White Paper of 1939 still dictated their immigration policy. That policy was too restrictive, limiting legal immigration of Jews to fifteen thousand per year.

The British were primarily interested in keeping their empire in the Middle East intact. They also wanted to retain access to the oil fields. That meant appeasing the Arabs, or at least not overtly challenging them. The Arabs did not want Jews in Palestine.

Many ships like the *Exodus* reached our shores. The British intercepted *Exodus* and sent the forty-five hundred Jewish passengers back to Europe. Other refugees were interned on the island of Cyprus or at the Atlit detention camp south of Haifa. The Jews who did make it in by sea had to be loaded into small boats and brought ashore at night. Between 1945 and 1948, about eighty thousand illegal Jewish immigrants made it into Palestine.

The fighting between the British and Jews was nasty and cruel. The Yishuv, the Jewish community committed to a homeland in Palestine, attacked British police stations, shops, and other facilities that were involved in catching illegal immigrants. The Etzel, also known as the Irgun Zeva'i Le'umi, carried out most of the reprisals.

Under Menachem Begin, it had been fighting the British in Palestine even before the end of the war in Europe. The Etzel rejected the policy of restraint favored by the Haganah. Their method was "an eye for an eye." After the British hanged four members of Etzel in the Acre prison, Etzel broke in and freed forty-seven of its people. Shortly after that, when the British executed three more Etzel members, Etzel captured and hanged two British sergeants.

The British were fed up with us and wanted out. They desired to turn responsibility for their Palestine Mandate over to the United Nations. The proposed solution was announced in November of 1947. It called for partitioning the land into Jewish and Arab enclaves, with Jerusalem a free city under UN supervision. Jews agreed with the arrangement. Arabs did not. Violence and rioting, a civil war between Arabs and Jews, immediately broke out across the country.

I re-enlisted in the Haganah in 1947. My group's command station was the police station on Dizengoff Street in North Tel Aviv. We carried rifles, handguns, and semiautomatic submachine guns like sten guns. Our primary mission was to guard the Jewish neighborhoods that faced Arab cities or villages.

We were sent to several trouble spots such as Sheich Munis, which today is Ramat Aviv, on the outskirts of Tel Aviv and bordering on Jaffa. Another was the Arab village of Salameh, about five kilometers from Jaffa. Arabs from Salameh had attacked the Tel Aviv neighborhood of Hatiqwa in December of 1947. In April 1948, as part of a Haganah offensive to the east of Tel Aviv, our group was assigned to capture Salameh. But the night before we moved in, the entire Arab population fled. There was no shooting or bloodshed on that occasion. Still, I may have escaped the war in Europe, but there was no escaping it in my new homeland.

So much else had happened to me in that year of 1947. There was a party at the home of an aunt of Dora Fisher, one of the girls who had survived the concentration camps along with Mary. The men who came to the party were mostly my friends who had graduated from the Technion. We thought we were brilliant—the elite. We were full of ourselves. We thought that any girl who could capture one of us would be very lucky.

They say that women's intuition is far superior to men's. That may be true, but my own intuition worked for me that night in a life-changing way. I met this shy girl, this survivor of the Holocaust, and I knew right away that I would marry her.

The first thing I noticed was her eyes. Her beautiful blue eyes. And she was prettier than all of the other girls too. But it was more than her good looks. I was ready to settle down. I wanted a serious relationship, one that would be different from all the others. And somehow I knew that she was the one for me.

It was not easy. The way I felt when I met Mary was totally different from any feelings I'd ever had for a woman. I tried hard to impress her, and I probably came across as a little arrogant and obnoxious. She rebuffed me initially and would not let me walk her home after the party. But I kept trying. Finally, she consented to go to a movie with me. That was our first date.

My Technion buddies told me that I was crazy. She was one of those people who had escaped the Germans, those survivors who had not fought back and had done nothing to resist. That is how they were viewed, at first, by the people who had made it early to Eretz Israel and who had not experienced the hateful deeds of the Nazis. Survivors were considered damaged goods. Few of them ended up marrying non-survivors. We would be the exception.

Maybe Mary believed that about herself. I suspect that she didn't think she had anything to offer to a highly educated, sophisticated electrical engineering school graduate—or to anybody else. She'd had no education beyond her teenage years, and when we met she had a menial sewing job in a pajama factory.

After what she had been through, I knew she could do better. She had it in her. We needed a telephone operator at the Standards Institute of Israel where I worked. I used my connections and got her the job. She didn't speak Hebrew, but she would learn it fast. I got my friend Ephraim to sit next to her and coach her.

Within a year, she was speaking Hebrew like a *sabra,* a native-born Israeli. She also knew Russian, Yiddish, Polish, and a little German. Later on, she would learn English. Mary had a knack for languages. She just never knew it.

Israel declared independence on 14 May 1948. The five Arab nations surrounding Israel immediately attacked, launching the War of Independence.

Two weeks later was our wedding day. Our reception was in Dora's aunt's house, in the same room where I had met Mary about one year before. Egyptian war planes attacked Tel Aviv that night. We had to douse the lights and finish the reception hastily. I donned my army uniform and reported back to my unit in the infantry. I was a married man at last, and on that day my life as an adult truly began.

Transitions —
Liberation to Palestine

In Charleroix, Belgium, with Eva and Dora. I am holding
my $200 pocketbook.

I DO NOT WISH to be known only as a Holocaust survivor. That is important, but it is not my whole story. I am a wife. I am a mother. I raised two children. I had a career. I have descendants. This, alone, is a victory over those who killed my family and were ready to kill me. This is my vengeance. I didn't just survive the Holocaust. I overcame it. And by doing so I fulfilled something that my mother always said.

She was a wise woman. So many of her sayings have stayed with me:

"All by yourself, your soul is clean."

"A new broom does it right."

"The crowd is stupid."

"When you hit somebody, it heals. When you say something, it never heals."

These sayings sound much more melodious—some of them even rhyme—when you say them in Yiddish. I remember them even today.

There was one of her sayings that always scared me. I don't know why. But perhaps it is fitting. For me, it was certainly prophetic.

"There is not a bad experience that you cannot overcome."

For more than four years, I lived in another world, a man-made hell. But I survived that hell and I overcame it, just as my mother had said I could. I feel it is my duty to pass along my story. Ever since that day when the chimney sweeps pulled me out of the river at Kaiserwald, I have felt that there was a higher power that wants me alive so that I can do that.

And how many times did that higher power intervene—making sure that the coin came up "heads" for me?

There are seven that I've told you about, in addition to the time at the river:

- In Vilna, I was dragged to the police station for not wearing the yellow star; they let me go.

- They liquidated the Vilna ghetto and sent my mother and sisters to the line on the left; they dragged me into the line on the right.

- I was in line for the gas van at Kaiserwald; someone pulled me away and the guards didn't see.

- I was next in line to enter the gas chamber at Stutthof, but they closed the door and sent me away because I was number 151 when the chamber could only hold 150.

- I was in the line for death at Stutthof; Lily, in the other line to be sent west to Magdeburg, slipped the guard a gold coin to let me in. I grabbed Bella and Dora and brought them with me, and the guard didn't bother to stop us.

- At Magdeburg, one more day of working in the choking, toxic fumes of Polte-Werke would have killed me. The supervisor was a decent man, not a fanatic. He took pity on Eva and me, and he let us go to another assignment.

- When Magdeburg was being evacuated and they were herding us toward the sports stadium, someone pulled me into a cellar and saved me from the bombardment and shootings at the stadium.

There might have been other times in which fate, or luck, or that higher power, intervened for me without my knowing. But I survived, I overcame, and I am here to tell of it.

I have said that my first life ended when the Germans started the war, and that I was "re-born" into a new life, my second life, in Israel. That is true, but it is too simple. When a child comes into the world, it is not ready to survive and prosper. When I finally escaped the clutches of the Germans and their horrible killing machine, you might have thought that I was prepared for anything. I wasn't.

In many ways, I was like a child again. I was starting over. A child cannot survive without parents, family, friends. My immediate family—parents, brother, and sisters—were all gone. I could not have made my way, in the new and "normal" world that I was entering at the age of twenty-one, without the love and help of so many who became my new family. They are all an important part of the rest of my story.

And I have already mentioned that Bella and Dora and I, being together all through the concentration camps, probably saved one another's lives. But soon I would find others—blood relatives, friends, and, most importantly, a husband—who loved and nurtured me and enabled me to flourish.

I knew that I would not be returning to my childhood home in Vilna. It would be either Israel or America. I had relatives in both countries. The end of the war did not mean the end of anti-Semitism in any country of the world. But the countries of Eastern Europe— Lithuania, Poland, Hungary, and the rest—were especially unwelcoming to any Jews who tried to return. Jews were almost always unable to reclaim property or businesses that had been stolen from them.

Hundreds of Jews were murdered by local mobs during the first two years after the Germans surrendered. The Soviet Union's government made it known that it would not be able to guarantee the safety of Jews in the face of the Polish-Lithuanian threat to their lives; Russian authorities urged that the Jews congregate in Vilna. This shows that the American soldiers who liberated us at Magdeburg and had feared for our safety at the hands of the Russians were correct.

Another memory comes back as my thoughts turn to Magdeburg. It was there, before we left the immediate area for Hillersleben, I had my first experience of interest in me by a man. It was anything but pleasant. I was far from ready for an exclusive relationship with any man, but even then I knew what I didn't want. My girlfriends and I stayed in a German house, enjoying the comfortable beds, eating from the well-stocked refrigerator. A Jewish man who occupied one of the other houses nearby came calling several times. He told Dora, "I want to marry her." I had encountered him in the camps, but I never liked him. He was crude and repulsive, so I told Dora and Bella that they should never let him into the house.

It was not the last I would see of him. Later on, he found where I was living in Palestine, and began pursuing me again. It took some doing to avoid him.

Hillersleben's accommodations were luxurious. It had been both a German Luftwaffe base and top-secret proving ground, housing a community of scientists. They performed research and testing of giant railway guns manufactured by the Krupp Steel Company. This base had several operations buildings, a number of two-story barracks, private homes for the officers, and a small hospital.

We stayed only a few days in Hillersleben. My girlfriends and I were in comparatively good physical shape, in contrast to the many Jews—more than two thousand of them—who had been freed from the train at Farsleben, near Magdeburg. Those prisoners needed extraordinary care from the U.S. Army medics; they had to be fed intravenously, because their malnourished bodies could not digest normal food. At least seventy-five of them died in the first month of their stay, mostly from typhus.

My Displaced Person's Index Card

In addition to the U.S. military, the Jewish Joint Distribution Committee, which was known as the Joint, was there to provide food, clothing, medical help, and emotional support. So, too, were Jewish soldiers, both from the American army and from the six-thousand-man Jewish Brigade that had fought as part of Britain's army.

By that time, the Bricha (also called Bericha) had been underway for almost a year. Meaning "escape" or "flight," it was an underground movement to help surviving Jews escape the clutches of Stalin's Russia and the anti-Semitism and pogroms of their former homelands. The goal was to bring them to the land of Israel, which was still British Mandate Palestine. Britain kept up its severe restrictions on immigration to Palestine, however, so a great portion of the refugees who made it there got in illegally.

The Joint supplied much of the funding for Bricha; the Jewish Brigade helped with the logistics of transport and security. My relative Abba Kovner was one of the prime movers behind Bricha. I will tell you more about his role shortly.

One day in Hillersleben, I was walking in the street when an American soldier came up to me and spoke in Yiddish. He asked me if I knew anyone in the United States. The only thing I was able to remember, from those family visits in Vilna more than a decade before, was my uncle Sam's name. He had changed it from his family name, Tabachowitz, when he moved to America. I replied, "Sam Share Syracuse."

The soldier said that I had told him all that he needed to know. He contacted a Jewish army chaplain who happened to be from Syracuse, New York. That chaplain passed my information along to the Jewish community in Syracuse, and in short order they located my father's brother and his family. It took several weeks for word of them to get back to me, but at least I knew that they were alive and they were excited to know that I had survived.

Eva and Lily Misrah left Hillersleben and were able to go directly to Palestine. Bella and Max had gotten married before they left Magdeburg; they ended up in America after first living with some friends in southern Germany for a few years. Edith, Dora, and I decided that we would prefer Palestine, but we needed to obtain the legal papers first.

Fortunately, we were in a sector that was administered by the Americans after the Germans surrendered. America was much more sympathetic and accommodating to Jewish refugees than Britain. The British did not allow any Jews who had crossed over from countries of Eastern Europe to stay in their Displaced Persons camps.

Additionally, President Harry Truman stepped up to do more for Jews than his predecessor, the deceased Franklin Roosevelt. Though he could not immediately get the American Congress to raise existing immigration quotas, he used diplomatic pressure on the British to accept one hundred thousand Jews into Palestine. That was nowhere near enough, but it was a start.

My certificate of identity for entry to Palestine. It also lists Warsaw as my birthplace.

President Truman also sent Earl Harrison, the dean of the University of Pennsylvania Law School, to Europe to inspect the camps holding displaced persons. Harrison asked Joseph Schwartz, the Joint's European director, to accompany him. Harrison's report on what he found—the deplorable overall conditions and the discrimination against Jewish refugees—called for separate Jewish camps. The United Nations Relief and Rehabilitation Administration (UNRRA) would administer them with help from the Joint. Truman agreed, and it was done.

My next stop was one of those Jewish-only camps. Dora, Edith, and I took a train to Brussels, Belgium. From there we were sent to Charleroi, a city of heavy industry about forty miles to the south. Other camps for Jews had been set up in Brussels and Liege. There had been a small Jewish community in Charleroi between the two World Wars, but most of its residents had been rounded up and sent to their deaths.

Our DP camp was clean and new. We had freedom of the kind that we'd never experienced before; we could travel about the country and go anywhere we wanted. We filled out papers and waited, hoping to get approval to emigrate to Palestine. On the applications, we lied about our city of birth; following the urging of the Jewish soldiers we had met, we all claimed that we had been born in Warsaw.

This was only the second lie I can remember that I ever told. The first was pretending that my name was Mila Kovner after she, my cousin, had been murdered at Ponary. We feared if the occupying forces knew we were from Vilna, we would be sent back "home" to a land that no longer welcomed us. This fear was reasonable. The British government believed that Jews who had survived the Nazi regime should simply return whence they had come.

One day the three of us were at the offices of the Joint. Dora was summoned into a separate room and was in there for a long time. Edith and I began to worry about her. Finally, Dora emerged with a big smile on her face. She was going to Israel. So were Edith and I. Because of an amazing coincidence, she was approved. And she obtained approvals for us, too.

It had happened this way. The intake officer, whose last name was Isgur, asked her where she had been born. She replied, "Warsaw."

"You are not from Warsaw," he said. "You are from Vilna, and you are my niece."

Mr. Isgur wanted to adopt Dora and have her come to live with his family. She refused his generous offer and insisted that she wanted to go to Palestine with Edith and me. Once again, those family bonds that we had forged during our time in the camps held firm. Mr. Isgur promised that we would have the proper papers within a few weeks. Not long after that, Dora learned that her sisters, Tanya and Rita, had also survived.

While we were waiting for our paperwork to come through, a telegram arrived from my father's extended family in Syracuse. There were many of them, the Shares and the Millers, all living in upstate New York. It was the first confirmation that I still had relatives in America. The Shares wanted me to come and live with them, and they could have made it happen. But by that time I had secured passage to Palestine and was determined to go there, where I would be reunited with my favorite cousin, Ber Kovner.

With that telegram came two hundred American dollars. I'd never had that much money before. My girlfriends and I thought that we could now do more than window-shop in Charleroi. But we got little more than a bitter lesson, both about the value of money and, more importantly, about human nature.

In the town, we saw three nice pocketbooks in a store window. I had never had one. So we went in and picked out one for each of us. I handed the storekeeper my two hundred dollars. He gave me no change in return. He had seen a chance to cheat a naïve and trusting girl out of a great deal of money. Yes, I did have a lot to learn about living in the real world.

After we received our immigration papers from the Joint, we took a train through France to the port of Marseilles on the Mediterranean Sea. I remember very little about that journey, other than that it took a long time. It was approximately six hundred miles through country that had been devastated by bombings, land battles, and other horrors of modern war. The train had to stop on many occasions so that the tracks, bridges, and railbeds could be repaired.

From Marseille, we went by ship to the port of Haifa. Again, my memories of that journey, of almost two thousand miles, are vague. It must have taken about two weeks. After we disembarked in Haifa, I was back in a place that felt like prison. The Atlit Refugee Camp, twenty miles south of Haifa, was in fact a prison. The British had built it in 1939 to incarcerate any Jews who had escaped Nazi Germany's clutches and had made it to their Mandate of Palestine without immigration papers. When I arrived, British authorities and representatives of the Jewish community were in charge of Atlit. Jewish policemen stood guard.

They processed my papers and gave me a physical examination. The doctor initially thought that I was ill; he detected an irregular heartbeat. It turned out to be a heart murmur. I had never known I had it, and it has never since then given me any trouble.

Before I left Atlit, I got yet another bitter lesson about people in the real world. Eva and Lily Misrah had been waiting for us to arrive. Eva came to the barbed-wire barrier on the first day and tossed over a "care package" for us. But we never laid hands on that gift. Another prisoner grabbed it and ran away, disappearing into the camp before we could stop him.

After two days in Atlit, I was free to go. My cousin Ber Kovner and Klara Bar, another relative from Vilna, came to get me. They had seen my name on a list of new arrivals that had been published. I stayed with Ber, who had taken the name Meir Vilner, and his wife, Esther, for a short time; they had a house in a citrus grove. Later I moved in with Klara in her apartment in Tel Aviv.

I was twenty-one years old. My second life had finally begun.

My Relative Abba Kovner, Post-War

Abba in his writing studio at Ein HaHoresh Kibbutz

*A*T THIS POINT I wish to return briefly to tell you some more about my relative, Abba Kovner. His story is not my story. But his career and deeds did have a direct and lasting effect, not only on me but also on the lives of many Jewish people of our times.

Abba had a strong early hand in organizing the flight of thousands of Jews from Europe and their eventual entry, by both legal and extra-legal channels, into the land of Israel. I was one who, through a series of fortunate occurrences and helped by the movement that

Abba launched, was able to gain legal entry to Israel, which at the time was still the British Mandate of Palestine.

His experience is also a good example of what Jews faced if they tried to return to their former homes in Europe.

I had just arrived in Stutthof and had more than a year of captivity still ahead of me when the Russians liberated Vilna in July of 1944. Abba returned to the city. With him were about two dozen members of Hashomer Hatzair, the Zionist youth group, who had fought along-side him as partisans in the forest.

When walking the streets of Vilna, he saw a woman and her young daughter emerging from a narrow alcove, their melina, where they had lived in hiding for months. The mother burst into tears when she saw Abba and the partisans. The little girl asked her, "Mammeh, may I cry now?"

Many years later, when testifying at the trial of Adolf Eichmann in Israel, Abba was asked about the first thing he had seen when he entered Vilna. He told the court the story of meeting the mother and her little girl.

Abba testifying at the trial of Adolf Eichmann

Abba went to his family's home at 7 Poplavska Street. No one was there. As he sat mourning on the sidewalk, a Christian woman who had been a neighbor approached him. When she recognized him, she said, "Are you still alive? We hate you. Go away."

That incident with the Christian woman, along with other anti-Jewish moves by the Russians who were now in charge, convinced Abba that there was no future there for him or for the few Vilna Jews who had survived. The Russian government in Moscow sent medals to the partisan brigades that had fought in the forest, but they ignored almost all of the Jews who had fought in those brigades. He tore up the recommendation for his own medal in front of the brigade commander, declaring that the Russians did not want to show that the Jews battled more and harder than non-Jews.

Abba also remembered with disgust the stories in *Pravda*, the Russian newspaper that had occasionally appeared at the partisans' camps with airdropped supplies. Articles about the partisans' missions said that Lithuanians had done the sabotaging, the fighting, and the dying. There was no mention of Jews at all; it was as if they had never existed.

He was also dismayed when he heard that a memorial service at Ponary, conducted by the Lithuanian civil government, included eulogies for the Poles and Russians buried there but did not mention the Jews, who were by far the most numerous of the victims at that place of slaughter. The Russians, Lithuanians, and Poles were already doing their best to write the Jews out of history.

Abba had been the first Jew in Vilna to recognize the true intentions of the Germans, and to speak up and attempt to fight back. Now he was one of the first to recognize that there was no place in Eastern Europe for its few remaining Jews, and he was determined to develop a plan to get them out of there and to Eretz Israel. As a first step, he dispatched members of the Hashomer Hatzair to other cities in Poland and Lithuania—Grodno, Bialystok, Kovno, Lvov, and Minsk—to look for survivors.

He also wanted to preserve the memory of Jewish Vilna for posterity. So he organized the collection of the books and papers that had been hidden in the ghetto by Herman Kruk's book brigade. His younger brother, Michael, had worked on that group before leaving for the forest and meeting his death at the hands of bounty-seeking Polish peasants.

Volunteers supervised by Abba spread the word of their work around the city. They intended to build a Jewish Museum in Vilna. In reality, it was to be a library or archive that both documented the deeds of the resistance movement and preserved the spiritual and cultural legacies of the thousands of Jewish lives ended by the Germans and their Lithuanian collaborators.

Abba knew that they only had a short time, perhaps just a few months, to collect and catalog their materials. The Russian government under Stalin, always hostile to Jews, would soon seal the borders and make emigration even more perilous. He also wanted to take some of the most significant items and documents out of the country, either to Jerusalem or to America, before leaving. So they worked feverishly at the task of collecting, but on at least one occasion other matters demanded their attention.

A Polish woman came to them one day with a handwritten letter dated June 26, 1944, just two weeks before Vilna was liberated. Headed "A Plea to our Jewish Brothers and Sisters," it had been thrown out of a truck that was transporting 112 Jews to Ponary to be murdered. Those 112, who included thirty children, had been hiding for nine months. Another Polish woman, the widow Marisia, had known of their whereabouts. She had given them food in return for extorting from them furs, silk, and thousands of German marks. When the Jews ran out of money and could not give her the five kilograms of gold that she demanded, she denounced them to the Germans.

The letter described how the German and Lithuanian police tortured those Jews for four days. They raped young girls in the presence of their mothers and sexually mutilated adult men. The letter ended with a plea for revenge against widow Marisia and gave her address, 34 Wielcka Pahulanka Street. It ended, "We bid farewell to you and the world. We call for revenge!"

Abba and his people investigated and found that the widow was then living as mistress of a high-ranking Russian security officer. They knew that there would be no way to have her arrested and put on trial. So they ambushed her on the streets of Vilna and killed her.

In the end, Abba's efforts to establish a museum in Vilna were in vain. The Lithuanian authorities and their Russian masters grew increasingly hostile. Most of the documents ended up in a local jail building that they called the temporary Jewish Museum. Those documents remained there through the long years of Soviet domination.

A few priceless items, such as the diaries of Theodor Hertzl, who was the founder of Zionism, and of Herman Kruk, were smuggled out by Abba's comrades and sent to the YIVO Institute for Jewish Research in New York. Kruk's diary is the source of much of the information in this book about the events that affected my own life in the Vilna ghetto.

Late in December of 1944, a friend in the Vilna police department told Abba that the Russian secret police were planning to arrest him the next day and charge him with stealing museum property. He donned a Polish army uniform and left on a military train, crossing the border into Poland and making it as far as Lublin.

At Lublin, Abba met with Jewish survivors of several camps and with representatives of the local Jewish community who seemed intent on cooperating with the newly constituted provisional government. He had little patience with such an approach, feeling that Jews would never truly be welcome, whether by a Polish government or by a Russian one.

He developed a three-part strategy that drove him for much of the upcoming year: *bricha* (the exodus from Europe); *hativa* (uniting the Jewish survivors); and *nakam* (revenge). He even committed that strategy to writing. Not many Jews burned for vengeance against Germans, but Abba was one who did.

According to the historian Dina Porat, Abba viewed the hativa as a temporary organization whose primary reason for existence was to make survivors' voices heard until they reached the land of Israel. The Jews of the Yishuv, those who were already in Israel, had not gone through the hell of Nazi-dominated Europe. They had no idea of what we had been through. They first needed to listen to our story, to understand us.

It took them a while to understand. On that, I can speak from experience. When I got to Israel, I felt shunned and degraded in the eyes of those who lived there. Many of them initially thought that we survivors had done nothing to resist, and that we simply could have fought back.

As I've mentioned, Abba was furious that, even as the war was still on, the Jews' contributions in the partisan battles were ignored. But there was even more to it. With his drive to collect all of those documents, religious items, and cultural artifacts, he was passionately determined to show both the Jews of Israel and the rest of the world just how much of our civilization had been lost.

Many years later, he founded the Museum of the Diaspora in Tel Aviv. That museum displays pictures, records, and documents from Jewish towns and synagogues from all of Europe. They were not just from Vilna, the religious and cultural center, "The Jerusalem of Europe." To him, the survival of the Jews was only part of the story. One of his mottoes was, "How can you know what we lost, if you do not know what we had?"

But in those whirlwind months of late 1944 and into 1945, the matter of bricha, the exodus, came first. Abba stayed in Lublin for three months. Knowing that the Jews had to get out of Poland before the war ended officially and the borders were closed, he sent comrades out to find escape routes through the mountains to Czechoslovakia or to Romania. They sought out bribable soldiers and guards who would assist the escapees. Abba arranged for forged documents and advised escapees on what they could carry and on what they should not have on their persons in case they were searched.

In March 1945, Abba and several of the leaders of the movement went to Romania. By then the trickle of migrating Jews seeking to flee Europe had swelled to thousands. Those who made it to Romania were hoping to find ships at a port on the Black Sea and to sail to Israel from there. In Romania, he first met representatives of the Yishuv and was disappointed that they had only one ship and one hundred immigration certificates to Israel. Romania was not going to be a suitable point of embarkation after all.

In Romania he also learned for the first time of the Jewish Brigade, which had fought under its own flag as part of the British army in northern Italy. The brigade was camped at Tarvisio on the Italian-Swiss-Austrian border. Abba sent messengers ahead to inform the brigade that thousands of Jews were fleeing Europe and needed their help.

Abba and his colleagues gave the one hundred certificates to the elderly and to pregnant women, and then they set out to find other means of escape. The best route was through Hungary and Austria and then to Italy; that would put them out of the clutches of the Russian government and its puppet states. Along that route he saw and heard of more cruelties against the Jews. Those who boarded trains, who sometimes had to sit on the roof because there were no seats, were robbed, extorted, and raped by Russian soldiers. When at last they crossed over into Italy at Graz, Austria, Abba turned back a final time and spat.

Refugees who made it into Italy found an enthusiastic welcome from members of the Jewish Brigade. Those Jewish soldiers, now that their combat days were behind them, embraced a new mission of escorting and protecting their people. Unlike the representatives of the Yishuv, these soldiers had been through the war and had put their own lives in peril. It was evident to them, as it had been to Abba and the partisans, that working through legal channels with newly established government authorities wasn't the answer. The flood of surviving Jews who needed help and a home far exceeded any numerical restrictions or quotas.

The British never wanted large numbers of Jews to emigrate to their Mandate of Palestine; their infamous White Paper of 1939 was still in effect. Even in Europe, they made things difficult for Jewish refugees. They did not welcome refugees from Eastern Europe into the displaced persons camps that they controlled. They closed the border at Graz, which forced twelve thousand Jews to camp out there and find ways to sneak across in small groups.

The Americans treated Jews very differently. In Italy, their soldiers never harassed or detained the refugees who flocked to the seacoast. General Dwight Eisenhower, their supreme commander, had required that his soldiers visit a concentration camp to see for themselves the cruelty of the regime that they had fought against. With the encouragement of the Americans, in the three years after Germany's surrender, 140 ships filled with Jewish refugees sailed from Europe to Palestine. I was on one of those ships, though I had come through the American sector in France, not Italy.

Abba arrived in Italy ahead of the rest. His appearance and his stirring rhetoric inspired the brigade members and ignited their determination to assist. Hanoch Bartov, a young soldier then serving in the brigade, wrote that Abba came alone, at night, his mane of hair tossed and his eyes burning. He greeted the pickets protecting the brigade headquarters, declaring,

"My brothers, blessings upon your heads . . . even if your chariots arrived late. . . . We will arrive and be on our way to you. Our brothers are waiting for me at the border. . . . Good bye, we'll get here."[1]

On July 15, Abba arrived back at the brigade camp at Tarvisio, at the head of a large group of refugees. The writer Yehuda Tubin pointed out that everyone "received A.K. with enormous enthusiasm, with hugs and kisses and cries of joy. Anyone in the Brigade who had any position at all was quick to welcome him."[2]

The following evening, Abba addressed a gathering of hundreds of soldiers and refugees. He spoke of his experiences in the Holocaust and about bringing the Jews of the Hativa to Eretz Israel and remaking the country into a Jewish state. He feared that the Holocaust was not over and that Jews had to struggle "against the hiss of the approaching knife, the knife lying in ambush in all corners of Europe."

More ominously, he spoke of vengeance: "If we do not take our revenge, who will take it for us?"[3]

That emotionally charged meeting ended with everyone singing "Hatikvah," which was then the anthem of the Zionist movement and which ultimately became the national anthem of the state of Israel. But when they were done, the partisans rose as one and sang their own anthem, "Say Not That This Is Your Last Journey."

Abba remained in Italy just two weeks more. The detailed work of bringing the thousands of refugees to Israel fell to others. Having inspired the bricha and convened the hativa, he was off to put into action the third part of his plan: nakam. Revenge. Fortunately for him and for millions of people, his nakam was largely a failure.

The bricha was not a failure. It was, rather, the largest mass migration of Jewish people since the Exodus from Egypt. Between 1944 and 1948, according to the U.S. Holocaust Museum, the people who left Eastern Europe numbered about 250,000, and "at least 80 percent came with the organized Berihah [bricha]."

Many more individuals and organizations, in addition to Abba Kovner, played key roles. Jan Masaryk, Czechoslovakia's foreign minister, opened his country's frontier to Jews from Poland, and in three months more than seventy thousand Jews fled through Czechoslovakia. A Red Cross "rescue train" carried five thousand Romanian Jews back to their country from camps in Poland. The Jewish Brigade set up a center, Merkaz la-Golah, for smuggling Jews into Italy from the liberated camps. The Joint Distribution Committee, led by Joe Schwartz, financed that center and distributed food. Jewish soldiers in the Jewish Brigade, the Red Army, and the American Army shielded the travelers from arrest and harassment.

The Jewish flight from Europe would have happened in any case. But it would not have begun as early as it did, and more people would have been trapped behind closing borders, without the vision, drive, and determination of Abba Kovner.

"It was a major accomplishment, which had begun in Lithuania and was realized in Italy, and although Kovner and the leadership he put together were no longer there, the movement continued, using routes and methods formulated by the exodus. . . . The beginning . . . and the momentum came from the forest in Lithuania about a year before the war was over."[4]

Abba testifying for Anna Borkowska, left, for enshrinement
in the Righteous Among Nations, 1984. Anna was formerly
Mother Bertranda, in whose convent outside of Vilna that Abba
and his family members were hidden.

Before he departed Europe for Palestine, Abba assembled a small group of like-minded Jews that he called the Avengers. He sent them to cities in Europe—Paris, Berlin, Munich, Nuremberg—to await his return. Abba went to Palestine to drum up support for his plan of revenge and to acquire a large quantity of poison to carry it out. He wore a British army uniform and carried false papers, pretending to be a Jewish Brigade member coming home on leave.

His plans were indeed horrific. Plan A was to poison the water supplies of several German cities and to kill six million people, matching the number of Jews murdered in the Holocaust. Plan B was to kill the SS men and other Germans who were then in prisons and awaiting trial.

After a month in Palestine, Abba was almost ready to give up. Almost all of the Jews who had made it there from Europe were not interested in continuing the fight or exacting revenge. Instead, they had a nation to build, and they needed the good will of other countries. The reaction of Meir Ya'ari was typical. Ya'ari had been in Palestine since 1920 after leading the Hashomer Hatzair in Vienna. He said, "I fear for you. You will never give up the War. You will never live a normal life. You will never trust. We have much to learn from you about how to die like a hero. But please allow us to teach you how to live a life we can give to our children."[5]

Abba was not yet ready to hear such a message. Finally, after a visit with the aging Chaim Weizmann, who was a chemist by training, he obtained cans of deadly poison and sailed back to Europe. He traveled under the false name of Benjamin Beit-Halachmi, a demobilized veteran of the Jewish Brigade who strongly resembled him. His Plan A was to introduce the poison into the water mains in four German cities. Had it succeeded, several million men, women, and children would have died horrible deaths.

When the ship approached the French port of Toulon, the captain's voice summoned him, calling out his false name over the loudspeaker. Someone in Palestine, quite possibly the Jewish leader David Ben-Gurion, wanted him detained. Abba threw the poison overboard and was arrested. He was sent to a British military prison in Cairo. The British did not know what he had been planning; the Jews had only told them that he was a threat.

Before going to meet the ship's captain, Abba gave a note to the young soldier who was escorting him. It was for his co-conspirator Vitka Kempner, who was in Paris. The note read, "Arrested. Proceed with Plan B."

Plan B was to poison the German prisoners in five different cities on a single day. They would infiltrate the bakeries supplying the prisons and would paint the bread with arsenic. Kempner bought the poison and distributed it to two confederates in each of the five cities. But something went wrong in four of the cities. Only in Nuremberg, at Stalag 13, did it work.

Two of the Avengers, Lebke Distel and Pinchas Ben-Tzur, hid in the bakery overnight on April 13, 1946. They painted nine thousand loaves of black bread with arsenic. They did not touch the one thousand white loaves. Those were for the American guards, who did not like black bread.

On April 24, the headline of a story in the *New York Times* read, "Poison Plot Toll of Nazis at 2,238." The story went on to say that it was a mysterious plot to target 15,000 former Nazi elite guard men. None of the 2,238 who fell ill had died, according to the paper. But other newspapers reported that hundreds had been killed, and hinted that the embarrassed Americans were trying to cover it up.

None of the Avengers were caught. Abba Kovner at last had a measure of revenge. He and the world were fortunate indeed that his Plan A was foiled. It was fortunate also that the nascent nation of Israel was never linked to the deed. He was kept in Cairo three months, then transferred to a British prison in Jerusalem and released.

In Israel, Abba lived the rest of his life at the Ein HaHoresh kibbutz, about fifty miles south of Haifa. He no longer thirsted for vengeance, and he turned more and more toward his writing. His poetry won him international acclaim. He won the Israel Prize for Literature in 1970. He conceived the Museum of the Diaspora, which is now the Museum of the Jewish People in Tel Aviv.

Abba Kovner is one of Israel's national heroes, a symbol of defiance and resistance. Our paths did cross again, after I arrived. And we both served in Israel's War of Independence, as did almost every Jewish person who lived there.

During the years I lived in Israel, I saw Abba only occasionally. He died in 1987 after a long battle with throat cancer. We were distant relatives and had never been personally close. And while his story touches my own in only a few places, I believe you should know it, too.

We Meet and Marry

*J*HAD BEEN LIVING in Palestine for about two years when I met Mort Wygodski, the love of my life. It was at a planning party. Dora's cousins included me with their local Technion friends to put on a party at their house in Tel Aviv. My first encounter with Mort was cordial, but we did not hit it off. He was sarcastic about my hometown; that turned me off, and I had refused his first request for a date.

But Mort was persistent. He was also smart enough to know that he had been less than a gentleman at our first encounter. Many years later, he told our son, Avi, that I was different from all of the women he had previously been with. He had had several affairs, and he was in a relationship with another woman at the time. But he was ready to settle down, and even then he saw some qualities in me that he wished for in a wife and mother for his children.

I was sitting on a bench, off to one side. He came up and introduced himself, then asked where I was from. When I answered, "Vilna," he made a sneering little face and said, "Oh, really? Vilna?" It was as if my home city was somehow below his beloved Bialystok. He didn't make me feel very special. And then he cracked some off-color jokes. When he asked if he could walk me home, I told him no. And I thought that was that.

The party was at Dora's aunt's house. The hostesses were two of Dora's cousins, and they were both quite beautiful. Dora was off in Jerusalem and didn't attend. Mort was one of the party's organizers. Many of the men there were graduates of the Technion. They had prestige and standing, and they knew it. In fact, all of them including Mort had large egos. Breaking the ice in such settings is often awkward, and that is how it was when Mort approached me.

At the party we danced and talked, and he gave me a kiss on my cheek. I allowed him to walk me home. He did not remember it that way; he said I refused his offer. In any case, I felt that he liked me and wanted to take me out. Our first date was a movie. He brought chocolate to share during intermission.

Perhaps his feelings for me were something completely new, and he tried too hard. Men often do that; they come across as being the exact opposite of what they really are. This is what happened with Mort.

A little background on the both of us, and on the society where we were living, will be helpful here.

After living with my cousin Ber Kovner and his girlfriend for a short time in their house by a citrus grove, I moved in with Klara Bar, my distant relative who was also from Vilna. She had a small apartment in downtown Tel Aviv.

I slept in the same bed with Klara, her husband, and their daughter. Eventually her husband went to sleep on a couch in another room. I was there for about a year. With my cousin Ber's help, I found employment, a sewing job in a pajama factory.

Those initial months were hard. I had no confidence in myself. I had no real education, no marketable skills. I didn't speak Hebrew. My circle of friends remained small—primarily Dora, her sister Tania, Eva, and Edith. I was probably pretty, but I didn't think so. And worst of all, I had that stigma—I was a Holocaust survivor, looked down upon by many of the Jews of Israel for not fighting back against the Germans.

Although no one ever said it to me, I had heard the awful term they had for us: *sabonim*. Soaps. It was a cruel reference to the widely-held belief—which some scholars of the Holocaust including those at Yad Vashem dispute—that the body fat of murdered Jews of Stutthof was used to make soap.

I was still carrying horrible memories that came back to me in nightmares. Sometimes I woke up screaming. One of those times I told Klara about standing in the line at Stutthof and seeing the door to the gas chamber close just before I was set to enter. That was the first time I ever talked about it to anyone. I had banished it from my conscious mind. But such memories never stay buried.

Klara believed in me more than I believed in myself. So did Mort, soon enough, but Klara was the first. After that first meeting, Mort found out where I lived. He came calling for me. Klara got to know him and warmed to him. I finally did agree to go on some dates with him. We would often take walks and sit on the beach together. We both spoke Polish and Russian, and we talked in those languages. She knew he wanted to marry me, and that he would be a good catch. But I was plagued with doubts. She heard all of my excuses.

I thought I could never be happy with someone who was so intelligent and knowledgeable. I wouldn't be able to talk to him about anything. I needed to go to school and prepare myself for this kind of a man. I wanted a taller man. I was only working in a pajama factory, after all. And on and on. She became furious with me.

Even as I became more comfortable and confident in being with Mort and in talking to him, I had to overcome other barriers: jealousy and prejudice. At those parties and other group gatherings, the men who were Technion graduates were considered very desirable catches. When Mort was drawn to me, a Holocaust survivor, some of the other girls who were on the prowl for husbands became envious and resentful. How could he prefer me to them? I compared myself with Dora's cousins. They were both gorgeous, and I didn't really think I was in their class in the looks department.

An even bigger hurdle was the peer pressure of Mort's friends. Almost all of them urged him not to marry me, but he never heeded their advice about me as we were becoming a couple.

There were some of his friends who made me feel very uncomfortable. I don't know why, because they tried to be kind. I could speak their language, but it didn't feel right. They would meet and listen to recorded concerts, and Mort wanted me to go and be a part of the group with him.

On one occasion, when he was trying to get me to one of this group's parties, and I said no, we argued. It came down to my saying, "It's them or me." At first he said, "It's them." And he walked away. But not far. He came back. And we didn't go to that event. I never dated anyone else. Nor did he, after that.

It was easier, somehow, for me to be friendly with the Technion graduates. Mort noticed this, so he initially kept our social circle small. When I became more confident and relaxed about speaking with others, he gradually brought me into events with more of his friends. He knew that I needed time to adjust and that there was no need to force things.

As I look back on my own doubts and on our little disagreements now, after so many years, they seem so small and laughable. Every young person who's in love for the first time has similar stories. But for me, at that stage of my life, it was serious and troubling. I was shy and insecure and wondering why someone like Mort would ever be interested in me.

Perhaps it is too dramatic to say that Mort "saved" me. But perhaps not. He didn't simply fall in love with me. He gently forced me to come out of my cocoon of shyness and insecurity. He saw talents and abilities that I never dreamed I had. His faith in me launched my working career.

When our group got together for parties or group activities, we liked to listen to popular music and go to the beaches on the Mediterranean. That was the carefree, fun part. But we would also talk about more serious and pressing issues.

There was the matter of my personal history, as a *Sh' erit ha Pletah*, a survivor of the Final Solution. It took a good deal of discussion and explaining what had really happened back in Europe. As I gained confidence in myself, I was able to do that. The Jews of the Yishuv, who had been living in British Mandate Palestine throughout the war, thought we could have fought back, that we should have been ashamed for allowing ourselves to be slaughtered. They had no idea of what we had been through, or about how hard it would have been to fight back. In time, most of them overcame that initial judgment of me and of people like me. Others never did.

Then there was the issue of politics. Palestine, still under the British Mandate, was anything but a peaceful and tranquil place. For the previous ten years, tension had reigned and violence frequently broke out; Arabs, Jews, and British authorities were all involved. Young adults like Mort and I could not ignore it. We talked a lot about what else might happen. We knew we had to be prepared. Even before he had arrived in Palestine in 1938, Mort had been recruited by the Haganah, the Zionist paramilitary organization. He was still performing neighborhood security patrols. I also became a part-time soldier, joining the militia reserves.

After about a year of living with Klara, it was time for me to go off on my own. I rented a room in a house at 2 Keren Kayemet Street. It was actually just a half of a room. Because the landlady needed the money, I had to share the room with another woman, a schoolteacher, who looked down upon me and did everything she could to make my life miserable. She would sweep the dirt from her side of the room to my side; she would put her cat onto my bed and pile trash there. She would comb her hair while standing on my side of the room and violate my personal space.

By that time I was dating Mort. When I told him about my living situation, he began to stop by after work. He would bring me a sandwich, and we would eat together every evening. He warned my roommate to stop harassing me. But he also urged me to leave my dead-end job and do something more worthwhile.

Mort worked as an electrical engineer at the Standards Institute of Israel. He inquired about positions there and found that they needed a telephone operator for the switchboard. That sounded like an ideal job. But there was only one problem. I didn't speak Hebrew. I had begun lessons in both English and Hebrew at a local Berlitz school, but I was nowhere near fluent.

He waved away all my objections, talked them into hiring me, and got his friend Ephraim to sit with me at the switchboard. Ephraim was an ideal mentor. He stepped in and interpreted or clarified when needed, but he insisted that I do it on my own as much as possible. And I flourished.

Within six months, people told me, I was speaking Hebrew like a native of Israel. I had an aptitude for languages that I never knew was there. And it was not just Hebrew that I could put to use. People were arriving in Israel from all countries of Europe. I could communicate with them in Russian, Polish, Yiddish, and even German.

I started work in the Standards Institute in the spring of 1947. That year was a difficult and dangerous one for all of us. In January, the British had announced that they were washing their hands of the Mandate and turning the territory over to the United Nations. This was in response to the violent, coordinated Jewish resistance they had encountered in 1946. I will describe that resistance in more detail shortly.

Before 1947 ended, the United Nations approved a resolution to partition the land into a Jewish state and an Arab state. Jews accepted this plan; Arabs rejected it. More intense fighting and rioting between the Arabs and the Jews broke out; the war for the Jewish homeland had begun.

That war had been a long time in the making. The British had been in charge of the region since the collapse of the Ottoman Empire in World War I. In 1936, a rising number of Jewish immigrants touched off a three-year revolt by the Arabs who lived there. The British wanted to placate the Arabs and keep that violence under control. They needed the Suez Canal to remain open for access to India, the place they considered the jewel in the crown of their empire. In the 1930s, not long after the ships of their navy switched from coal power to oil, they also began taking millions of barrels of Middle East oil each year out from the port of Haifa.

Germany had been abusing and mistreating Jews ever since Hitler came to power in 1933. Many tragic events showed that Jews were not welcomed anywhere in the world. By 1939, when World War II broke out, the Jews' situation had already become desperate. There was Kristallnacht in Germany and Austria: on the 9th and 10th of November, 1938, 267 synagogues were burned; 7,500 Jewish businesses were destroyed; thugs of the Hitler Youth and SS invaded Jewish homes, plundering and raping; 26,000 Jews were sent to concentration camps.

Many students of Jewish history consider Kristallnacht as the beginning of the Holocaust. The Germans' practice of mass murder, their Final Solution, had not yet begun. But the Jews of the Yishuv recognized what was happening. They described it for the first time with the word Shoah, taken from the biblical book of Zephaniah (1:15): "That day *is* a day of wrath, a day of trouble and distress, a day of devastation and desolation, a day of darkness and gloominess, a day of clouds and thick darkness."

In May 1939, the refugee ship *St. Louis*, with 937 passengers aboard, sailed from Hamburg to Cuba. The refugees had Cuban visas, but the Cuban president, Federico Laredo Bril, would not let them disembark. The U.S. State Department refused to let them land in America. Eventually the ship sailed back to Europe, and 254 of the passengers ended up dying in the Holocaust.

Tragic events like Kristallnacht and the voyage of the *St. Louis* told Jews that they had few real friends in the world. They needed a country of their own; Britain's Balfour Declaration of 1917 seemed to indicate that at least the British would favor it. The Declaration read, in part, "His Majesty's Government view with favour the establishment in Palestine of a national home for the Jewish people, and will use their best endeavours to facilitate the achievement of this object."

But that never happened. Rather, the opposite took place. In 1939, Britain gave in to most of the Arabs' demands and issued its infamous White Paper. This government policy document severely restricted Jewish immigration to fifteen thousand people per year for five years. It came at a time when Jews most needed someone, anyone, to allow them a place to live in peace.

Germany started World War II when it attacked Poland in September of 1939. Jews wanted to join in the fight against Hitler. That meant allying with Britain and France. But Britain had also become an enemy because it was keeping Jews out of Palestine. That contradictory situation prompted the famous declarations of Jewish leader David Ben-Gurion, who said, "We must help the [British] army as if there were no White Paper, and we must fight the White Paper as if there were no war."[1]

British Prime Minister Winston Churchill opposed the White Paper. In a speech to the House of Commons in 1939, he said that the paper's limitations on Jewish immigration were wrong and should be lifted. But he did not succeed. The paper remained in force throughout the war. Between 1934 and 1939, about forty-nine thousand Jews had made it into the country illegally. Fewer than sixteen thousand succeeded in getting in between 1940 and 1946, when millions would have come if given the chance.

The British tightened the restrictions even further in 1942 when their War Cabinet stated, "All practicable steps should be taken to discourage illegal immigration to Palestine." Their coast guard intercepted ships carrying refugees, and sent those refugees to squalid internment camps—Atlit, south of Haifa; and the islands of Cyprus in the Mediterranean and Mauritius in the Indian Ocean.

The Jews' response to British immigration policies came at the Extraordinary Zionist Conference in New York in May 1942. At the conference, David Ben-Gurion issued the Biltmore Declaration, calling for an end to all limitations on Jewish immigration and the establishment of a Jewish Commonwealth in the land of Palestine. The Declaration also rejected the White Paper, labeling it cruel and indefensible and a repudiation of the original intent of Britain's Balfour Declaration in 1917.

When I arrived as one of the few legal immigrants, the British were still in charge. Their White Paper was still official policy. But the Jewish immigrants, legal and illegal, kept arriving. The British could not stop them all. Nor could they stop the escalating violence. Jews around the world kept that ultimate goal of having their own country in sight, and the British were the enemy.

At that Extraordinary Zionist Conference, Ben-Gurion also said that the Jews had no alternative but to respond with "constant and brutal force." The Haganah and two other armed groups, the Irgun and the Lechi, joined forces and established the Tun'at Hameri Haiviri, the United Resistance Movement. They began planning attacks on "infrastructure and symbols of power that legitimated the British Mandate."[2]

It did not take long to ramp up the attacks and to bring on brutal reprisals from the British. In June 1946, eleven coordinated bombings destroyed road and rail bridges and damaged the railway system. The British retaliated twelve days later in an operation called Black Sabbath. They placed Jerusalem, Haifa, Tel Aviv, Ramat Gan, and Netanya under lockdown. They sent seventeen thousand soldiers out to search for resistance fighters, weapons, and documents. They arrested twenty-seven hundred Jews.

A month later came a bigger and more violent response. Using large tin milk canisters, members of the Irgun smuggled bombs into the King David Hotel in Jerusalem, the British Mandate's military and administrative headquarters. Warning calls to the hotel, twenty minutes before the detonation, were ignored. The blast had the force of a five-hundred-kilogram aerial bomb. Ninety-one people were killed.

The attack dissolved the uneasy partnership between the Haganah and the Irgun. The Haganah was a "mainstream" army while the Irgun and Lechi had been further to the right-wing side of politics and more radical in their tactics.[3] The attack prompted outrage in both Britain and America and weakened support for the Zionist cause. Ben-Gurion and the Haganah falsely denied any knowledge or involvement. But the attack succeeded, in the end. The British had had enough. They were exhausted from fighting World War II. They had one hundred thousand soldiers, one-tenth of their empire's army, stationed in Palestine. On January 22, 1947, more than a year after I had arrived there, the British announced that they would leave. The United Nations could decide the fate of the Jews and Arabs in their Palestinian Mandate.

America's president, Harry Truman, was in favor of the United Nations General Assembly's plan, announced in November 1947, to partition the British Mandate of Palestine into a Jewish state and an Arab state. The Mandate was to cease no later than August 1, 1948. He overruled the recommendations of both America's State Department and its Central Intelligence Agency, which thought that Israel would not prevail in the war that was sure to follow. Russia also supported the partitioning, but for different reasons. They wanted to weaken

Britain's influence abroad, and they hoped that Israel would become a Socialist or Communist country.

Truman's support helped to bring in thirty-three votes in favor. There were thirteen votes against, which included all of the countries of the Arab League. There were ten abstentions, including Britain. Almost immediately, the Arabs launched a war of annihilation against the Jewish state as they set up a blockade of Jerusalem. For the next six months, there were riots, skirmishes, road ambushes, bombings, and massacres that were instigated by both sides and that provoked retaliation.

I volunteered for guard duty. Guarding was part time, only a few nights a week. I was stationed on the roof of a building, and I would watch for planes. I had never held a rifle before, but I was excited and eager for the opportunity to help. I still had my job at the Standards Institute of Israel. I was the only one of my circle of friends and relatives that I remember who performed that guard duty.

Mort, with his engineering background, was in the scientific forces of the military. He lived with a roommate named Gedi, in an apartment in Sderot Chen, which is near the center of Tel Aviv. The apartment was owned by Mrs. Kaufman and her son Moshe, who was an architect and Mort's Technion classmate.

Mort and I had been dating for a little over a year when Mrs. Kaufman suggested that we get married. She asked Gedi, his roommate, to find a new place so that Mort and I could be together in the one room. Gedi moved, and we decided that we were ready. But during that tumultuous time, there was only one day available to us for our wedding: Lag Ba' Omer. It was the thirty-third day of the Counting of the Omer, which by Jewish tradition is the forty-nine days of harvest between Passover and Shavuot. Since the ninth century of the Common Era, those forty-nine days have been a time of mourning for forty-nine thousand students of Rabbi Akiva, all of whom died during a plague. During the Counting of the Omer, traditional Jews observe mourning rituals, which include a ban on shaving, getting haircuts, or getting married. The only day when weddings are permitted to Ashkenazi Jews is Lag Ba' Omer, which fell on May 28 that year.

Two weeks before that date, on May 14, history again intervened. The British announced the ending of their mandate and began pulling their military out. Israel immediately issued its Declaration of Independence.

May 14 was a Friday. The announcement and signing ceremony was a brief one. It had to be done in advance of the Sabbath. Security considerations precluded having a large, well-attended affair that would have been appropriate for such a momentous occasion. Jerusalem was inaccessible due to the fighting, so the ceremony took place in the Tel Aviv Museum. The United States immediately recognized the new nation, and Russia followed suit three days later.

My cousin Ber Kovner, by then known as Meir Vilner, helped to write Israel's Declaration of Independence. At age twenty-nine, he was the youngest person to sign it. He had joined the Palestine Communist Party, and by the time of the declaration was the party's leader. Though he was not a committed Zionist, he supported the UN partition plan and the country's independence because he was an ardent foe of the British.

The Declaration of Independence ignited the second phase of the war. Five Arab nations—Egypt, Saudi Arabia, Syria, Lebanon, and Jordan—all declared war against Israel. The first six months had been more of a civil war, waged by local Arab fighters and militias against the forces of the Yishuv. But now it would be an all-out international conflict, pitting the standing armed forces of Israel against the armies of five invading countries.

Mort and I were still able to hold our wedding on May 28. Our ceremony was in the rabbinate (Vad Ha Keyla) with a *chuppah*. Dora's sister Tanya and her husband, Itzchak Shine, were the only witnesses at the ceremony. The reception was in the house in Tel Aviv where we had met, at the planning for the party hosted by Dora's aunt and cousins. Dora was not there. She also was getting married that night, in Jerusalem.

We had just emerged from the chuppah, the canopy that symbolized the new home we would build, when all the lights went out. The Egyptians were bombing Tel Aviv. We concluded the evening's festivities by candlelight, with window shades drawn. At midnight, Mort changed into his army uniform and reported back to his unit for duty.

Our life as a married couple had begun, with my new husband off fighting for our country on our wedding night.

Life in Israel, the War of Liberation, & Aftermath

With my favorite cousin Ber Kovner, who was then known as
Meir Vilner, in Palestine. Ber retrieved me from the camp at
Atlit, near Haifa, shortly after I arrived.

A T THE END of British Mandate Palestine and the start of
the War of Liberation, there were about 630,000 Jews in
the land and almost 1.2 million Arabs. In the first year of our married

life in Israel, now a real country and our adopted homeland, approximately 6,000 of our fellow citizens died in the War of Independence. Of these, about 4,000 were members of the military and 2,000 were civilians.

With the simultaneous attacks by five Arab nations came this declaration of intent from Azzam Pasha, Secretary-General of the Arab League: "It will be a war of annihilation. It will be a momentous massacre in history that will be talked about like the massacres of Mongols or the Crusades."[1] There was no escaping reality—we Jews were in a fight for our lives. No one was exempt.

The Arab nations launched the war and took responsibility for doing so. They attacked from all sides: Egypt from the south; Transjordan from the east; Syria, Lebanon, and Iraq from the north. Palestinian Arabs had already been fighting the Jews within the borders, in the civil war prior to May of 1948.

One day before Israel declared independence, local Arab bands supported by the Arab Legion overran and destroyed four kibbutzim, collectively known as the Etzion Bloc and located in the Hebron Hills south of Jerusalem. The settlers had no choice but to surrender, and 127 of them were murdered.[2]

The United Nations Security Council, led by the United States and Russia, condemned the Arabs' violations of the partition plan. The UN's Palestine Commission had never been permitted, by either the British or the Arabs, to go to Palestine to implement the resolution of the UN General Assembly for partitioning. The UN had already declared an embargo on armaments shipments in 1947. Despite that embargo, the Arab nations had little trouble obtaining arms. Britain rejected the embargo and kept sending shipments to the Arabs.

Israel's military, newly named the Israel Defense Forces, had twenty-five thousand troops. It had to get its armaments by smuggling them in, mostly from Czechoslovakia. A shipment of more than twenty-five thousand rifles and five thousand machine guns arrived during a ceasefire in July 1948. In an ironic twist of fate, many of those guns had been produced for the German army in munitions works that Germany seized from Czechoslovakia in 1937. Some of the guns used by Jewish soldiers even had come with German markings and swastikas.[3]

Israel also had no military aircraft at the start of the war, and few trained pilots. Czechoslovakia again came to the rescue. Germany had built its Messerschmitt fighter planes there. After the war, the Czechs continued to build them. Jewish-Americans who had flown for the United States flew those German planes to Israel to join the battle. They wore surplus German pilots' uniforms with Luftwaffe patches. Other Jewish-American flyers secretly purchased surplus American planes, in violation of American law, and brought them to Israel.

Jan Masaryk, the foreign minister of Czechoslovakia, signed the sale contract in January of that year. One of the few national leaders willing to defy the arms embargo, he died under mysterious circumstances—probably assassinated by Communists—in March 1948. His father, Tomas, had been a great supporter of Zionism and the cause of Israeli statehood.

The first month of the war went badly for the Jews, especially in the Old City of Jerusalem. The residents and a small group of defenders surrendered after a two-week siege. Major Abdullah Al-Tell of the Arab Legion, who became the military governor of the Old City, wrote in his memoirs, "I have seen in this defeat of the Jews the heaviest blow rendered upon them especially in terms of morale, since they were evicted from the Western Wall and from the Jewish Quarter, for the first time in 15 generations."[4]

Morale among the Jews was indeed low after the loss of Jerusalem. The killings at the Etzion Bloc were another discouraging blow, but they caused a change in tactics by the Haganah. Previously, it had followed a policy of "restraint," targeting only individual Arabs who were known to have taken part in attacks. After Etzion, the Haganah sought revenge and reprisal on entire Arab villages if attacks had emanated from them. That made the conflict a total war in which the entire population was imperiled. Casualties among both soldiers and civilians increased dramatically.

At the war's outbreak, the better-equipped Arab armies outnumbered the Jewish forces. But the Arabs had no coordinated plan of attack. Nor was there ever a plan to build their own Arab nation on the land. They only wanted to prevent the Jews from having their own country. Their goal was a massacre of Jews, as Azzam Pasha had boasted.

Tel Aviv's population was almost exclusively Jewish, unlike Jerusalem, Tiberias, and some other cities that had a mixed Jewish-Arab population. Therefore, the city itself experienced little or no combat. But we were always tense and apprehensive. The land of Israel is so small that no city was safe from air raids or from ground attacks from unfriendly nearby villages. Mort was a member of the scientific forces of the Haganah. He was in a unit that protected the city from possible attacks from Arab enclaves. I was a lookout, watching for enemy planes from rooftops and armed with a rifle just in case of trouble in the streets below.

Tel Aviv did come perilously close to becoming a battleground. The fledgling Israeli Air Force, and then the Givati Brigade, saved us. Almost immediately after they arrived, the volunteer American pilots were told that the Egyptian Army was just six miles from Tel

Aviv. Four of them took off immediately in primitive, hastily repaired German Messerschmitt fighter planes, and turned the Egyptians back.

Those pilots numbered 190 out of a total of 3,500 people from around the world, many of whom were not Jewish, who came to Israel to help with the war effort. That boosted our morale considerably. Even though their governments were not officially our allies in the war, we knew that we were not totally alone in the world.

The Egyptian Army, the biggest of all the Arab nations' forces, attacked from the south, through the Sinai Peninsula and the Negev Desert. The Givati Brigade, the largest brigade in the Israel Defense Forces, marched out to meet them. The Givati Brigade had 9,500 soldiers, 20 percent of them women. My relative Abba Kovner, with the rank of captain, served as the brigade's information officer. That position uniquely suited his talents as a leader and motivator for the Zionist cause.

The Givati Brigade's commander, Shimon Avidan, sent for Abba in the middle of May 1948. Abba had been living on the Ein HaHoresh kibbutz. His son Michael had been born three days before the war broke out. I would like to cite the account of his critical role at some length here. As historian Dina Porat tells it,

> Kovner arrived at the Givati Brigade's most difficult hour, after a series of defeats and many casualties, sometimes dozens of men killed and wounded in a single battle, a heavy blow for a state that numbered 600,000 citizens. . . . The brigade's morale had been undermined, as had its ability to defend the 27 communities under its command, including Tel Aviv. The fate of the entire campaign was in doubt. . . .

> "Through Abba Kovner, the commander made each soldier feel that the fate of the entire brigade rested on his shoulders," wrote Givati veterans in retrospect. . . . On the eve of battles Kovner often went with the units to their departure points and stayed with them until the last minute, explaining how each individual battle

was important to the war in general and trying to ease their anxiety. On the eve of the battle for Ashdod, when Egyptian tanks, armored vehicles, and artillery were about to pound their way north, Kovner explained the tanks' limitations and how, during World War II, the partisans had overcome them using simple weapons, making them less daunting. . . .

Ashdod fell only two months later, after much bitter fighting and bloodshed, but "the soldiers came back and went out the next night, and the third, and the tenth, and the hundredth. The force propelling them was . . . internal. It was the same force to which the voice appealed . . . because nobody could speak as [Kovner] could.[5]

After being checked by the Israeli Air Force, the Egyptian Army occupied the village of Ashdod, twenty miles south of Tel Aviv, on May 29, 1948. The Givati Brigade suffered many casualties and failed to capture the town, but they were able to stop Egypt's advance and force it into a defensive strategy. The northernmost point of their advance was a bridge over the Lachish River on the north side of Ashdod. Israelis halted the Egyptians by blowing up that bridge, which is known as *Gesher ad Halom* (Bridge of Until Here) to this day.

Egypt never thereafter regained its offensive momentum. In October 1948, after three days of bombardment by the air force and fearing encirclement, the Egyptian forces retreated to the south and most of the town's three hundred occupants fled.

After initial setbacks in other areas of the country, the Israeli armed forces grew in strength and began its own offensive drives. The United Nations Security Council declared a détente in June, which lasted a month, and another in July, which lasted officially until October but was violated sporadically by Egypt, Jordan, and Israel. Each of the pauses in the fighting benefited Israel more than they did the Arab countries, giving Israel more time to acquire arms and train their forces.

The United Nations sent in Count Folke Bernadotte, a Swedish diplomat, in an attempt to mediate a truce and negotiate. His proposal was rejected by both Jews and Arabs. It was similar to the boundaries that had been proposed and rejected by all sides before the partition vote. The Jews had by that time seized the momentum and were expanding their control over territories even outside the partition boundaries.

Bernadotte was assassinated in September 1948 by members of LEHI (Lohamei Herut Israel), a far-right terrorist group. Before he was killed, he had written in his diary:

> The Palestinian Arabs had [sic] at present no will of their own. Neither have they ever developed any specifically Palestinian nationalism. The demand for a separate Arab state in Palestine is relatively weak. It would seem as though in existing circumstances most of the Palestinian Arabs would be quite content to be incorporated in Transjordan.[6]

The fighting on all fronts continued until the end of 1948 when Israel's forces attacked Egypt's in the south and succeeded in driving most of them back over the international border. Britain threatened to invoke its military treaty with Egypt, so the Israelis pulled back. The Egyptians were ready to negotiate at that point. They did not want to be rescued by Britain.

A ceasefire went into effect on January 7, 1949. Just a few hours before the ceasefire, Israeli aircraft shot down five British fighter planes. Israel and Egypt reached an armistice in February. Israel signed separate armistice agreements with Jordan, Lebanon, and Syria by June of that year.

Israel gained about 50 percent more territory than was originally allotted to it by the UN Partition Plan. But much of the land lay in waste, especially the citrus groves that had been the basis of the prewar economy. The war created about 726,000 Palestinian refugees who fled or were evicted from Jewish-held areas. Gaza fell under the jurisdiction of Egypt. The West Bank of the Jordan and East Jerusalem were occupied by Jordan.

But the war was finally over. Mort and I had done our parts, as did almost every one of the Jews in Eretz Israel. We had been glued to the radio, waiting for the announcement that Israel had at last won its independence. I was twenty-five years old then, and I had been caught up in war of one kind or another for almost all of the preceding ten years. Peace at last. And we were eager to begin building a life together.

The War of Independence had also unleashed a wave of anti-Zionism and persecution of nearly one million Jews who had been living for centuries in Arab countries like Algeria, Egypt, Iraq, Syria, Libya, Morocco, and Yemen. Some nine hundred thousand Jews, with their lives endangered and their wealth stolen, became refugees. Approximately six hundred thousand of them settled in the state of Israel, and three hundred thousand migrated to Europe or America. The descendants of those who came to Israel during that time now make up more than half of the country's total population.

Of my blood relatives who were still alive, Ber Kovner (Meir Vilner) was my favorite. He always was, even back in those long-ago days in Vilna. He was the one who came to pick me up from the Atlit detention camp when I got to Israel.

He had come to Israel from Vilna when he was very young, in 1938, to study at the university there. Back in Vilna, he had left Hashomer Hatzair, the Zionist youth organization to which Abba belonged, became involved with the local Communist Party, and eventually became its leader. It was in this capacity that he signed Israel's Declaration of Independence.

Ber had a long career in Israeli politics. He was elected to the Knesset, Israel's parliament, on three different occasions. When he resigned from the Knesset in 1990 as part of a seat rotation agreement, he was the third-longest serving MK after Tawfik Toubi and Shimon Peres. He passed away in 2003 and was the longest-surviving signatory to the Declaration.

Unlike his cousin Ber, Abba Kovner had no interest in politics after the War of Liberation. But he remained a towering figure in Israeli society and around the world. Until his death from laryngeal cancer in 1987, he resided at the Kibbutz Ein HaHoresh with his wife, Vitka Kempner. He was a prolific poet, and his only prose work, *Face to Face*, was for many years the authoritative book on Israel's War of Independence. His son Michael took up Abba's mantle as both artist and warrior. He is an accomplished painter, and he served in the IDF commando unit that freed 103 Israeli hostages at Entebbe, Uganda, in 1976.

Abba wrote three inscriptions on the wall of the Museum of the Diaspora, inscriptions that sum up his passion and his life's work.

The first inscription speaks of the unity of the Jewish people for all time in all places. The second inscription notes, "No Jew is alone on his Holy Days," reminding visitors that each individual belongs to the whole nation. The third inscription, "To remember the past, to live in the present, to have faith in the future," invokes the understanding that the history of the Jewish people, which is one entity, and the history of the many individual Jews within it, make an unbroken chain which no one can sever.

Speaking at Abba's funeral, the great poet Abraham Sutzkever stated that Abba "was a person in whose presence one felt the eternity of the Jewish people."[7]

Ber Kovner and Abba Kovner were my two heroes. They had grown apart when they were young men in Vilna, and they did not get closer again during their later lives. They were very different, and they did very different things. But they were both giants in Jewish life and in the formative years of the state of Israel.

Life quickly got back to normal for us after the War of Independence. Our landlady was Mrs. Kaufman. She painted, and she had a son who was an architect. Such a wonderful woman. When we began dating, Mort and a friend lived in a room in her house. I used to come around to the house and got to know her. The roommate was one of his many friends who tried to persuade him not to get involved with me, a Holocaust survivor. Mrs. Kaufman would have none of that. She told Mort, "She is such a nice girl. You should marry her. We'll get your roommate out and you can live here."

When we moved into her house, Mrs. Kaufman insisted that I come and use her kitchen whenever I wanted. That might not seem like much, but it really was kind of her to let me into her family's living space. I sometimes took her up on the offer, but I also didn't want to impose on her. So I got a little portable stove and kept it in the corner of the porch of our room so that the wind didn't get at it and blow the fire out. I know that she didn't really like that, but she loved me a lot and didn't make me remove it either.

Our social life revolved around our friends at the Standards Institute where we both worked. We also saw my Kovner relatives, Ber, Abba, and Genia. I had not known Genia, who was Abba's brother, very well back in Vilna. He and his wife, Neuta, had made a harrowing escape from the Nazis during the last days of the Vilna ghetto. In Israel, Mort and I often socialized with them.

I also was welcomed several times at the luxurious home of my friend Eva Misrah and her mother, Lily. As I mentioned previously, they were members of the wealthy family that made Wolfschmidt vodka. I remember how amazed I was to be in a house that actually had a refrigerator of its own.

Lily is the one who had saved my life in Stutthof, when she bribed the German guard with a gold coin and got me, Bella, and Dora out of a line headed for execution. Lily offered to adopt me in Israel. She and Eva tragically both died early deaths from cancer that was due to smoking.

When life got back to something resembling normal for Mort and me, I kept learning about human nature. Sometimes my life lessons were good, and sometimes they were not.

There was a woman, the mother of one of the young people at the party where I met Mort, who was going to America shortly after the War of Liberation ended. I thought she was such a nice lady. I gave her the names of my family members in America. They were excited to speak with someone who had met me, and they gave her two hundred dollars so that Mort and I could buy a refrigerator. She took the money and bought things for herself, and when she came back, she gave us Israeli money, which was worth much less. I couldn't imagine how she could do that to me.

Many years later I got another hard lesson about human nature. We were living in America, and our Tel Aviv apartment was vacant. Two members of that same family, whose last name was Schein and one of whom was the son of my old friend Tania Fisher, asked if they could stay there. Naively, I agreed to let them use the place for a low rent and without a lease or any contractual arrangement. Mort warned me not to, but I ignored him.

When we returned to Israel several months later, we found that many of our personal possessions from the apartment had disappeared. They had either been sold or given away. Because the whole arrangement was done on a handshake, with nothing in writing, we had no legal recourse or leverage to make them vacate immediately or to reimburse us for our lost property.

Overall, however, all of the years we spent in Israel were happy ones. We lived with Mrs. Kaufman for about three years. An organization of engineers, Beit Hama'andes, built an apartment house on the outskirts of Tel Aviv, at a location where Germans used to live. We went to live there, and though we didn't have much money saved at that point, Mort was able to get us a loan. The building was soundly constructed and its foundation properly reinforced because most of those who would live there were trained engineers.

By the time we moved in, I was pregnant with Avi, our first child. On our first night there, we could hear the jackals howling out in the nearby desert. Now, the building is well within the city and not far from the central business district. We never sold that apartment, and for many years after that I would go to Israel during the summer with my children and stay there.

After Avi was born, I had to take a leave of absence from my job at the Standards Institute. They expected me to come back after my maternity leave, but I stayed at home to raise Avi. When he was old enough to be in nursery school, I felt ready to resume my working career, but Mort was against it.

Soon came a life-changing event, though we didn't know it at the time. Demand for engineers had been growing in the United States. In 1952, two hundred engineers from Israel were candidates to go to America and work there for two years. Only two were chosen, and Mort was one of them.

The Standards Institute had partnered with Electrical Testing Laboratories of New York on a top-secret project related to electric power for nuclear energy plants. Mort was assigned to that project.

His friend Barzilli was also selected; he worked at another American company. For Mort, it was a unique opportunity to distinguish himself even further in his career.

During that first visit to America, Mort stayed with a well-to-do uncle, Jack Vernon. He was able to save enough money to buy a ticket for me and Avi to come to America. His first letter to me told of something marvelous and unbelievable. The Vernons could actually open their garage door without getting out of their car. Such technological wonders awaited us! Back in Israel, I was still without a refrigerator and using an old-fashioned ice box.

At the end of those two years, Mort returned home to Israel. But he had impressed his colleagues and would soon be asked to come back. That would be the start of another new life for us, in America.

Coming to America

With Polaire Share in Syracuse; she helped me a great deal in
transitioning to life in America.

E OFTEN JOKE that my extended family in the United
States Americanized me. That is not quite true. No one
could ever do that.

The Shares of Syracuse, Bill and his wife, Polaire, especially, did
teach me much about living in America—its customs, its idioms and
expressions, its technical wonders like refrigerators and automobiles,
its expectations for table manners. In Israel, as in Europe, you hold
your two utensils in your hands. In America, you put the knife down

first. In time, I learned all those things. I was a willing and eager student.

But I never became like most of the people I met in America. That is because I have no censoring gene.

Even my mother said that about me, back in Vilna. She used to say, in Russian, "What you have here," as she pointed to her head, "should be here," as she pointed to her tongue. I heeded her advice throughout my life.

I say what is on my mind. Israelis and Europeans are like that. Americans are not. My son, Avi, who was born in Israel, is like me in that way. My daughter, Charlene, who was born in America, is different. She became Americanized.

If somebody comes to me and says, "Do you like my dress?" and if I don't, I say, "No, I don't like your dress." I will never insult somebody deliberately, and will never say what will hurt somebody, but I will always tell the truth. I suppose that if I were less open and blunt, some things might have gone more smoothly along the way. But it would not have been the real me.

When we first came to Florida, I joined a book-review club at our synagogue. I was giving a comment, my opinion about something, and I forget what it was that I said. I never forgot the response.

The discussion leader said, "Mary, here in the United States, we don't say it. We don't talk like that."

I answered, "It's a really beautiful country. So why wouldn't I say what I think?"

She didn't answer me, but a year later she saw me again. She took my arm and said, "Mary, I'm so sorry. Everything has changed. It is so different now. The psychiatrists are telling people, lying on their couches, 'Tell the truth. Get everything out.' It wasn't that way before."

I didn't know what to make of all that. I asked her why wasn't it always that people could speak what was really on their minds. I realized then that I had learned something that made America different. People were not saying what they were thinking. That is unfortunate. Keeping your feelings and opinions bottled up can lead to depression and all sorts of other difficulties.

Being myself and saying what I think has made me successful with friendships in my life. It also helped with my school teaching. My students of Hebrew used to tell me that whenever they wanted to know the truth about something, they could come to me.

Mort with brother Chaim and their parents in Chile, where we
stayed before moving permanently to America.

We had not decided to move permanently to America when we made our first visit as a family in 1953. We came to America for the second time in 1958. That year, Electrical Testing Labs wanted Mort to come back to New York and finish the nuclear power plants project. He agreed to, but told them that he wanted to get there in six months so we could come by way of South America. His parents had settled in Santiago, Chile. That country had been one of the few to open up to Jews fleeing from Europe after World War II. His brother was getting married there, and his parents had not yet met me.

Avi was six years old when we arrived in Chile. We came by ship to Montevideo, Uruguay, and took a train to Santiago. Mort's parents wanted us to stay and live with them there, and we considered it. We stayed for six months. Avi started school there at a private Jewish school, and he had a terrible time with it at first because he didn't know the Spanish language. Finally, one of the Jewish teachers who was from Israel and knew Hebrew was able to communicate with him.

I became pregnant with our second child. My mother-in-law said, "I am going to the synagogue and pray for you, that you will have a little girl." She was the only one of the family who went to synagogue. Her prayers were answered. Charlene was on the way, but she would be born in America.

We came to Syracuse and lived for six months with my uncle and aunt, Hy Miller and his wife, Fanny. The house was within walking distance of my cousin Bill and Polaire Share's house. Bill's father, Uncle Shimon, gave us our first car, a 1950 Studebaker with a column shift. Hy Miller was a member of the New York State Assembly. He helped me to obtain a visa to come to America with Mort, but at that point, we still did not know if we would stay in America or would eventually go back to Israel.

Bill Share was a doctor with a thriving practice, but I didn't want him to be the one who delivered my baby. He arranged for one of his friends to be on call. But there was something about Syracuse that I never realized, and which foiled those plans. The city is in the snow belt of Upstate New York. You never know when heavy blizzards will swoop in from the Great Lakes to the west. And a terrible snowstorm struck on January 24, 1959, right when I went into labor.

Bill's friend never made it through the snowstorm, so Bill delivered Charlene there, in the Irving Cross Hospital. Polaire came over in the morning when I woke up. She told me, "Mary, you have a beautiful girl with big blue eyes." Then they called Mort, 250 miles away in New York, where he had already begun working at his job. They woke him up from a sound sleep. I can still remember that phone call too.

"Mort, you have a little girl."

"Huhh? What?"

After Mort found an apartment, we relocated to New York City and stayed there for six years. But we came back to Syracuse every summer to be with my family. America was more appealing to me than it was to Mort. All of his personal friends as well as his professional contacts were still in Israel. I had more family members in America than he did, and the Syracuse area reminded me in many ways of my childhood.

In the summers, we would spend many days at the Share family's lakeside home in the town of Cazenovia. With the boating and swimming and family gatherings, it was like our dacha in Pospieszki, a day's drive by *droschka* from Vilna. Bill taught Charlene how to swim. When she was two years old, he threw her into the water. I started screaming, but he just said, "That's the way we teach them here."

Bill's wife, Polaire, worked so hard in those summers. She did every bit of the work for all the family members. I remember one thing she always reminded me about Avi. He would repeatedly say to her, "Ima Tai" in Hebrew, which means "Mother Tea."

It was there, after reminiscing with Maurice and Rosalind Sinuk, my cousins who had emigrated to Canada in the 1930s and who came to Syracuse frequently, that I determined to bring music back into my home.

Music had been missing from my life ever since I stopped taking piano lessons as a girl, something I have always regretted. Maurice remembers me hiding behind the piano in Vilna. I don't remember that. But I do recall how my father loved music and the arts. I also remember the violin that hung on the wall. I don't know why, but I never heard him play that violin. Perhaps he gave it up when his children arrived. Years later, his two sisters told me that he had played the violin when he was a child.

Maurice also told me that he had heard my father play it many times, and that his playing was beautiful. So I resolved that my children would learn both piano and violin.

Violin is a hard instrument to play. You've got to have a good ear for music while you're angling the bow and using your fingers. Avi started his lessons when we were in New York. First we had a teacher come to our apartment. It didn't work out with him, so we found a graduate from the Juilliard School. She had two small children, so Avi took his lessons at her home. He liked working with her and he made good progress.

When we came to Florida, I went to the symphony here and asked for a violin teacher. The conductor's wife, who was the symphony concertmistress, took Avi on, and I would drive him to Eckerd College, where she taught. She was German and quite strict and demanding about practicing. He didn't like practicing as she wanted, so they parted ways. He found another teacher, the mother of one of his friends. Her son was an excellent violinist who later played in the symphony. Avi worked with her and continued with the violin through his high school years. Avi's son, Elan, also played with the Tallahassee Youth Orchestra.

Charlene still plays both violin and piano. We were lucky to find two teachers that she loved. The violin teacher was concertmaster in the orchestra. I would drive her to lessons and wait for her in my car, because his house had no air-conditioning.

Charlene encouraged both her kids to play violin. And they both ended up playing piano as well. I am very happy that our family's musical tradition, which began at least 120 years ago with my father, and possibly even before that, will continue through the next generation.

One of Mort's bosses in New York was Mr. Schmidt. He said that Mort was the first Jew that he'd ever met. No other Jews worked there. He said he couldn't believe that Mort was Jewish, or how good Mort was at his job. As a child, he had been taught all sorts of horrible things—that Jews had horns, that they were not capable of honest work, and so on. He and Mort became great friends.

At Electrical Testing Laboratories, Mort rose to the position of Supervisor of Technical Operations. But after about six years there, he felt that his prospects for further advancement had become too limited. We had always held open the possibility of returning to Israel. But some of Mort's friends urged him to try to get into the aerospace industry. He was a desirable candidate for that field; he already had high security clearance from the American military, from his work at Electrical Testing.

So he began to look around and received some attractive job offers. He took the one in Saint Petersburg, Florida. The company, Electronic Communications Inc. (ECI), put him up at the Buccaneer Hotel in Saint Petersburg Beach. The sunset, as he looked westward over the Gulf of Mexico, reminded him of our years and our many beach dates in Tel Aviv. That was the deciding factor for him.

When we moved to Florida in 1963, we first had an apartment near where Mort worked as principal engineer for reliability at ECI. He would come home to have lunch with me every day. I was still young enough to have another child, and Mort wanted to have one. He felt that our surroundings were so beautiful, even though we did not have our house yet. But I felt that it was enough for me to take care of two children. Besides, I wanted to get back into the working world. We also became American citizens that year.

Working in the aerospace industry during the 1960s and 1970s had its peaks and valleys. Funding for government projects like the Saturn Rocket was ample, and jobs were plentiful and well-paying, as long as the projects were underway and a government priority. President Kennedy had set the stage for Saturn in 1961 when he declared that America would put a man on the moon by the end of the decade.

That did happen, and Mort played his part in it. His company made the communications systems for the Saturn Rocket. Mort's job was to subject the company's products to extreme conditions to be sure that they would hold up under inordinate vibrations, liftoff stresses, and the excessive temperatures of space.

The Saturn program produced a total of thirty-two rockets launched between 1961 and 1975. There was another ironic twist here. It turned out that Mort was working for a program that was led and named by Werner von Braun, who had been in charge of military rockets for Germany during World War II. We never entirely escape from history.

Mort (center) at Electronic Communications, Inc., where he
worked on quality control for the Saturn Rocket program.
Astronaut Dave Scott, whose autograph appears
on the photo, is at left.

When aerospace projects wound down and ended, or when the companies working on them lost their contracts, technical professionals like Mort had to find other work. After seven years, the company's contract expired and they laid him off.

Mort landed a similar job at Honeywell. After seven years there, the same thing happened. That time, he went back to Israel for nine months and worked at the Standards Institute. They gave him a promotion and his own office, but the money was about half of what he'd been paid in America. A move back to Israel was also less attractive because Avi would have had to drop out of college and enter the army. I was working in a day care center at that time.

One day Charlene came home from middle school and told me that the father of a neighbor of one of her classmates knew of a job that would be a good fit for Mort's background in quality assurance. It was with HowMedica, Inc., in the medical field, a subsidiary of the Pfizer Corporation. HowMedica had one of its largest factories in our town. They made millions of ostomy bags as well as creams that were used in abdominal surgery. Product failure would be disastrous there, just as it would have been on the Saturn Rockets.

Mort got the job and returned to America, and this time we knew it was for good. We had bought our house lot on the Intracoastal Waterway in 1967, thinking that it would bring good resale value if we ever wanted to return to Israel. Bill Share had found the house lot for us, and he planned to buy one himself and spend his final working years in Florida. But that was not to be. Bill died of cancer in that same year.

When Pfizer joined an international consortium of testing consultants, they named Mort to be the company's representative. He traveled to many countries in Europe, staying for a week or two at a time. I went with him occasionally, when I could get time off from my own work. Mort was such a history buff. He knew about every castle in England. Traveling with him was an education in itself.

Mort stayed with Pfizer's HowMedica subsidiary for the rest of his career. When Pfizer sold the subsidiary, he decided to retire.

One more thing about Mort, the former ladies' man from Bialystok. He never followed the crowd, never strayed, when it came to me and our marriage. Just as he ignored his friends' warnings about me back when we met in Israel, he laughed off any suggestions about going astray after we were married. On one occasion, there was a business meeting with his Vernon cousins at a fancy resort in the Catskills—big-moneyed clientele, lots of Jewish people there. They were all given separate rooms. Mort was escorted to his room, and when they opened the door, there was a woman waiting for him.

At a function in 2008, a little over a year before Mort's death

"She's yours," they said. "You must be kidding," was his reply. "I have a beautiful wife at home." The guys on the trip made fun of him. He didn't care, and they all got the message. Then he came home and told me all about it.

It took me more than forty years, but I finally became what I had aspired to be, long ago in Vilna: a teacher. At our Temple Beth-El, the teacher of Hebrew left and the rabbi asked me to take his place. When I protested that I had had no training in education, he brushed my concerns aside and said, "You will become a teacher. You speak Hebrew better than he did."

So I took the job and taught all grades the Hebrew language, Jewish studies, the holidays, and preparation for the bar mitzvah. I loved the work and took courses at a local junior college to get certified in preschool education.

I taught part-time at the temple and synagogue for many years. When a private Jewish day school opened up, first in St. Petersburg and then moving to Clearwater, they asked me to come there and teach. I was reluctant to do it at first and said that I would just give it a try. But I stayed there for nineteen years, until the school closed. Then I went back to our synagogue to teach Hebrew for a few more years before retiring.

*

One day came the final, official word of what had happened to my father and brother. I had been seeking information on them from the Soviet Union for years, and I never got a response. They completely ignored me. So I asked the Red Cross for help. They called back one day when I was at school, and they said they had some information that could not be delivered over the phone.

They said they would come to school, and that I had to have somebody with me. I knew right away what it would be. Sure enough, they had a verification form on two men who had died in the brutal labor camp at Klooga, Estonia. It was my father and brother. German records said that they had tried to escape and were shot, two weeks before the end of the war in the East. They had survived all the way to that point, and were killed in one of the Germans' final atrocities. The Germans fled the advancing Russian army, but on their last days before evacuating they killed almost all of the prisoners and burned the bodies.

People call this sort of news "closure." I hate that word. There is no closure, no ending, when you lose loved ones to ruthless murderers.

Mort and I both were smokers for many years. I had begun when the American soldiers were passing out cigarettes on the day they liberated me in Magdeburg. One of those soldiers, years later, told me that they had also given out chocolates. I responded that I didn't get any chocolates, but that I did get cigarettes, and from then on I regularly smoked two to four a day.

I finally quit after going to a doctors' dinner one night with Bill Share. He saw me light up after the dinner, and first asked me to look around and tell him how many doctors were having a smoke then too. There were none. Then he had me exhale my smoke into his white handkerchief. He pointed to the stain that the smoke had made, and said that I was doing that same damage to my lungs.

I never smoked after that, and I persuaded Mort to stop smoking the next year. But it was too little, too late. In 2002 they found a tumor in one of his lungs after he had experienced stomach pain. Surgeons removed one lobe of his lung to get the tumor, and told him that he could consider himself cured if it didn't come back in seven years.

Seven years later, he went for a checkup and they discovered another tumor. This one was close to his heart, and the doctors did not want to risk operating. Finally a young female radiologist conducted a biopsy and confirmed the tumor's malignancy. Mort underwent radiation and maintenance chemotherapy with a medicine that was usually given to patients with asbestosis. That treatment worked for a time, but then his weakened lungs filled with fluid and he developed pneumonia. He passed away in January 2010, just four days before his ninety-first birthday.

A gathering of my extended family in Tel Aviv, 2017

But back to those trips Mort and I took, and that history we took in. . . . In all those years, I was carrying around some history of my own. It was on a visit to Vienna in 1988 when that history came roaring back and the direction of my own life changed again. We were near the Vienna Opera House, and we walked by a group of people, arguing loudly. "It never happened!" was what I heard.

"It" was the Holocaust. The man was a Holocaust denier. I could not let that pass. Remember, I have no censoring gene. I barged into that group, looked him in the eye, and told him he was dead wrong.

That was the first time I spoke up, and spoke out in public, about what had happened to me, and to six million Jews of Europe. It would not be the last time.

$\mathscr{S}$peaking $\mathscr{U}$p $\mathscr{E}$ $\mathscr{S}$peaking $\mathscr{O}$ut

Television interview outside Mauthausen
Concentration Camp, 1988

EFORE I TELL you about my late-in-life vocation as a spokesperson for Holocaust survivors, I must clarify something. The encounter with the deniers on the street in Vienna was not the first time that I talked to groups of people about my experiences. There had been several other occasions.

But in Vienna, it was the first time that my words about the Holocaust were fighting words. I had heard the lies, and I was angry. I wasn't just telling a curious audience about my own life. I was striking back against the hateful prejudice that killed six million of my Jewish brothers and sisters. I was striking back against the outrageous falsehood that it "never happened" or that not so many Jews died and what was the big deal.

That prejudice, that virus—or, perhaps, that cancer—of anti-Semitism is still with us. It did not die out after Germany's military defeat. Left unchecked, it will claim even more victims. When I tell my story, I am no longer just speaking about myself. I am speaking on behalf of the six million who died. I am speaking on behalf of those who survived, like me, but cannot bring themselves to talk about it. I am also speaking on behalf of those, even possibly still unborn, who in the future could fall victim to crimes of hate.

It took me many years and several tentative steps before I came to this point, where I realized that mine would be one of the voices to refute those who deny the truth of the Holocaust.

Right after the war, when I finally made it to Israel, with Germany behind me, and all the danger past, I could not bring myself to talk about what had happened to me. Many people including my future husband asked me about it, but I talked very little.

Still, sometimes it was impossible to put it behind me completely. In Israel, I first stayed at the home of my cousin Klara. At times I would wake up screaming, in the middle of the night. It was Klara who first told my son, many years later, that it was one of my nightmares that made me recall standing in the line at Stutthof, expecting to go to the shower, and just escaping death because I was the 151st person in the line.

I was able to tell Klara of some of my other memories, but only on a few occasions. The rest of the time, it was just too painful for me. As time went on and life got better, I was able to be what I always wanted—a wife, mother, teacher. I didn't forget what had happened. I remained friendly and in touch with Bella, Edith, Dora, and several others who had made it through the Holocaust along with me. But I didn't let those awful years define me. I didn't dwell on them, and I didn't talk much about them.

That quiet period lasted about thirty years. Then one day in the early 1970s, my daughter, Charlene, came home from school. She had mentioned in history class that her mother had been in concentration camps and had survived the Holocaust. The teacher was a little skeptical, but was interested in hearing more. He had never met a Holocaust survivor. So he asked her if I would come in and speak to the class.

I didn't know what do to. I had never spoken in public before. I didn't know what I could possibly say, especially to a group of twelve-year-olds. But I went. I didn't have a prepared speech, so I simply told the students a few things about my life and what had happened to me. Then I did my best to answer their questions.

Addressing students at Plant High School, Tampa, Florida in 2019

My son, Avi, was away at college when I spoke at Charlene's school. When he learned of it, he was upset with me. He had known of the Holocaust, but he had not known any details about my time in the concentration camps. He had never asked, and I had never thought to tell him.

I surely was not the first Holocaust survivor to speak openly, to people outside of family, of that evil time. But there were not yet many who did. And I was not ready to bear witness regularly, although there had been a few times when I spoke to groups of adults in various organizations and Jewish Community Centers.

Still, it took almost another twenty years before I would make telling my story a central part of my life's work. The first turning point was in Vienna. It was in 1988 that Mort and I took the trip to Austria and encountered the Holocaust deniers.

You must understand something about Austria in 1988. It was not a place for discussion of the Holocaust. Kurt Waldheim, the former Secretary General of the United Nations, was the country's president. During his UN days, he had concealed and lied about his past as a Nazi, a loyal and hardworking lieutenant to Adolf Eichmann.

That past finally came to light shortly before Austria's presidential election in 1986. Rather than disqualify him, it provoked a nationalist backlash that got him elected in spite of his misdeeds. Austria had always been enthusiastically in the Nazis' camp, and Vienna had long been virulently anti-Semitic.

Though I didn't know it, I was plunging into a perilous stew when I challenged the man who yelled, "It never happened. It's a lie."

As I walked right over to the two who were arguing, Mort tried to hold me back. It could be that he realized that I would meet with hostility, but I was furious and determined and I broke away from him.

"Don't you say it didn't happen. I was there. I am a witness. I am a concentration camp survivor."

The other man in that street-corner tiff was Peter Ochs, an American writer who had been a BBC correspondent. He asked me if I would consent to be interviewed about my life. In fact, he pleaded with me.

"Please, please tell me your story. I am a freelance reporter from Britain."

I told him that Mort and I were there for only a day, and that there were undoubtedly many people there who had been in the concentration camps. But he was almost desperate.

"I know. But they are afraid. They are in hiding. They won't talk to me."

At first, we were wary about doing something like that. But we checked with the American embassy and found that Mr. Ochs was who he said he was.

So I agreed to be interviewed, but I wanted it to be at an actual concentration camp. We went to Mauthausen, which is about one hundred miles east of Vienna. At least one hundred thousand Jews had perished at that place. On the ride to Mauthausen, I told him my story. He said to me that there were young people, young German people, who want to hear what really happened.

When we got there we walked around inside the camp. I told my story again, on camera. I knew exactly where the ovens, the crematories, were. It was hard for me to do, but I was able to get through most of the day without breaking down emotionally.

At one point, though, the pain came flooding back. A group of students was touring the camp that day. They wanted to hear more about me. They spoke German, and my German was not very good. But I tried, and they and Mr. Ochs helped me find the words. Talking to those young people brought back all the pain of my childhood. I thought of that awful day in Vilna when they pulled me away from my family and sent them all to their deaths and me to the labor camp in Latvia.

Not everyone who was there that day believed me. Some didn't even want the subject brought up. A couple approached me and said that this was not the place to talk about it.

Perhaps they were anti-Semites. But if they were natives of Austria, they were probably typical and they should have been ashamed. Austrian support for Hitler had been loud and enthusiastic, right from the beginning. It was only two weeks after the 1938 Anschluss with the Third Reich that they began to build the Mauthausen camp. Austria was nothing like it seemed in the movie, *The Sound of Music*.

Mr. Ochs was surprised that I had been able to remain calm while I told my story. When we were finished, he went up to put his hand on the wall of the camp. And he cried.

He asked what he could pay me. I told him that I would not even think about any kind of payment. All I wanted was a copy of a picture he had taken outside the concentration camp gates, and a copy of the interview tape when it was finished. Later on, he told me that my story and many others were in a book he had written for use in British schools.

I also have some pictures that Mort took that day. One of them was of me with two young girls. I got a letter from one of them later. She wrote, "You have no idea what you did for us."

Those two days in Vienna were a revelation for me. They were satisfying in a way that I hadn't known before. I felt good about doing my part to dispel the lies and to break down the wall of silence in Austria. But I still wasn't ready, or comfortable, with speaking in public about my life.

About two years later, Rabbi Jacob Luski of our synagogue, Congregation B'nai Israel, asked me to accompany him on a visit to the Bay Pines Veterans Hospital in St. Petersburg. I didn't want to go. A group of war veterans was a much different audience, and the prospect of speaking to them made me nervous. But the rabbi persisted. And he was persuasive.

The rabbi reminded me that the people I would see there were those who fought in World War II because of people like me. He said they deserved to see me, to hear from me, to know that their sacrifices had not been in vain.

So I went. And I had not been speaking very long, in the presence of so many wounded veterans, before it became too much for me. I broke down and wept. Rabbi Luski was so right. Those men needed to hear from me. And I needed to be in their presence too. I needed to face them and to thank them.

I knew then, finally, that I could and must continue the work that they and their fellow soldiers, those who made it back home and those who gave their lives, had begun. This was the reason I was spared in Kaiserwald. This was the reason that, on so many other occasions, my life could have ended in a moment, but did not.

Rabbi Luski also urged me to tell my story to young people. With his help, I wrote a formal speech and began my speaking to high school students. Word got around, and invitations began to arrive. When the Florida Holocaust Museum was established at Madeira Beach in 1992, I was very happy to become involved when asked by its late founder, the philanthropist Walter Loebenberg. I spoke at the opening ceremony.

In 1994, the Florida Legislature passed the Holocaust Education Bill (SB 660), which amended existing statutes and required all school districts to incorporate lessons on the Holocaust as part of public-school instruction. Florida became the fourth state in the United States to mandate Holocaust education in elementary and secondary schools. I had spoken to the legislature in Tallahassee before that law was passed.

In addition to addressing students in person, in four counties of western Florida, I have spoken via Skype videoconferencing to schools in the Florida Panhandle, where there are no known Holocaust survivors. We still own our old apartment in Tel Aviv, so on trips to Israel I've talked to young people there. I made the last of those trips in 2017, at the age of ninety-two.

I have tried to accommodate requests from everyone: high school students, college students, adult groups, and members of the military who are currently serving. They all must be told about it. They all need to hear it from someone who was there.

Speaking to students at Florida Holocaust Museum, 2016

The Florida Holocaust Museum moved into larger quarters in St. Petersburg in 1998. They acquired a boxcar that had been used by the German National Railway throughout the years of the Holocaust. I had been thrown into one exactly like it on September 24, 1943, the worst day of my life. A boxcar transported me, Bella, Dora, and hundreds of others from Vilna to Kaiserwald. Ten months later, another one carried us from Stutthof to Magdeburg.

I wrote the following speech and delivered it when the Museum Boxcar Exhibit opened:

BOXCAR 1130695-5

Years ago I saw a movie from the Israeli War of Independence entitled "Hill 68 Does Not Answer." The hill could not answer because all of the defenders were dead.

Boxcar 1130695-5, could you answer? Tell us about the people you carried to the concentration and death camps. In how many trips and convoys were you used? How many people were in each transport? What were your destinations? Auschwitz, Treblinka, Majdanek, Sobibor, or Belzec? How many innocent men, women, and children did you carry, who later perished in the camps?

We know that you will remain silent, but we also know that you were employed by the Nazis, and you were actively involved in atrocities as a vehicle of—and to—death. Convoys of locked cattle cars and freight cars, like you, were the transport vehicles of the Shoah. You were used extensively and often. In one direction you carried the Jews and others to extermination camps, and in the other direction you carried their money, valuables, extracted gold teeth, hair, and clothing to Germany to help the Nazi war effort and enrich the Fuhrer and his henchmen.

There were about forty boxcars in each convoy and over one hundred people were jammed like sardines in one car. The boarding of the trains was supervised by police and the SS. The openings were secured by barbed wire and locked from the outside. For the entire journey there was no food or water. Many of the elderly and children died during the transfer. There would be no need to gas them later.

Polish railroad workers, who operated the trains, received written transport orders on which route and destination were indicated. Auschwitz, Treblinka, Majdanek, and so on. . . . These killing sites were chosen because of their closeness to rail lines and the location in semi-rural areas, so very few people would know what was happening there.

At the final destination the trains halted and the human cargo was discharged for extermination, at first by carbon monoxide from gas engines and later by Zyklon gas, specially developed for this pur-·pose. The bodies were either buried in mass graves or incinerated in crematoria.

Boxcar 1130695-5, you did a very good job for the Nazis. You cannot tell us much yourself, but I know because I was there. And maybe it was you that I was in. I was transported in such a boxcar from the ghetto to the labor camp Kaiserwald in Riga.

We want to keep you as a reminder of the horror of the Holocaust in which six million Jews and five million others perished.

Now you will be on permanent display at the Tampa Bay Holocaust Museum as a symbol of evil.

Your display at the museum will also serve as a warning to us and the future generations that another holocaust of such a magnitude and ferocity may occur again, if we will not be on guard to prevent it.

NEVER, EVER AGAIN.

Over the years I have addressed many of the museum's gatherings and programs, both at the museum itself and offsite, as a member of the Speakers' Bureau. I and both my children and their spouses are life members of the museum. For me, the museum is a memorial for all of my family who perished.

After he retired, Mort became a researcher and translator at the museum. He threw himself into this volunteer work with energy and enthusiasm, and he quickly became a beloved member of the museum's staff. He specialized in interpreting and explaining historical documents that were in Polish, German, Yiddish, and Hebrew.

In 1996 I was one of the Holocaust survivors interviewed by researchers for filmmaker Steven Spielberg's Shoah Foundation. There were approximately fifty-five thousand individuals who agreed to have their interviews filmed and made part of the permanent historical record.

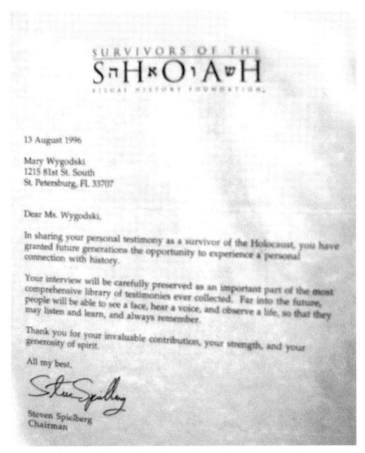

Letter from Hollywood producer Steven Spielberg, thanking me
for my interview with his foundation, 1996

Every year, from 1999 to 2011, I would address teachers from all parts of Florida who had come to Florida State University's Holocaust Institute for Educators and the University's Center for Professional Development. My speaking usually came on Survivors' Night. In 2015,

I was keynote speaker at the International Holocaust Remembrance Day event in Tampa.

It has also been heartening to know that a third generation of my family has taken up the task of keeping the story of Holocaust survivors alive. My grandson Elan's documentary project for his high school history fair was named Best in School in 2019.

When I speak to young people, especially, I let them know that I don't have all of the answers to the wrongs of the world. I particularly recall one boy, of junior-high-school age, asking me why so many people hate Jews. I thought for a long moment, and then I answered, "I don't know. Why do you think that people hate Jews?"

I must also tell you that I have frequently become saddened and discouraged. I have seen the persistence and the staying power of anti-Semitism and hatred. I have visited Poland and Lithuania and some concentration camps, along with members of my family, and sometimes being in those places proved too much for me.

On one occasion I went to Poland with Avi. I walked into Auschwitz, and after being in the first room I could not continue. Even I, who had been through those things that were on display, was not immune to the horrible realizations of what the Germans had done.

Our family organized another trip on the occasion of my oldest grandson's, Matthew's, Bar Mitzvah. In addition to our children and two grandsons, our entourage included Eddie Share, the brother of my dear cousin Bruce Share. The plan was to visit all of the places where I had been, as well as other famous and infamous places in Holocaust history.

Again, when we came to Auschwitz, I could not bring myself to go. I stayed in the hotel and took care of Matthew's younger brother, Jeremy. I also did not accompany Mort and Charlene on day trips to Bialystok and to the killing camp of Majdanek. We also attended a soccer match while we were on the trip, and I was distressed when I saw the graffiti painted on the walls of the stadium. It said, in Polish, "Jews belong in the ovens." How they could do this today? I could not understand. Anti-Semitism has never gone away and probably never will.

Nevertheless, I remain optimistic. I have found that people of all ages are most interested in learning about my experiences and about the Holocaust in general. At the University of South Florida in February of 2019, I was scheduled to speak to a group for about twenty minutes. Instead, I was with them, answering their questions, for four hours. Anti-Semitism and hatred cannot triumph as long as there are people, like that audience, who are willing to listen and to know the truth.

In April of 2021, I participated in a five-day filmed interview for Dimensions in Testimony, a project of the University of Southern California's Shoah Foundation. It employed the latest technologies in filmmaking, video displays, and language processing to create an interactive biography. For many years after I am gone, people will be able to ask me questions and receive real-time responses. They will be able to learn the truth about the Holocaust directly from me and from others who were eyewitnesses to history's greatest organized crime. I was pleased to be a part of this latest endeavor of the Shoah Foundation.

There are some Holocaust survivors, like my lifelong friend Bella, who do not talk of their lives and experiences in those awful years. They prefer to put it all in the past. I understand and respect that. Such memories are too painful for some; they are surely painful for me. But I do feel that I was spared so that I could tell the truth to those who come after me.

CHAPTER 20

Bella

I DON'T USUALLY TALK about what happened. If you ask me, I will try to answer. But I am one of those people who has buried the past.

How it all happened, the details of it, I honestly don't remember. We were all thrown together in the railcar. We stayed together. We worked together, and Mary and Dora and I slept together, in the same little place in the barracks.

It was extraordinary, in that regard. People did stick together. It was a full-time occupation, in the camps, just to stay alive. We didn't have much hope, and there was no time to think about it.

Mary saved my life in the camps. She was a very practical girl, and I was not. She came from a large family, so she was the responsible one. She knew how to talk to the guards. She knew how to sew. She would keep the clothes that we were wearing looking a little bit better, a little more acceptable than the others.

We got our bread rations in the morning. If we ate it all then, there was nothing left for the afternoon. Mary made sure that we didn't eat it all right away. "Not now," she would say, "we are going to save it." It was things like that, which she would do, that pulled me through.

Mary has beautiful blue eyes. I always wanted eyes like hers. When we were in school, we sat on the same bench together. The school days would run from eight or nine to two or three, and then there would be homework. We didn't play very much in the streets.

She would come to my house, most of the time. I would also go to their apartment. It was a very large one, and her mother was always there, taking care of the children. She was a good-looking woman, very tall. I thought she was beautiful. She was also very pragmatic; Mary was like her.

Mary's parents were religious. Mine were not. In my house there was a lot of Jewish tradition, but not much religion. My mother, who was born Berta Leskes, was a dentist. That was very unusual. My grandfather had sent her to Prague for her education.

My father, Hirsh Klok, was an agent for Electrolux, a Swedish company. He sold vacuum cleaners, which were almost unheard of in those days. It was the Depression, so times were bad. My mother was the actual family breadwinner.

I was the only child, so I was spoiled. I played the piano, but only because I had to. My father had to pay me to sit down and play it. But I used to read a lot. I loved books. I love visual art, and I have come to love music, opera, and the theater. I have no creative ability. That is something I wish I had.

My late husband, Max Funkelstein, was from Riga, Latvia. I met him there in Kaiserwald, the first camp where they sent us. He also was sent to Stutthof and Magdeburg. At the time of liberation, when we were fleeing from the Germans, Dora and I got separated from Mary, and Max got shot in the leg. We initially took refuge in a cemetery.

When the Americans arrived, they looked like such strange creatures. We went back and found Mary, and the first place we all went was back to the camp. At that point we had nowhere else to go.

Magdeburg is on the Elbe River. That is where Max and I were married. The Americans pulled their forces back from there and let the Russians come in. When we knew that the Russians were coming, Max and I left. He had friends in Bavaria. We went to a little town not far from Garmisch-Partenkirchen and lived there for three or four years.

It was difficult to get into the United States at that point. They had a quota. Max applied, and waited, and finally got his papers. So he went to America first, and I went to live in Israel. Later on, I applied for my own visa. Because we were married, I was able to get one and join him in New York. That was in 1952.

We had a wonderful life in America. Max went to work selling women's sunglasses and hair accessories. He was good at it, and the company, Riviera, did very well. Its founder was Boris Kliot. He was also from Riga and was in the camps with us.

Riviera eventually grew to where it sold its products all over the country. Boris wound up selling the company for several million dollars. He became a devoted philanthropist. The Kliot Neurosurgery Wing of Ichilov General Hospital in Tel Aviv was named for him. He also built a memorial in the Rumbula Forest near Riga to honor the twenty-seven thousand Jews who were murdered there in 1941 by the Nazis. Boris lost his parents and four sisters in those massacres.

I went to work in the office of ASCAP, the American Society of Composers, Authors, and Publishers. We paid royalties to performing artists.

I still live in our original apartment in Astoria, Queens. After living there for a little more than twenty years, we planned to move to the West Side of Manhattan. But in 1973, Max was diagnosed with cancer. He passed away in 1974. So I stayed put here, and it's fortunate that I did because my unit is rent-controlled. I wouldn't be able to afford to live in Manhattan today.

I have loved New York—the theaters, the museums, the opera. Italian opera especially—Puccini, Verdi. As long as I was able to climb the subway stairs, I would go in to Manhattan to take advantage of everything it has to offer.

And I love this country. Lately, though, I have been upset with the politics—so much distortion.

As for the speaking out about the Holocaust, about what happened—I cannot do it. I give Mary a lot of credit for being able to do it. And if it were not for her, and how she watched out for me back in the camps so long ago, I would not be alive today.

CHAPTER 21

Edith

*J*DID NOT KNOW Mary during our childhood years in Vilna. We attended different schools. I believe that the first time we met was at Magdeburg, the third concentration camp. It may have been at Stutthof, though. It is so long ago now that I don't remember exactly. But we have been friends ever since.

There is one thing about Mary that I will never forget. She was always optimistic. She never lost hope for the future, no matter how bad it was in the camps, no matter how cruelly they treated us. She was so unlike me in that way. I don't know how she was able to do it.

My family lived in Nova Vilejka, just outside of Vilna. My younger brother and I used to come in to Vilna for school.

My father was in the lumber business. They would bring in trees from the forests and make wooden boards and planks for buildings. In 1939, just before the war broke out, my brother died in an awful accident at the lumber factory. It was on a Sunday, and few people were around. He and a friend were playing on one of the lorries that carried the trees. Somehow, the lorry tipped and fell on him.

When the Russians came in, the lumber factory closed. Some of my parents' friends asked us to come into Vilna, where it would be safer, and to live with them. We did, for a time, until my parents found an apartment just for us. When the Germans attacked and bombed Vilna, one of the bombs came into our apartment and destroyed it. We were not injured, and we moved back with our friends until the Nazis forced everyone into the ghetto.

The Nazis took both of my parents from me. My father was snatched from the apartment and brought to Ponary, where he was shot. One of the neighbors, a Polish family, had informed the Nazis that he could be found at the apartment.

When the Nazis liquidated the Vilna ghetto, they sent a group of us to the slave labor camp at Kaiserwald. My mother and I were both in that group, so we were spared immediate death. But death came soon for her.

Even though Kaiserwald was a work camp, the Nazis were constantly conducting "cleanings." They would select people who were old, or sick, and take them away to be shot or to die from carbon monoxide in the backs of closed vans.

I don't know why my mother was selected. But one night, after work ended, she did not come back to the barracks. I searched for her and found the man who was in charge of the place where she worked.

I don't believe he was an evil man or a cruel man. But he said to me, "I don't know where she is now, but I can send you there if you want."

I still did not believe that she was gone and kept searching through that work area. Finally, I found her clothing. I found her sweater. It was still there. Then I knew that I would never see her again.

There was one time at Kaiserwald that I thought I was going to die. The camp commandant summoned me to his office. A letter had come to me at the camp from a friend who had been taken away to work in Estonia. The commandant had the letter. I thought I was going to be punished with death. But he let me go. I am from Latvia, where his girlfriend was from. Maybe that was the reason.

After the Americans liberated us at Magdeburg, I ended up at Charleroi in Belgium with Mary and Dora. The three of us stayed together and visited the offices of the Jewish Federation every day, hoping to get the certificates that would allow us passage to Israel. We had been told to say that we had been born in Warsaw; if they knew we were from Vilna we would have been placed in the hands of the Russians.

One day, while we were waiting, Dora was called into the office. She was in there for a long time. Mary and I were both worried about her. But finally she came out and told us what had happened. The man who interviewed her was her uncle, who knew that she was from Vilna.

Dora's uncle and aunt were wonderful people. They were childless, and they wanted to adopt her. Then they said that they would adopt all three of us. Those adoptions did not happen, but we did get our certificates and were off to build our new lives in Israel.

I met my husband, Shlomo, in Israel. His father had moved him and their family there in 1934. They had lived in Berlin, where he managed a business. He decided to leave after some Nazi youths brutally murdered one of his employees. They took him out one night after work, got him drunk, and beat him to death. They were never punished.

That young man was not Jewish. But Shlomo's father knew that if such a thing could happen to him, it could happen to anybody. So he and his family got out in time.

We met in Israel and were married in 1947. He worked in management for Solel Boneh, which was one of the largest engineering companies in the world. We came to America in 1959. Shlomo's skill as a machinist got him a good job at the Owens-Illinois company. We have a son, Joel, and a daughter, Arna.

We lived in southern New Jersey for many years. In 2016, we moved to California to be closer to our daughter and grandchildren. We have loved America. It has been wonderful to us. I do miss Israel very much, however. I wish we had not sold our beautiful apartment, which was high up on Mount Carmel overlooking Haifa.

I have loved and admired Mary ever since we met. While I am not reluctant to talk about my own experiences during the Holocaust, I would not be able to speak out in public the way she has done.

CHAPTER 22

Generations Two & Three

At the taping sessions for Dimensions in Testimony, April 2021. Grandsons Matthew and Jeremy in front. Son Avi, grandson Elan, daughter Charlene, standing.

Avi Wygodski

THOSE OF US in the Second Generation, like Charlene and I, are alive today because our parents were able to survive when millions of others did not. It's a profound realization that we represent the survival of families that would have died out completely, and that many other families totally vanished. To us, the Holocaust is not some abstract historical phenomenon or table of statistics. It is our past. It is my mother's life, and it is the deaths of my aunts, my uncles, and my grandparents.

Second-Generation children have no family tree to climb. The Holocaust disrupted and erased much of our family history. We therefore have a special responsibility. Just as the survivors themselves must do, we must make sure that the Holocaust is remembered by future generations. Whatever we write, post, and videotape now will become a public record for the future. Whatever information we overlook or ignore will be lost forever. That must not happen.

My mother felt that way. But it took her many years to begin speaking about what she endured and survived. Once she did, that was not the only thing she would speak about. She believed and reminded those who heard her that there were larger lessons to be learned from the Holocaust—lessons about humanity and inhumanity, about tolerance and intolerance, about truth and lies, about justice and injustice.

The Holocaust is just as important as other seminal events in Jewish history—the Exodus, Purim, Chanukah, the destruction of the two Temples—and its story must be passed on from generation to generation. The world must remember this deliberate attempt to annihilate the Jewish people. And our generation must also succeed in our own lives and make the world a better place.

It took me a while to realize just what my own place is in the world. I was born in Tel Aviv. When I was six years old, I thought the whole world was Jewish. When we moved to Forest Hills, New York, I thought that just half the world was Jewish. When we moved to St. Petersburg, Florida, when I was twelve, I finally understood just how few Jews there are in the world. I was suddenly different. I felt the sting of anti-Jewish harassment.

When I told my father about the snide remarks and threats that I heard in school, he said respond to it, stand up to it and defend yourself, don't hide from it, or they will continue to torment you. If someone hits you, get even if you can. Be proud of who you are and of your people. He was speaking from experience. He had been in the British police force when living in the Palestinian Mandate. Later on, he fought in the Haganah, the precursor of the Israel Defense Forces (IDF) that reclaimed the Jewish ancestral homeland.

My mother also spoke from her experience. She urged me to be positive. She made me believe that if I set my mind to accomplish a specific goal, it would be achievable as long as there is persistence and patience. She never let me give up or quit on anything.

It wasn't just my mother's words that showed what she meant. I remember one example of her persistence during a trip to Vilna in 1992. We flew to Berlin, took a train to Warsaw, and then tried to take another train to Lithuania. But we needed a visa to pass through Western Belorussia, so we went to the Russian Embassy.

There was a long line at the embassy, waiting for approvals after filling out lengthy applications. We waited a couple of hours, and then they told us to come the next day. My mother was furious. Since she spoke Russian, she went to the teller window and demanded to see the director immediately. We were escorted to the ambassador's office in the back, and he asked my mother what she wanted.

She didn't just mention the visa. She proceeded to criticize the whole country of Russia, on how unorganized the place was and how it was no wonder that the Russians don't have a successful tourism industry because of their bureaucracy. The guy quickly signed the visa documents that we needed to get onto the train.

After what my mother endured during the Holocaust, she showed no fear in traveling in that countryside, where there were few travelers at that time. She showed me how assertiveness and fearlessness will achieve the desired goal.

As for my own knowledge of the Holocaust, and my becoming involved in supporting my mother in her mission as a spokesperson, that came much later as well. It wasn't until I was in college, at the University of Florida, that she spoke to an audience at the local Jewish Community Center about her experiences, and that I realized I wanted to know more. I knew some of her stories from home but not all of them.

About ten more years went by. I was well into my career as an architect in Tallahassee, Florida, when I took a class at Florida State University with Professor Richard Rubenstein, a Holocaust scholar. He taught the gruesome details of how that horror of horrors happened, of its immense scale, and of how little was done to stop it. We learned that around 1942–43, approximately 80 percent of the total European Jewish population was exterminated in about a sixteen-month period. Even though my own mother had survived the Holocaust and was already speaking about it, I needed that course to immerse myself into the history and the theology of the subject.

After the Florida Legislature passed the Holocaust Education Bill, requiring that the history of the Holocaust be taught in public schools, Florida State established a weeklong summer institute for teachers to learn how to present the Holocaust to age-appropriate students. Thursday evening was dedicated to a survivor's presentation; during the first couple of years the speakers were German Jews who had left Europe before the war after experiencing anti-Semitism. I knew that my mother's story would have a big impact on the classes of forty to fifty teachers. So I asked her, and she was willing.

For about fifteen years, she would make the trip up from St. Petersburg, first with my father and later with my sister. She would read her abbreviated story for thirty minutes, and then stay for a question-and-answer period that often ran for more than two hours. The reviews after the seminars would usually say that her presentation was the highlight of the whole week of classes. A couple of times she was the featured speaker on Sunday evening, where about two hundred community people were invited for the institute's opening night.

My mother never hid her past. She openly spoke about her experiences when asked, and she only wished that she could remember more details. She believed that she came "back to life" after the war, and she has lived her precious life to the fullest, many more years than most people.

When it comes to making decisions, my mother is very clear on what was right and wrong and what was appropriate to do. She respects other people's views, as long as they will respect hers. She believes strongly in fighting for the protection of human rights and freedoms for all individuals. Jews in Poland under German rule did not have the right to "life, liberty and the pursuit of happiness."

My mother also believes that truth must—and will—win over falsehood. She is just as passionate speaking about Holocaust denial as she is about Israel's right to exist. The negative portrayal of Israel by the media really troubles her. It is reckless and false. The Jewish people have been victims for thousands of years of displacement, expulsions, and discrimination. In the last century they have faced multiple wars and terrorism because they want to live in their ancestral homeland. She says that if there had been a country of Israel in 1939, there would not have been a Holocaust.

Charlene Wygodski

When I was growing up in St. Petersburg, attending the elementary, junior, and public high schools, I don't remember any other kids whose parents were in the Holocaust. Nor did I meet any when I went with the other Jewish kids to Hebrew school or Sunday school. My history was different from theirs.

Many family members perished, on both my mother's side and my father's side. There are whole branches missing. I try to imagine them and their lives, through my parents' stories.

Each survivor's story is unique. So are the ways in which their stories impact their children's lives. We members of the Second Generation are a living connection to the ghosts of the past. The hatred, prejudice, and apathy that Holocaust survivors endured forge a legacy that comes to be embodied in the lives of the Second Generation and their children. I feel that I am a product of my family's legacy, but in the best possible way. My parents both worked hard so that my brother and I could achieve our highest goals and dreams. In their eyes, there was nothing we couldn't do, and education was foremost. They provided the means for me to attend college and dental school, and I am very grateful for that. She always told us that no one can ever take our education away from us.

I like to tell the story of my first encounter with my mother's legacy, outside of our home. It was in the seventh grade. The teacher mentioned World War II and the Holocaust. I raised my hand and said that my mom was a survivor of the concentration camps. He had never met anyone like that, and I'm not sure that he fully believed me. He invited her to come in the next day so that he could ask her a few questions.

She turned out to be the best show-and-tell in my class. It was then that I started to have the feeling that I had a responsibility to help keep her story and her memories alive.

My mother started out small, with her speaking out, but she soon became a megaphone for the Florida Holocaust Museum. I and my family are proud of the phenomenal job she has done keeping her story alive, passing on her lessons learned in the Holocaust and responding emphatically to deniers.

Survivors like my mother, who can speak about the atrocities they suffered and witnessed, are now few and far between. They are in their eighties and nineties, and the window is rapidly closing. I have always admired her sheer tenacity and willingness to continue as long as she can. Due to travel limitations, she has kept active by taking advantage of technologies like Skype and Zoom.

It was an amazing experience for all of us to see Mom take part in Dimensions in Testimony with the USC Shoah Foundation. It was not easy on her, at the age of ninety-five; she pushed through a full week of filming, telling her story and responding over and over to specific, detailed questions. I think that may end up being her biggest contribution to future generations.

Besides her story, I want people to know that despite all of the cruelty Mom endured and all of the losses that she suffered, she has kept a positive and inspirational attitude towards life. She believes that God left her on earth for a reason. The chain of memory will be broken by the passing of time, and history and its lessons will become more important. My role, as her daughter and as a Second-Generation member, is to keep her torch burning and to pass it along.

Matthew Bloom

My grandmother played a large role in my early impressionable years. Some of my earliest memories are with her, including as a student in her kindergarten class. As I got older, we began talking about the Holocaust and she later shared her story with my class at Baypoint Middle School. When I was in high school, we traveled together to Vilnius, Lithuania, the city of her childhood before she was forced into the ghetto and concentration camps.

She instilled in me a love for learning and education, something she was deprived of for many years due to the Holocaust. My passion for musical instruments also came from her constant encouragement and support—she has always said the violin reminded her of her father, even though she had never heard him play it at home in Vilna. She has taught me to stand up for what I believe in, to say what I think, and to never be a bystander.

Jeremy Bloom

My grandmother always said that her greatest revenge on the Nazis was having a happy family that continues the Jewish legacy down through the generations. I am happy to say that I am doing that. As I write this, I am living in my grandparents' apartment in Tel Aviv, the same one that she and my grandfather built right after the War of Liberation. I plan to continue this mission and to keep the stories of her Holocaust experience alive into the future.

I'm fortunate to have grown up with a close connection to my grandmother. Out of her own circumstances, she supplied many stories and morals that instilled my cherished life values within me. She taught me to endure and to power through the hardships that I have encountered. She has been a fierce advocate for me—to think about what I say, to say what I think, to be unafraid to respectfully speak my mind, and to be true to myself and to others.

Elan Wygodski

I am keeping alive a family tradition that my grandmother, my Sapta, always wanted me to pursue. I play the violin, just like her father, my father, my aunt, and my cousins. I know that she's proud of me for that. And one of her greatest wishes was to come to my Bar Mitzvah, which she was very thrilled about.

All through my childhood, she has taught me many life values and lessons. She has told me stories, read stories, sung songs, and conversed with me for hours in Hebrew. My grandmother has always wanted me to read books and to constantly be learning. She has a great saying: "Everything you possess can be taken from you except knowledge and education." She has also taught me to never lie or cheat, as this would have a much greater consequence than telling the truth.

My grandmother has also shared her experiences of life in Poland before and during the War. I have always cherished every moment with her, and I especially remember when we visited Israel together. She told me what life was like in Israel, how Israel was created back in 1948, and what it was like for her during the War of Independence. It is still difficult for me to comprehend how lucky I am to be her grandson.

I have done what I can to pass on her story to my own contemporaries. For school, I created and submitted a History Fair documentary project based on her Holocaust survival story. I discussed and presented her experiences, from going to the ghetto to being sent to three concentration camps to being liberated by the American army. The school judges were impressed by this project, giving me first place for our school's fair and sending my work on to the regional level of competition.

One evening, while working on homework, I decided to write this poem for her:

> Six million that died with complete despair
>
> everyone sat watching with no help to spare
>
> burned and gassed up into the air

still, no one that seemed to care

burning of blood and flesh let by

the smell of death arises in the sky

for the six million that died, and their lives stolen away

we will never forget how we were left in dismay.

They shall be remembered.

In dedication to Mary Wygodski, and in honor of my great-grand-parents, who perished in the Holocaust.

Final Words

I LIKE TO WALK the streets at night. All by myself. I talk with Mort. I talk with my mother too. Her sayings come back to me.

"My little girl yesterday. My daughter today. And my friend forever." I do hope that I have been the kind of mother to my children that my mother was to me.

"All by yourself, your soul is clean."

And then, "There is not a bad experience you cannot overcome." I hope that I have proven the truth of that.

I also ask God to please help me remember how much that I have loved and enjoyed this life. I ask him to not let me complain about my bodily aches and pains, so that I will not take away from my children their own enjoyment of their lives.

I feel very peaceful on those evening walks. But part of that inner peace has to come from knowing that, for most of my life, I have been at war and done my part.

For me, war never ended. Long ago in Vilna, I did not choose to go into the forest and join my courageous relative Abba Kovner and the resistance warriors. But I did become a fighter. I did resist the monstrous legacy of hatred that Adolf Hitler spawned. It took much for me to break my silence and join the fight. But I did it. I embraced my calling.

My near-death experience and vision of my family, as I was sinking into the river at Kaiserwald, was the true beginning. I did not think about telling my story to anyone at that time, but I did know even then that some higher power wanted me to remain alive. For what purpose, I didn't know.

Life went on and I got everything that I ever wished for—a loving husband, beautiful children and grandchildren, good health, good friends, and a satisfying career in a peaceful and prosperous country.

But I eventually realized that there was something else that I had to do. I needed something to make me grasp, at long last, just what the higher power's purpose was in keeping me alive. That power was the God that I had rejected for taking my family away from me.

God works his will through the people he sends into our lives. The people he sent to me brought me back to the fight, and back to him. I had to see the looks on the faces of Charlene's schoolmates. I had to behold Mr. Ochs bursting into tears, and to hear the thanks of the German-speaking Austrian children, when I spoke at Mauthausen. I had to feel the gratitude welling up within me as I looked into the eyes of those wounded veterans at the Bay Pines Veterans Hospital.

I couldn't remain silent. I had to rejoin the battle against Adolf Hitler and the monstrous evil that he perpetrated on my six million Jewish brothers and sisters. He is long dead but his vile followers remain abroad in all countries of the world.

The great American author John Steinbeck wrote the following in a letter to a friend just when World War II was breaking out: "All the goodness and the heroisms will rise up again, then be cut down again and rise up. It isn't that the evil thing wins—it never will—but that it doesn't die."

Mr. Steinbeck was right. The evil thing doesn't die. But we all must do our parts to make sure that it never wins. I hope and pray that my story has helped.

Shalom Aleichem

Mary Wygodski
November 2021

Author's Note
on Sources

$\mathscr{A}$s I UNDERTOOK the writing of this book, my intent was to relate Mary Wygodski's story in her own words while also putting that story into a full and proper historical context. This required research on the Jewish people; on the lands of Eastern Europe and Israel; and on the Holocaust, World War II, and the War of Liberation. I sought information particularly on those historical events that had a bearing on the lives of Mary and her family.

I drew upon many sources. The materials that pertain to Mary's direct experiences were taken almost exclusively from her personal memories and from the Wygodski family archives. She spent many hours with me, retelling the story that she has shared with thousands of people over the years. Her son, Avi, and her daughter, Charlene, were frequent participants in those meetings and contributors to many aspects of Mary's story.

For the chapters on Mort Wygodski's life, the primary source was his own handwritten personal history. It spanned the years of his childhood in Bialystok up until the time he met Mary and immediately fell in love with her, in British Mandate Palestine.

Bella Funkelstein and Edith Goodrich graciously consented to meet with me at their homes and to tell of their memories of Mary and of their own experiences in the years of the Holocaust and afterwards.

Additional family members who shared their recollections of Mary, especially of her years in Syracuse, New York, included Bruce Share, Mary's cousin, who asked me to take on this book project; Bruce's sister, Rene Wolpin; his brother, Eddie Share; and Mary's cousins Maurice Sinuk and Philip Miller.

Sid Handler, like Mary a native of Vilna, spent several hours with me, recounting his own experience of life in Vilna and of his survival. His mother was working as a seamstress in the city's Kailis slave labor camp, making winter clothing for the German military. When the Nazis' summons came for all children to assemble for what became the Children's Aktion in March 1944, she shoved him into a lumber-storage bin, returned for him at night, and then hid him under piles of coats for three months, until the Red Army liberated Vilna.

World War II and the Holocaust are both subjects of a vast and ever-expanding body of literature. This literature encompasses traditional works of history, personal memoirs, and works of historical fiction that can give readers and students a nuanced appreciation and understanding that may not come through in straight factual accounts.

All of the books and sources that I read and consulted in the course of researching and writing this book appear in the bibliography. Of these, a few bear special mention here because they were particularly useful in reconstructing the history and events recounted in certain chapters.

Laimonas Briedis's *Vilnius: City of Strangers* (Central European University Press, 2009) was the chief source of the turbulent early history, detailed in the Preface, of that city where Mary was born and spent her childhood.

Several books supplied excellent details of the Nazis' implementation of their Final Solution in Vilna and the country of Lithuania. These events are described and discussed in Chapters 3, 5, 6, and 8.

Herman Kruk's diary, *The Last Days of the Jerusalem of Lithuania* (Yale University Press, 2002) is a day-by-day account of events from September 1939 to September 1944 when Krug was imprisoned in Klooga, Estonia, where he perished along with Mary's father and brother just days before the Russian army arrived. *Stronger than Iron: The Destruction of Vilna Jewry 1941–1945, an Eyewitness Account* (Gefen Publishing, 2009) by Mendel Balberyszski is another close-up view of Vilna Jews' ordeal.

Yitzhak Arad's *Ghetto in Flames: The Struggle and Destruction of the Jews in Vilna in the Holocaust* (Holocaust Library, 1982) gives both a wealth of detailed information of those difficult days as well as a historian's analysis. Dr. Arad also edited the chilling *Ponary Diary, 1941–1943: A Bystander's Account of a Mass Murder* (Yale University Press, 2005) by Kazimierz Sakowicz, who lived near the gate of the Ponary killing fields and recorded in understated, factual language the horrors that he witnessed.

David Fishman's *The Book Smugglers: Partisans, Poets, and the Race to Save Jewish Treasures from the Nazis—The True Story of the Paper Brigade of Vilna* (University Press of New England, 2017) is a chronicle of the work of a team of Jews, led by Herman Kruk. They hid and preserved a portion of Vilna's cultural and religious treasures from the Nazi plunderers who were under the overall supervision of Adolf Hitler's fellow traveler and sidekick, Alfred Rosenberg.

Mary's cousins Abba Kovner and Michael Kovner are mentioned prominently in Fishman's book. Many facets of Abba's life and accomplishments appear in Chapters 1, 3, 6, 7, 8, and 15 of this book. In *The Fall of a Sparrow: The Life and Times of Abba Kovner* (Stanford University Press, 2010), Dina Porat tells the full story of Abba and his place in Jewish history, both during and after World War II in Europe and in the new state of Israel from 1948 on. *The Avengers: A Jewish War Story* (Vintage Books, 2001) by Rich Cohen tells of Abba's leadership of Vilna's partisan youth group in the ghetto and the forests.

Israel: A Concise History of a Nation Reborn (Harper Collins, 2016) by Daniel Gordis is the source of much information about that land and its War of Liberation, which appears in Chapters 13 and 17.

Online sources that I frequently consulted for dates, statistics, and fact-checks included the Jewish Virtual Library (www.jewishvirtuallibrary.org) and the website of Yad Vashem (www.yadvashem.org).

Chapter Notes

Preface: Vilna

1. Briedis, Laimonas. *Vilnius: City of Strangers.* (Baltos Lankos, 2009), 199–200.
2. Ibid., 208.
3. Ibid., 208-209.
4. Ibid. 195

Chapter 3: Mary: Vilna, 1939–41

1. Arad, Yitzhak. *Ghetto in Flames: The Struggle and Destruction of the Jews in Vilna.* (Holocaust Library, 1982), 10.
2. Ibid.
3. Ibid., 36.
4. Ibid., 11.
5. Yad Vashem. *Chiune Sempo Sugihara.* https://www.yadvashem.org/righteous/stories/sugihara.html

Chapter 5: Mary: Vilna, 1941, the Nazis Invade

1. Baker, Nicholson. *Human Smoke: The Beginnings of World War II, the End of Civilization.* (Pocket Books, 2009), 344.
2. Sakowicz, Kazimierz. *Ponary Diary, 1941–1943: A Bystander's Account of a Mass Murder.* (Yale University Press, 2005), 11–12.

3. Arad, Yitzhak. *Ghetto in Flames*, 103.
4. Ibid., 169.
5. Ibid., 170.

Chapter 6: Mary: Vilna, the "Quiet Period," 1942–43

1. Kruk, Herman. *The Last Days of the Jerusalem of Lithuania: Chronicles from the Vilna Ghetto and the Camps, 1939-1944.* YIVO Institute for Jewish Research, 2002, 300.
2. Ibid., 152.

Chapter 7: Mary: My Kovner Relatives

1. Porat, Dina. *The Fall of a Sparrow: The Life and Times of Abba Kovner.* (Stanford University Press, 2010), 10.
2. Ibid., 71.
3. Cohen, Rich. *The Avengers: A Jewish War Story.* (Vintage Books, 2001), 97.
4. Porat, Dina. *The Fall of a Sparrow.* 165.
5. Ibid., 46.
6. United States Holocaust Memorial Museum. *Songs of the ghettos, concentration camps, and World War II partisan outposts.* https://www.ushmm.org/collections/the-museums-collections/collections-highlights/music-of-the-holocaust-highlights-from-the-collection/music-of-the-holocaust/never-say-that-you-have-reached-the-final-road.

Chapter 8: Mary: Vilna, 1943, Final Months and Liquidation

1. Arad, Yitzhak. *Ghetto in Flames.* 341.
2. Kruk, Herman. *The Last Days of the Jerusalem of Lithuania.* 389.
3. Ibid.
4. Arad, Yitzhak. *Ghetto in Flames.* 358.

5. Porat, Dina. The Fall of a Sparrow. 139.
6. Arad, Yitzhak. *Ghetto in Flames*. 401.

Chapter 11: Mary: Magdeburg

1. Medick, Hans and Selwyn, Pamela. "Historical Event and Contemporary Experience: The Capture and Destruction of Magdeburg in 1631." History Workshop Journal, No. 52 (Autumn 2001), pp. 23–48. Oxford University Press, 2001. Cited by Military Wiki, in "Sack of Magdeburg." military. https://en.wikipedia.org/wiki/Sack_of_Magdeburg.
2. Towers, Frank. "Magdeburg Revisited—30th Infantry Division." Studylib.net, https://studylib.net/doc/8637766/ magdeburg-revisited---30th-infantry-division

Chapter 12: Mort: Palestine, 1941–45

1. Center for Israel Education. "British White Paper Restricts Jewish Immigration and Land Purchase." https://israeled. org/resources/documents/hmg-white-paper-statement-policy

Chapter 15: Mary: My Relative Abba Kovner, Post-War

1. Porat, Dina. The Fall of a Sparrow. 202.
2. Ibid., 203.
3. Ibid., 205.
4. Ibid., 209.
5. Cohen, Rich. *The Avengers: A Jewish War Story*. 201.

Chapter 16: Mary: We Meet and Marry

1. Center for Israel Education. "British White Paper restricts Jewish Immigration and Land Purchase." https://israeled. org/resources/documents/hmg-white-paper-statement-policy/

2. Gordis, Daniel. Israel: A Concise History of a Nation Reborn. (HarperCollins, 2016), 141.
3. Destiny Foundation. "The Conflict Between the Irgun and the Haganah." www.jewishdestiny.com/destinys-projects/faith-fate/a-new-beginning/educators-guide/instant-lessons/the-war-of-independence-the-first-stage/the-conflict-between-the-irgun-and-the-hagannah-the-altalena-story-the-formation-of-the-idf/.

Chapter 17: Mary: Life in Israel, the War of Liberation, and Aftermath

1. Barnett, David. "Azzam's Genocidal Threat." Middle East Forum, www.meforum.org/3082/azzam-genocide-threat.
2. Gordis, Daniel. Israel: A Concise History of a Nation Reborn. 153.
3. Ibid., 176.
4. Jewish Virtual Library. "Israeli War of Independence: Background and Overview." https://www.jewishvirtuallibrary.org/background-and-overview-israel-war-of-independence
5. Porat, Dina. The Fall of a Sparrow. 240–243.
6. Jewish Virtual Library. "Israel War of Independence: The Bernadotte Truce Plan" https://www.jewishvirtuallibrary.org/the-bernadotte-truce-plan.
7. Porat, Dina. The Fall of a Sparrow. 336.

Bibliography

Arad, Yitzhak. *Ghetto in Flames: The Struggle and Destruction of the Jews in Vilna*. Holocaust Library, 1982.

Arad, Yitzhak. *The Operation Reinhard Death Camps, Revised and Expanded Edition: Belzec, Sobibor, Treblinka*. Indiana University Press, 2018.

Baker, Nicholson. *Human Smoke: The Beginnings of World War II, the End of Civilization*. Pocket Books, 2009.

Balberyszski, Mendel. *Stronger than Iron: The Destruction of Vilna Jewry 1941-1945: an Eyewitness Account*. Edited by Theodore Balberyszski. Gefen Publishing House, 2010.

Barnett, David. "Azzam's Genocidal Threat." *Middle East Forum*, www.meforum.org/3082/azzam-genocide-threat.

Bauer, Yehuda, and Nili Keren. *A History of the Holocaust*. Franklin Watts, 2001.

Briedis, Laimonas. *Vilnius: City of Strangers*. Baltos Lankos, 2009.

Center for Israel Education, 9 Oct. 2020, israeled.org/.

Cohen, Rich. *The Avengers: A Jewish War Story*. Vintage Books, a Division of Random House, Inc., 2001.

Destiny Foundation. "The Conflict Between the Irgun and the Haganah." *The Destiny Foundation*, www.jewishdestiny.com/destinys-projects/faith-fate/a-new-beginning/educators-guide/

instant-lessons/the-war-of-independence-the-first-stage/the-conflict-between-the-irgun-and-the-hagannah-the-altalena-story-the-formation-of-the-idf/.

Falbaum, Berl. *Shanghai Remembered: Stories of Jews Who Escaped to Shanghai from Nazi Europe*. Momentum Books, 2005.

Fishman, David E. *The Book Smugglers: Partisans, Poets, and the Race to Save Jewish Treasures from the Nazis*. ForeEdge, an Imprint of University Press of New England, 2017.

Fishman, K. Heidi. *Tutti's Promise: A Novel Based on a Family's True Story of Courage and Hope during the Holocaust*. MB Publishing, 2017.

Fogelman, Eva. *Conscience and Courage: Rescuers of Jews during the Holocaust*. Anchor Books Doubleday, 1995.

Good, Michael. *The Search for Major Plagge: The Nazi Who Saved Jews*. Fordham University Press, 2006.

Gordis, Daniel. *Israel: A Concise History of a Nation Reborn*. Ecco, 2016.

Gross, Jan T. *Neighbors: The Destruction of the Jewish Community in Jedwabne, Poland*. Penguin Books, 2001.

Hackett, Joyce. *Disturbance of the Inner Ear*. Little, Brown, 2003.

Hayes, Peter. *Why? Explaining the Holocaust*. W. W. Norton & Company, 2018.

Hilberg, Raul. *The Destruction of the European Jews*. Martino Fine Books, 2019.

Hunter, Georgia. *We Were the Lucky Ones*. Penguin Books, 2019.

Israel Gutman, ed.; Sara Bender and Pearl Weiss, associate eds. *The Encyclopedia of the Righteous Among the Nations: Rescuers of Jews during the Holocaust. Europe (Part I) and Other Countries*. Yad Vashem, 2007.

Israel Gutman, ed.; Sara Bender and Pearl Weiss, associate eds. *The Encyclopedia of the Righteous Among the Nations: Rescuers of Jews during the Holocaust: Europe (Part II): Albania, Bulgaria, Greece, Romania, Former Soviet Union (Belarus, Estonia, Latvia, Lithuania, Moldova, Russia, Ukraine), Former Yugoslavia (Bosnia-Herzegovina, Croatia, Macedonia, Montenegro, Serbia, Slovenia).* Yad Vashem, 2011.

Jewish Virtual Library. www.jewishvirtuallibrary.org

Kelly, Martha Hall. *Lilac Girls: A Novel.* Ballantine Books, 2020.

Kruk, Herman, et al. *The Last Days of the Jerusalem of Lithuania: Chronicles from the Vilna Ghetto and the Camps, 1939-1944.* YIVO Institute for Jewish Research, 2002.

Labson, Gabriella Auspitz. *My Righteous Gentile: Lord Wedgwood and Other Memories.* KTAV Publ. House, 2004.

Langmuir, Gavin I. *History, Religion, and Antisemitism.* University of California Press, 1990.

Langmuir, Gavin I. *Toward a Definition of Antisemitism.* University of California Press, 1996.

Larson, Erik. *In the Garden of Beasts: Love, Terror, and an American Family in Hitler's Berlin.* Broadway Paperbacks, 2012.

Loridan-Ivens, Marceline, and Judith Perrignon. *But You Did Not Come Back: A Memoir.* Atlantic Monthly Press, 2016.

Lowe, Keith. *Savage Continent: Europe in the Aftermath of World War II.* Penguin, 2013.

Military Wiki. "Sack of Magdeburg." military.wikia.org/wiki/Sack_of_Magdeburg#cite_note-8.

Mokotoff, Gary, et al. *Where Once We Walked: A Guide to the Jewish Communities Destroyed in the Holocaust.* Avotaynu, 2002.

National Geographic. "Revenge on the Nazis." www.nationalgeographic.com/tv/movies-and-specials/revenge-on-the-nazis.

Orringer, Julie. *The Flight Portfolio*. Random House Large Print, 2019.

Porat, Dina, and Elizabeth Yuval. *The Fall of a Sparrow: The Life and Times of Abba Kovner*. Stanford University Press, 2010.

Rees, Laurence. *The Holocaust: A New History*. Public Affairs, 2017.

Reichental, Tomi, and Nicola Pierce. *I Was a Boy in Belsen*. The O'Brien Press, 2011.

Sakowicz, Kazimierz, and Yitzhak Arad. *Ponary Diary, 1941–1943: A Bystander's Account of a Mass Murder*. Yale University Press, 2005.

Sands, Philippe *East West Street: On the Origins of "Genocide" and "Crimes against Humanity*. Vintage Books, 2017.

Sands, Philippe. *The Ratline: Love, Lies and Justice on the Trail of a Nazi Fugitive*. Weidenfeld & Nicolson, 2020.

Shaer, Matthew. "The Holocaust's Great Escape." *Smithsonian.com*, Smithsonian Institution, 1 Mar. 2017, www.smithsonianmag.com/history/holocaust-great-escape-180962120/.

Snyder, Timothy. *Black Earth: The Holocaust as History and Warning*. Tim Duggan, 2015.

Snyder, Timothy. *Bloodlands: Europe between Hitler and Stalin*. Basic Books, 2010.

Towers, Frank. "Magdeburg Revisited - 30th Infantry Division." *Studylib.net*, studylib.net/doc/8637766/magdeburg-revisited---30th-infantry-division.

United States Holocaust Memorial Museum, www.ushmm.org/.

Wachsmann, Nikolaus. *KL: A History of the Nazi Concentration Camps*. Farrar, Straus and Giroux, 2015.

Weinstein, Eddie, and Noach Lasman. *17 Days in Treblinka: Daring to Resist, and Refusing to Die*. Yad Vashem Publications, 2008.

Wittman, Robert K., and David Kinney. *The Devil's Diary: Alfred Rosenberg and the Stolen Secrets of the Third Reich*. Harper, an Imprint of HarperCollins Publishers, 2017.

Wygodski, Mary Tabachowitz, and Cynthia Waddell Stone. *Mary's Story: A Survivor's Memoir of the Holocaust*. Sentry Press, 2010.

Photos

Cover photo and photo of Mary Wygodski on p. 297 by Matthew Burke.

Photos of Mary and family on p. 263; of Mary speaking at Florida Holocaust Museum on p. 272; of Bella on p. 279; and of Edith on p. 283 by Tom Burke.

Photo of Abba Kovner at Eichmann Trial on p. 210 downloaded from encyclopedia.ushmm.org.

Photo of Abba testifying on behalf of Anna Borkowska downloaded from yadvashem.org.

All other photos courtesy of Mary Wygodski and family.

Acknowledgments

I N   T H E   N E A R L Y five years that it took me to research and write this book, I leaned on many people for help in addition to Mary Wygodski and her family members and others who are mentioned in the accompanying note on sources. No one was more important to me along the way than my wife, Mary Ellen. At approximately the same time that I set to work, she began to show symptoms of the Alzheimer's Disease that took her life in December of 2019. She was a beloved school teacher for more than thirty years, and she realized perhaps even more than I that preserving and telling Mary's story for future generations was profoundly important. She consistently encouraged me and prodded me to keep working. Even as her mental and physical capacities weakened, she insisted that nothing I was doing was more important than to finish Mary's book. Without her by my side—and our children Matthew, Andrew, and Emily echoing her sentiments—I might not have been able to see the work through to its conclusion. I was able to bring Mary Ellen from Boston to Florida to meet Mary in person before she became too ill to travel. That visit is an especially cherished memory.

As someone who grew up in a conservative Catholic home and attended Catholic schools and college, I knew few Jewish people and had never discussed the Jewish faith or customs with anyone. That had to change if I were to do full justice to the stories of Mary and her family members. The lone exception to this was the late Hy Slavet, whose enthusiasm for his religion and for the land of Israel piqued my curiosity and helped to widen the tunnel of my vision. That was during many conversations we had back in the 1960s, in our adjoining seats as season ticket holders for the Boston Bruins in the old Boston Garden.

Hy's niece Amy Slavet Glaser is one of many Jewish contemporaries who took a great interest in my work on the book and who offered tips and insights on Jews and Judaism, as well as suggesting additional readings and sources of information. Others who helped and inspired me in like manner are Teresa Brugman, Lynne Kosofsky Moore, Karen Mack, Denise M. Mahoney, and Andrea Lincoff and her mother, Rose Brown. I also am indebted to Dave O'Brien, my Gridiron Club of Greater Boston colleague, for arranging my interview with his client and Holocaust survivor Sid Handler, who is also mentioned in the note on sources.

Those who reviewed the entire manuscript and offered invaluable edits and suggestions are my sister, Margaret Burke Lee, Ph. D.; Catherine Marenghi, poet and author of the beautiful memoir *Glad Farm* (CreateSpace Independent Publishing Platform, 2017); Ann Haendel, Holocaust educator and docent at the Florida Holocaust Museum; and Kate Auspitz, Ph.D., historian and author of *The Radical Bourgeoisie: The Ligue de l'Enseignement and the Origins of the Third Republic* (Cambridge University Press, 2002) and *Wallis's War: A Novel of Diplomacy and Intrigue* (University of Chicago Press, 2015).

About the Author

TOM BURKE'S CAREER stops included educational fund raising, banking, and corporate communications, but all along the way he was a freelance writer and sports historian. His byline has appeared in *The Hockey News, Boston Globe, Hockey* magazine, the *Sunday New York Times,* and several program editions of the Beanpot Tournament and the NCAA Hockey Championship Tournament. He is co-author of *Tales from the Boston College Hockey Locker Room: A Collection of the Greatest Eagles Hockey Stories Ever Told (2014).* A native of Winthrop, Massachusetts, he now lives in Boston.

'Tom Burke, an American, too young to have fought in World War II, did not personally save Jews, Roma, or partisans from the Nazis. Yet, he must be counted as one of

"The Righteous among the Nations" because he preserves a remarkable story of Jewish resistance and survival. *The Life of Mary Wygodski* celebrates her determination to live in freedom and dignity. His book inspires us, as she inspired so many, never to forget suffering but never to abandon hope. Tom and Mary together insist that to be human is to defend our rights and the rights of others.'

—Kate Auspitz, Ph.D. edited a Holocaust memoir, *My Righteous Gentile: Lord Wedgwood and other Memories,* by her mother-in-law, Gabriella Auspitz Labson.

Made in the USA
Middletown, DE
08 January 2022

57891380R00191